The Labour of Words in Higher Education

# The Labour of Words in Higher Education

*Is it Time to Reoccupy Policy?*

By

Sarah Hayes

BRILL SENSE

LEIDEN | BOSTON

All chapters in this book have undergone peer review.

The Library of Congress Cataloging-in-Publication Data is available online at http://catalog.loc.gov

Typeface for the Latin, Greek, and Cyrillic scripts: "Brill". See and download: brill.com/brill-typeface.

ISBN 978-90-04-39536-7 (paperback)
ISBN 978-90-04-39535-0 (hardback)
ISBN 978-90-04-39537-4 (e-book)

Copyright 2019 by Koninklijke Brill NV, Leiden, The Netherlands.
Koninklijke Brill NV incorporates the imprints Brill, Brill Hes & De Graaf, Brill Nijhoff, Brill Rodopi, Brill Sense, Hotei Publishing, mentis Verlag, Verlag Ferdinand Schöningh and Wilhelm Fink Verlag.
All rights reserved. No part of this publication may be reproduced, translated, stored in a retrieval system, or transmitted in any form or by any means, electronic, mechanical, photocopying, recording or otherwise, without prior written permission from the publisher.
Authorization to photocopy items for internal or personal use is granted by Koninklijke Brill NV provided that the appropriate fees are paid directly to The Copyright Clearance Center, 222 Rosewood Drive, Suite 910, Danvers, MA 01923, USA. Fees are subject to change.

This book is printed on acid-free paper and produced in a sustainable manner.

# Contents

**Preface: What This Book Is Not**   VII
**Acknowledgements**   XIII

**Introduction**   1
The Political, Social and Economic Constructs Shaping Higher Education Policy   1
Human Performance   22

1 **The Labour of Words and Academic Labour**   27
Academic Labour   27
Rationalising Human Activity   40
A Deficit Model Ignores Human Strengths   47

2 **The Words of Labour**   57
Progressing Rationalisation via Rational Policy Discourse   57
Reflecting on What Neoliberalism Has Taught Us   63

3 **The Labour and Delivery of Buzz Phrases**   71
Packaged Consumption   71
Increasing Consciousness of the Labour of Words   76

4 **Technology Enhanced Learning McPolicy**   89
The Value of Technology Enhanced Learning   89
The Labour of 'the Use of Technology'   102

5 **Student Engagement McPolicy**   113
The Value of Student Engagement   113
The Labour of Student Engagement   117

6 **Employability McPolicy**   129
The Value of Employability   129
The Labour of Employability   136

7 **Re-Writing Human Labour into HE Policy**   144
What Might Be Learned from the Labour of Words in HE?   144

**References**   151
**Index**   166

# Preface: What This Book Is Not

### Noticing and Resisting McPolicy

Let me begin with what this book is not. This is not a book about linguistics, though certain linguistic approaches have been borrowed and applied in order to illustrate the topics under discussion through analysis of UK Higher Education (HE) policy data. Where linguistic terminology is needed, clear explanations are provided for accessibility to a wide audience of readers. This book is thus an attempt to offer worked empirical examples that go beyond theorising alone, to support a practice of noticing, and indeed resisting, certain dehumanising forms of policy discourse. These can now be observed on a grand scale and so I refer to this form of written discourse as McPolicy: a McDonaldisation of HE policy. My exploration of HE policy as McPolicy is inspired by the work of George Ritzer on the McDonaldisation of Society (1992, 1997, 2008, 2018) and by others who have examined Ritzer's work, in relation to HE, including Dennis Hayes and Robin Wynyard (2002) and Dennis Hayes (2005, 2017). McPolicy aptly describes a rational method of writing policy across UK universities that relies heavily on repetitive statements that frequently obscure who is enacting the processes described. As such, there is a widespread failure to attribute the human academic labour of staff and students, to the actions discussed.

Whilst it is easy to shrug and question whether written HE policy has much impact on work in universities anyway, it is important to look at McPolicy in a wider global context. We live in times where we are happy to employ a workforce to complete simple focused tasks where training is swift. Yet these are people who are also easily deskilled and replaced. HE policy texts can transmit implicit meanings in relation to the 'value' of human labour. They can powerfully invoke reactions in readers, but I suggest this is a 'trouble free' language that is akin to George Ritzer's discussion of a 'globalization of nothing' (Ritzer, 2004). Just as globalisation has been discussed by Ritzer as involving the spread of forms that are centrally conceived, and devoid of distinctive content, these documents are curiously similar to each other in structure and lacking in diversity. A contradiction perhaps, when considered alongside many university marketing claims of distinctive institutional values for student learning. Furthermore, the ever-growing volume of HE policy of this nature shares a logic that could alter people's perceptions concerning the ways that human labour, in relation to learning and teaching, is evaluated. Whilst providing an explicit analysis in this book won't eliminate the implicit, it could help to 'displace it' (Savage, 2013: 17). Such a displacement offers new conceptual space to re-imagine alternatives to vacuous knowledge claims, such as the validity of 'best practice', or empty buzz phrases such as 'the student experience', 'Technology Enhanced Learning', 'student engagement' and 'employability'.

This book is written for anyone who has an interest in noticing and making connections within and around political developments in HE. In noticing, I suggest that we each might develop a 'sociological imagination', wherever we are based in the world. Just as C. Wright Mills urged his students to research the world around them as part of life, using their imagination across all political contexts and not confining this to a narrow field of study (Mills, 1959), this is a practice all can engage in. As such, there will be liberal references in this book to consumer culture and the media, alongside academic references and linguistic examples. This is intended to provide analogies that connect – rather than divide – human academic labour and experience. With this in mind, I make no apology for appearing flippant on occasions, particularly when I draw the reader's attention to examples of the irrationality, of rational McPolicy.

### The University Is the People

The book is framed from the perspective that a university is formed from its people (students and staff) and that a university relies on the academic labour of these people, as creative individuals with home and family commitments and diverse identities (Hayes, 2018a, 2018b). The people within a university are what make it distinct, yet government, institutional and media rhetoric often drowns out the value and relevance of this observation. At the time of writing, a new regulatory body, the Office for Students (OfS) has been formed in the UK. A key goal of OfS is that: 'every student, whatever their background, has a fulfilling experience of higher education that enriches their lives and careers' (Hayes & Wilson, 2018). One way to further such aspirations, is to connect both students and staff with the process of writing policy in HE institutions and demonstrate how these texts connect with university activities. This means calling into question the way in which many written HE policies are currently constructed. Frequently there is no explicit reference to the very humans who will enact the tasks stated, and in many cases, no reference to those who authored said policy documents either (Bartholomew & Hayes, 2015). At a time of parliamentary HE review in the UK, in relation to value for money and strong attention on HE globally also, universities are perceived as a means to address countless social and economic issues. This includes even the global threat of technological unemployment, due to rapid automation. Therefore, when such wide ranging expectations are at stake, the methods

PREFACE: WHAT THIS BOOK IS NOT

by which HE policies are created and communicated, is a fundamental area inviting reform.

## Limitations

The focus for analysis is largely HE policy since 1997, to date. The empirical data referred to is derived from UK policy alone, though it is expected that readers from across the globe will be able to draw their own comparisons. Additionally, the critical theorists who inform this work are both contemporary and classical, with the notion of 'rationality' as a prominent theme, explored reflexively throughout the book, as it appears to play out within recent HE policy. The book provides a critical (and sometimes an ironic) sociological account of a phenomenon worthy of our attention via interdisciplinary research into HE policy. A sustained and ongoing tendency to marginalise academic labour, by attributing human actions to particular words and phrases, rather than to people, needs to be confronted.

This is not however a pessimistic account! A critical appraisal can yield new, fruitful ways to resist oppressive trends that might otherwise go unnoticed. It is important also to acknowledge the academic injuries and anxiety that many colleagues now report (Gill, 2009; Hall & Bowles, 2016), due to the extremes of rational approaches, such as restructure, a persistent audit culture and a pursuit of efficiency in HE that can at times take rationality towards irrationality (Ritzer, 1998). A fundamental way to resist dehumanising processes is to restore human voices (Couldry, 2010; Hayes, 2018b). This book therefore provides powerful empirical data through a corpus-based Critical Discourse Analysis (CDA), alongside relevant theory to expose a lack of human presence, and ultimately voice in university McPolicy.

Finally, I suggest some routes of resistance that are based in and drawn from my own experience and practice as a critical pedagogical educator in HE. I call for others to develop these arguments through further research into new ways that HE policy might be constructed, ways that fully acknowledge and attribute the human labour involved, enabling each of us to creatively reoccupy our HE policies.

## A Tale of Two Globes

I offer an illustration of two globes to demonstrate how the concerns raised so far might be linked to wider cultural changes. The first globe, pictured below, is an institutional installation that sits outside of a university in Birmingham, in the UK. This globe is beautifully constructed and inscribed with values that this university endorses. The globe is pristine, a statement of what the institution stands for. It is not though a vehicle for further human expression. It is a finished artefact, a complete statement.

*The Globe, Newman University, Birmingham*

I contrast this globe with another that has resided in a street in the centre of the city of Zagreb in Croatia since 1994. The second globe is a bronze sphere entitled *The Grounded Sun,* the work of Croatian artist Ivan Kožarić. Again, it is beautifully constructed, but it is not the craftsmanship that I am comparing, as I contemplate these two material artifacts. Rather it is their ownership and function as a means for human expression. The globe in Zagreb bears the inscription of years of graffiti, where passers by have made their mark, in the labour of adding their words.

In noticing these two globes, I find myself questioning *why now,* do humans feel the need to make their mark in so many ways, as material expression?

PREFACE: WHAT THIS BOOK IS NOT                                              XI

*The Grounded Sun, Ivan Kožarić*

Whether it is by ink on their skin in the form of a tattoo, that speaks to personal identity and belief, or by attaching padlocks to bridges to signify their presence and their regard for a lover (in the form of 'love locks'), or by social media comment and prolific personal images. Humans (it would seem) seek to preserve something of themselves across both the digital and material world.

*Infinity Tattoo*

### Displacement of Humans

The practice in HE policy discourse of displacing humans from their own labour, and instead attributing these processes to a range of non-human entities, is a relatively recent change that I draw attention to in this book. Whilst there has been a natural tendency over time for new technological innovations to displace people, this has not always been mirrored in HE policy language. So, it is worth questioning *why now?* What is it about recent decades that has effected such a change in the way that HE policy discourse is now structured? Even when the New Labour government first came to power in the UK, the idea of a strong, 'enterprising self' was being put forward in rhetoric as something to aspire to. Yet there was also an implication of everyone in the legitimation of government policy decisions, via a subtle form of hegemony that redrew the lines of individual and collective responsibility (Mulderrig, 2011: 575). Over twenty years later, authors are questioning a widespread 'snowflake' society, where students and staff in HE are increasingly shaped in public opinion and policy to be deficient and needy (Fox, 2016: 178). Worse still, at a time when we all appear to be working harder than ever before, any references to human labour at all in HE policy, are few and far between.

# Acknowledgements

For my family: *David, Calum* and *Joe Hayes*. Thank you for your continual love, encouragement and constant belief in what I do. Together with our cat, *Jasmine*, we sustain each other, as a proudly dysfunctional unit. You are all present throughout the pages of this book, having shared my ideas, contributed your own, and celebrated with me, the completion of *The Labour of Words in Higher Education*.

Thank you to *Petar Jandrić* for his wonderful friendship and for all that we have written together over the years and continue to work on. Thank you also to *George Ritzer* for undertaking his recent interview with Petar and I (Ritzer, Jandrić, & Hayes, 2018) and for providing the inspiration for the label of McPolicy, through his enduring McDonaldisation theory. I express too, my thanks to *Dennis Hayes*, for his insights into the rise of both McDonaldisation and therapeutic culture in the Higher Education sector.

Finally, this book is dedicated to all of the human beings who are the living and breathing 'body' of our universities and whose labour really enacts the processes discussed throughout these pages. Higher Education is often a labour of words, but still there are real bodies behind these texts. We owe it to each other, not to let McPolicy get routinely accredited, with our academic labour.

# Introduction

**The Political, Social and Economic Constructs Shaping Higher Education Policy**

*When Did the Academic Labour of Teaching become 'Best Practice'?*

It started by noticing (with a growing irritation, if I am honest) an abundance of references to something called 'best practice', when I first began to work in Higher Education (HE) back in 1998. It was at a time when, following the Dearing Report of the National Committee of Inquiry into Higher Education (1997), successive UK government policies declared a need to respond to the demands of a 'knowledge-based economy' (KBE), to be ready for an 'information age': to develop 'lifelong learning' and to ensure competitive advantage in the 'global marketplace'. The notion of best practice, discussed in the context of teaching in Higher Education, HE hereafter, concerned me because I wondered why the word 'best' was being placed in the setting of academic practice. My perception of teaching practice in academia is that this refers to an ongoing development (or practice) of instruction, as a craft. To discuss 'critically reflexive practice', rather than 'best', would therefore seem to suggest practitioner self-awareness and routes for ongoing learning as a lecturer. To describe practice as 'best', appeared to remove the learning (or practicing) element, indeed to extract even the *human* element. This was my impression anyway, that academic labour, whether in teaching or learning, would always concern an ongoing, contextual and ever-developing practice.

*If My Teaching becomes 'Best' Practice, Do I Cease to Be a Lifelong Learner?*

Originally an art student in Edinburgh in the 1980s, my practice back then involved working with visual and tactile elements in a creative manner. Learning to be creative is not though, the monopoly of the arts. Creative practice of any kind suggests that imagination is involved in shaping something. Best practice would seem incongruous in artistic labour too, as it implies something finished, complete, and therefore no longer in need of human imagination, perhaps also, something not ever quite attainable. After spending two lean years as a self-employed artist, following my graduation, I then spent the next four years working in finance. As such, I was no stranger to the smiling world of customer services and consumer culture. Consequently, my move into an increasingly marketised HE sector in the late 1990s did not feel like as much of a change as I had at first been expecting.

Yet, as I adapted to working in a university, completed an MSc, followed by a PhD, and taught both students and staff over the years that followed, new terminology for forms of academic labour grew thick and fast across the HE sector, and indeed beyond. I soon found out that others had written extensively, about so-called 'buzz phrases', or fashionable forms of jargon, such as 'market forces', for example (Philpott, 1999; Mautner, 2005; Cornwall & Eade, 2010), that transmit certain 'truths', but mask other alternative forms of understanding. Indeed, at times these terms seemed contradictory to each other, with a rational argument leading into irrationality, as one buzz phrase encounters another. For example, if I display 'best practice' in my work as an academic, is there room left for me to also practice 'lifelong learning'? Or is lifelong learning a term aimed only at my students?

### *Examining the Rise of 'McPolicy' in Higher Education*

As HE has come to be valued for its contribution to the global economy, the political discourse about academic labour in particular, has reinforced these values. By academic labour, I refer to the endeavours of both students and staff. I highlight the way in which HE policy texts have reduced the visibility of human labour by discussing the activities of people as if these were enacted by strategies, technologies and a range of socially constructed phrases, that are attributed with the efforts of individuals (Hayes & Jandrić, 2014; Hayes, 2015a, 2015b, 2016a, 2016b; Hayes & Jandrić, 2017b; Peters, Jandrić, & Hayes, 2018). Many authors refer to the 'neoliberal' university, where a strong prioritisation has been placed on meeting the needs of industry by providing a better workforce. This perspective emphasises the role of a degree in HE to secure future material affluence alone, rather than to study also as an on-going investment in the self (Molesworth, Nixon, & Scullion, 2009: 280). As universities have rationalised their approach to adapt to these changes, students have been treated primarily as consumers, where through their tuition fees they purchase a product in the form of a degree, rather than benefit from the transformative potential university education as a process offers for the whole of life (Hayes, 2015). Furthermore, in university employability strategies, students are frequently referred to in terms of 'graduate attributes', 'skills', 'assets' and 'components'. Academics are urged to develop 'best practice' to increase 'student engagement' and 'employability' and to attend to the ever-increasing volume of social issues that are now crammed under the faceless banner of 'the student experience'.

However, Feek (2010) argues (in the context of global development language) that human practice is not uniform and cannot be reduced to component parts for replication across different contexts. Therefore, rendering the diverse experiences of students as one 'student experience' may be convenient for politicians, but it is vague and problematic in what is assumed to be included. Feek raises concern too that the criteria for what constitutes 'best practice' are at best unscientific and tend to discourage diversity and local experimentation (Feek, 2010: 231). Czerniewicz (2018: 3) points out the absence of any reference to equality, inequality, diversity and access in university strategies for e-learning and technology enhanced learning. The same concern could be levelled too at employability and student engagement strategies. Repetitive statements assume that learning, technology and employability are experienced universally, rather than individually.

Thus, to borrow a fast food analogy from the work of George Ritzer, whose theories I draw on throughout this book, terms like 'best practice' and 'the student experience' can come to resemble a form of 'linguistic ready-meal'. Digest these too often and I suggest they may hamper critical thought, just as a frozen chicken korma may discourage an appreciation of creative cooking. A little flippant perhaps, but later in the book I will explain in some detail my choice and analysis of linguistic examples from policy texts and expound on why I refer to these as 'McPolicy' (a McDonaldisation of HE policy).

*Measuring 'Value for Money'*

Linguistic labels like 'best practice' and 'the student experience', when attached to human academic practice in policy, are rarely clearly defined. Such imprecision leaves them open to manipulation across many contexts as my analysis will reveal. In the UK, a recent addition to a growing menu of HE buzz phrases is the term 'value for money', now shortened to VfM in popular policy bulletins. Like other buzz phrases, VfM has become a 'thing' that can be referred to, shaped and reshaped in different contexts and even placed in discourse where it has power to 'act' to supposedly achieve things. Now that VfM has been written into the Higher Education and Research Act and has become the subject of an inquiry by the House of Commons Education Committee, it is regularly in the news. However, with much media attention, VfM is now also deeply entrenched in a public discourse regarding the merits of HE. Whilst an important topic, given the fees that students pay in the UK, confusion concerning this term is leading to widespread 'judgements that now hold the potential to redraw the landscape of English higher education' (McRae, 2018). The treatment of a degree as a commodity suggests a one-way transaction, where students are expected to make a judgement on the value of what they purchased. Yet the success of a student 'is dependent as much on their own commitment as that of their lecturers' (McRae, 2018). Therefore, the shared labour process that has for centuries closely interconnected academics with their students is effectively eroded away through this discourse. A series of judgements inferring that universities are simply 'ripping off' students (Boles, 2017) or offering 'threadbare' degrees (McKie, 2018) needs much more contextual detail. Otherwise it risks excluding the collective academic labour of both lecturers and students.

### *Nominalisation Commodifies Academic Labour Processes into 'Things'*

My research into HE policy developed my interest in how written texts are constructed around popular buzz phrases, particularly in order to communicate processes of academic labour. By examining how policy statements are formed through nouns and verbs, it is possible to notice where the person, or people, who would normally enact a process of human labour are obscured, through 'nominalisation'. Nominalisation offers 'a less specific representation of an action' thus 'eliding those involved in the process' (Simpson & Mayr, 2010: 6). This may not always be a conscious form of deception by the author, nor is it confined to the writing of policy, but it has wider effects in how, for example, the labour of students and academics comes to be viewed over time. For example, instead of writing: *students' raised money by auctioning items for charity,* I could instead write: *the charity auction raised money.* The verb *auctioning,* which expresses an active process of human labour, has been nominalised into *the charity auction.* So, in the first example, it is clear that the raising of money was accomplished by a group of students, through the process of *auctioning.* In the second example, we are told only that a non-human entity described as *the charity auction* achieved the raising of money. This particular change may not matter unduly, but when this form of writing is over-used in a manner that persistently deletes the academic presence of staff or students in HE policy, a persistent pattern of rationalisation emerges that is worth a closer look.

### *Scrutinising McPolicy in the McUniversity*

I began to notice that nominalisation, as an 'efficient' form of writing in HE policy discourse, displays some similar features to the phenomenon of McDonaldisation, as discussed by George Ritzer (1992, 1997, 2008, 2018). Ritzer's McDonaldisation thesis provides a contemporary paradigm to explain a continuation, and even an acceleration of Max Weber's theory of rationalisation, through the substitution of non-human for human technology in consumer culture. Whilst workers in McDonalds and other fast food outlets engage in repetitive, compartmentalised tasks, making them easily replaceable, discourse in HE policy consists of monotonous statements where the labour of academics and students is routinely replaced with de-personalised terms like 'best practice' and 'the student experience'. In companies like McDonalds or Starbucks, rationalisation means that the same products and experience can be accessed in branches across the globe. The construction of HE policy has taken on comparable qualities.

Across many UK universities, collections of institutional strategies on similar topics can be found, for example: *student experience strategy, employability strategy, technology enhanced learning strategy, quality enhancement strategy, widening participation strategy, lifelong learning strategy, wellbeing strategy*. This may not be so surprising, when alongside the core work of universities, many other social issues are 'educationalised' into HE, via government agendas. The concept of educationalising various social and economic concerns implies simply that more education can resolve societal problems (Peters, Jandrić, & Hayes, 2018). As this expectation on universities has grown, recurring, rational statements about each of these topics has been captured in institutional policy texts. The result is that there is now little to distinguish one university approach from another in terms of policy, but surely this is also problematic in relation to demographic diversity? It can hardly be consistent with the marketing campaigns of universities that seek to stand out from each other in terms of their offerings and opportunities for students.

These strategies appear to share all the predictability of uniform choices on a Starbucks or Costa menu. However, this is not to suggest that all universities do this to the same extent, or that all arrangements of the McDonaldisation process are considered equal. Ritzer argues that there are 'degrees of McDonaldization' and such variation can take a number of forms (Ritzer, 1998: 5). McDonaldisation theory has already been critically applied to universities in general, dubbed the 'McUniversity' (Ritzer, 1996; Hayes & Wynyard, 2002; Hayes, 2017), but here I argue for a much closer scrutiny of what I call 'McPolicy' in HE. I introduce the idea of McPolicy primarily to describe recurring analogous statements about academic labour found in HE policy texts where, through nominalisation, human agency is now routinely obscured. Whilst the approach I have adopted for analysis of the discourse is a corpus-based Critical Discourse Analysis (CDA), some further productive observations can be made, if these worked examples are also considered within wider consumer culture.

### *Analogies in Consumer Culture*

Indeed, HE policy texts share features of the four key elements that Ritzer attributes to McDonaldisation: *efficiency, predictability, control, calculability*. Firstly, non-human buzz phrases in McPolicy offer an *efficient* way of writing for policy makers and university management alike. Referring to 'the student experience', for example, this is a recognisable buzz phrase which can be 'ordered' in most universities as easily as a Big Mac or a pizza. In its nominalised form, 'the student experience' is efficiently packaged for ease of textual and verbal McDelivery. This can be noticed in the example below, drawn from the many student experience strategies I analysed:

> This student experience strategy delivers the student experience ambitions of the university.

I discuss other similar statements in Chapter 3, but briefly here, I invite readers to notice that a 'strategy' (not a human) 'delivers'. When you consider what is being delivered, it is the 'ambitions of the university' (not those of students) for 'the student experience'. This also a *predictable* buzz phrase, now found on university websites and at conferences across the sector. It may be an ill-defined label, but 'the student experience' is easily *controlled* in a system where it can be inserted into *calculable* processes, such as staff annual performance reviews and student module evaluations. As an academic working in the McUniversity, I can be asked: 'what have you done to enhance the student experience?', to which I might reply, 'here are my examples of best practice this year'.

I write this with something of a wry smile, but in Chapter 3 the analysis of McPolicy is explained in more detail. Then in Chapters 4 to 6, I provide many more examples, alongside analogies with Ritzer's ideas on the globalisation of 'nothing' (Ritzer, 2004). A proliferation of this way of writing policy in HE is a less obvious form of McDonaldisation. Nevertheless, it needs to be met with close scrutiny and strong resistance, not least because it has been sustained over decades. These are the decades in which academic labour has been increasingly, rationally audited for quality and performance (Shore & Wright, 1999; Ball, 2003). Yet somehow, rather irrationally, we have failed to quality assure or enhance, the very language of McPolicy in which we write our strategies for enhancement.

### *Rationalising 'Safe Spaces'*

Ritzer argues that over-rationalising any process may eventually lead to a form of irrationality (Ritzer, 2011). As one recent example, in the case of the McUniversity, institutions have sought to provide 'safe spaces', in response to student demands. Yet these sanctuaries that were intended to be without discrimination, now threaten the very free speech that they sought to enable: the free speech that universities have endeavored for centuries to preserve. Furedi expresses concern with regard to how academic freedom now appears to be 'rationed' (Furedi, 2016). He argues that though we have seen radical transformations during the 1960s in universities, today almost 50 percent of young people participate in HE. Therefore, what occurs in universities matters directly to the whole of society, including growing trends of banning speakers (Furedi, 2016). Other topics in HE that have wider social relevance include, for example, decisions by student unions on whether to restrict audible clapping on the basis of greater inclusion of students with certain disabilities in the democratic process (Khan, 2018). Such considerations firstly, raise a broader question of what adjustments to social conventions on behalf of one group, may mean for others. Secondly, these efforts, whether we agree with them or not, reach the media and then become somewhat distorted. Khan argues that politicians may then place their attention on addressing a fabricated wording in the press for political point-scoring, rather than turning their attention to the real issues that students face (Khan, 2018).

In calling this book *The Labour of Words in Higher Education*, I have sought to show how words themselves within HE McPolicy (and by association in the press too) now routinely enact academic labour on behalf of people. Words also speak and think on our behalf, as worked examples of texts will demonstrate. All of these recent changes can be understood within a larger rationalisation of HE. What is written in McPolicy is not in isolation from the wider conditions in which the academic labour of students and staff now takes place. Ritzer discusses other forms of rationalisation in the McUniversity, such as integrating features of shopping malls to become 'cathedrals of consumption'. Institutions extend their campuses to encourage student consumers to apply to study, but also to shop, eat and undertake leisure activities alongside. However, whilst HE institutions are increasingly conceived of as a means of educational consumption, Ritzer points to the issue that the university is a 'creaky, highly traditional institution that pales in comparison to all of the sparkling new means of consumption' (Ritzer, 1998: 10). This includes forms of consumption now augmented through the Internet. Perhaps here then, there is a role for new forms of McPolicy, that we write to enable greater human critical engagement with the commodified HE we now inhabit. We are, after all, the 'body' of the university.

### Human Commodities

I have noticed with interest though, that I can visit the supermarket and purchase a bottle of wine that has more 'body' attributed to it, than a student or a lecturer within an HE policy. Frivolous though that may sound, in a book that explores rationality and irrationality through nominalisation in university policy documents, cultural texts of different kinds are not separate from each other. What we read from a label on a commodity may have no obvious connection to a university strategy, yet both exist within a shared political economic culture. Furthermore, there are always alternative ways to construct strategic institutional narratives, just as there are alternative ways to advertise products, or to teach classes.

The linguistic reduction of humans into component parts in McPolicy shares some interesting similarities with advertisements for consumer goods. For example, in consumer culture, there are copious examples of a use of language to personalise commodities, by attributing human characteristics to products, in the ways that these are marketed. In the examples below, the human qualities of 'ambition' and 'growing old' have been applied to vehicles:

> The Vauxhall Grandland X lacks ambition. (Top Gear Magazine, 2017 issue 303, p. 61)

In respect of a Jaguar XJR 575:

> Another jag grows old disgracefully. (Top Gear Magazine, 2017 issue 303, p. 57)

Non-human products marketed globally in this way are often deemed, through a use of language, to have human properties and qualities. Purchasers may not really believe that a car can have ambition, but this use of language for marketing a product can play to the image that consumers have of their car, or it could be a response to information that a company has derived from consumer feedback. Despite being a set of mass produced artifacts (probably no longer even produced by human labour, but via automation) there seems to be few problems associated with attributing human features to consumer goods in advertisements or on product labels. A bottle of Budweiser for example states on the label the date on which the beer was 'born' (Dove, 2014), which mischievously begs the question as to why the 'best before date' is not then replaced with a statement about when the beer should 'die'. Perhaps that offers less appeal to consumers…From human characteristics to human actions, in the next example a hairbrush is attributed with the ability to 'coax', a quality that would usually involve the human skills of persuading or arranging something:

> The Charlotte Mensah Hairbrush coaxes knots out of European and afro hair alike. (Stylist, 2018 issue 401, p. 6)

Coaxing, in this instance, would involve the action of a human hand, in a technique of applying the hairbrush to the hair, yet in the statement above, the inference is that the Charlotte Mensah Hairbrush alone, performs the process that 'coaxes knots out' of human hair. The omission of a reference to the human labour involved in brushing hair may not seem too problematic. However, if millions of words of HE policy persistently reduce the labour, speech and thoughts of academics and students to actions that are said to be performed by 'a strategy', 'graduate attributes', 'student engagement', 'learning gain' or 'Technology Enhanced Learning', for example, when is it time to argue that a hairbrush coaxing knots is not the same thing as a lecturer coaxing learning?

### *Discourse, Power, Legitimation and Persuasion*

Whatever the language that is chosen to market consumer goods or to write McPolicy, it forms part of an argument or a proposition from which a reader or a consumer can draw conclusions. Such arguments have connections to social and political mechanisms of power, as they offer a form of reasoning that people are expected to buy into. This is an important point to make early in this book, given that I argue it is worth paying attention to the mechanisms around nominalisation in McPolicy. The topic of nominalisation has already been explored in many contexts by linguists, who argue that it has important ideological functions, such as deleting human agency and reifying labour processes. Some analysts have cited an over use of nominalisation in newspaper headlines (Fowler, Hodge, Kress, & Trew, 1979) and others point to examples in economics (Muntigl, 2002; Mautner, 2005).

In Chapter 3, nominalisation is explored in detail as a practice of academic writing that, with a little effort, could be avoided. Billig (2008) draws attention to the habits that writers fall into, even pointing to a use of nominalisation by the very authors who are writing critically about it: 'it requires extra effort to turn the passives into actives, or to resist the technical vocabulary. When writers do so, they must fill in blanks, supply extra information and consider more carefully the social relations that they are describing' (Billig, 2008: 797). With this caution in mind, I have made every effort in this book to write simply and explicitly and to try to clearly ascribe labour actions to the human beings whom I am discussing. Without doubt, I will have failed in places, but I hope I will have demonstrated that repeatedly choosing noun phrases to credit with academic labour needs to be questioned. If the human agents of the actions described are systematically omitted, then what is the status of the buzz phrases that replace them? Fowler et al. (1979) argue that the creation of such new terms has the effect of 'control through the one-way flow of knowledge' (Fowler et al., 1979: 33). If this is the case, then we ignore this form of writing HE policy at our peril.

Whether in the context of consumer culture or in HE (and it could be argued that these contexts are now much more closely aligned than they used to be) the 'attempt to persuade has a rational basis' (O'Halloran, 2017: 13). When a reader aligns with any point of view proposed, this is because they have been 'rationally persuaded' by the form of reasoning presented (Bowell & Kemp, 2015: 226). An argument may be rationally persuasive for a person at one particular time, but not necessarily at others. People are in different states of influence from the information that they have access to, at different times (Bowell & Kemp, 2015: 228). Perceptions of 'value' are also a function of language (Graham, 2001: 764). I define language therefore in the first instance, as a system of communication based on words and combinations of words into sentences. These patterns of words (whether spoken or written) enable 'exchanges' to take place in which values are present, for example, as forms of knowledge, opinions, beliefs and commands. However, language is much more than simply a channel for these expressions. Language is a systematic resource for constructing meaning in context. According to Halliday, linguistics is the study of how people exchange meanings through the use of language (Halliday, 1994: 15). Indeed 'language is a machine that generates, and as a result also constitutes, the social world' (Jorgensen & Phillips, 2002: 9).

### *Discourse as Compliance or Common Sense*

At this point an early distinction between 'language' and 'discourse' is helpful. Language is discussed by Simpson and Mayr (2010: 5) as an 'abstract set of patterns and rules which operate simultaneously', whereas discourse is quite simply what happens when language gets 'done' in real contexts of use. Therefore, discourse operates 'above the level of grammar and semantics to capture what happens when these language forms are played out in different social, political and cultural arenas' (Simpson & Mayr, 2010: 5). In recent decades, scholars in English Language and Linguistics have become increasingly interested in how powerful groups exercise control, via access to language, and in how people contest such discursive power (Simpson & Mayr, 2010: 2). Simpson and Mayr highlight two broad traditions of research on power, both of which are relevant to discussion about McPolicy. Firstly, the notion of power as dominance, through routes where others are required to comply is drawn from Weber's work on authority of the state and institutions (Weber, 1914). The legitimation of these processes is often via language, where rational statements justify the official actions of a body or institution (Simpson & Mayr, 2010: 2). Secondly, the concept of hegemony (Gramsci, 1971) refers to the mechanisms through which power is not so much exercised coercively as routinely, with dominant groups putting forward beliefs that appear 'natural' and 'common sense' (Simpson & Mayr, 2010: 3). In short, people may consent to the prevailing social order if it is effectively presented through a discourse that sounds plausible and legitimate.

McPolicy discourse often sounds just this. The arguments can appear rational and convincing, therefore why protest?

This form of 'commom sense' writing is a feature of what some authors have described as 'new capitalism'. This refers to contemporary transformations of capitalism characterised 'by a "restructuring" of the relations between the economic, political and social (Jessop, 2000). Norman Fairclough (1992) describes a 'technologisation of discourse', where as resources and toolkits, discourses can be used to pursue a wide variety of strategies in many diverse contexts (Fairclough, 1992: 215). This means it is not at all unusual now to find functions related to teaching and learning discussed in policy as if these were detached marketable entities, rather than the processes of human academic labour. The effects of marketisation around students and staff in HE might be considered complex and cumulative. Forms of negotiation take place constantly at different levels through material artefacts, as well as language. However, for the purposes of this book. I understand language as a 'principal means' (Mumby & Clair, 1997: 181) through which the social reality of the buzz phrases explored has been created, performed and enacted via the discourse around them, adding once more that these are not constituted *only* by discourse.

### Academic Identity and Labour in the McUniversity

As an educator in HE, it is my belief that people's personal academic identity has become a site of struggle. This is a topic I return to in Chapter 1, in relation to the neoliberal context surrounding academic work that many authors now discuss. Much criticism has been levelled at the marketisation of HE, within wider neoliberal agendas (Bertelsen, 1998; Olssen & Peters, 2005; Molesworth, Scullion, & Nixon, 2011; Ball, 2012), and also the ascendancy of buzzwords (Mauntner, 2005; Cornwall & Eade, 2010). Others have argued that 'both research and, critically, pedagogy are now governed by a language rooted in productivity and organisational development' (Hall & Bowles, 2016: 31). Furthermore, the aggressive reorganisation of the HE sector to subordinate the labour of learning to the free reproduction of capital has led to 'anxiety as the normalised response of a radically altered academic identity' (Hall & Bowles, 2016: 41). Strong emphasis on benchmarks, regular audits, greater entrepreneurial skills and measures to enhance research output and achieve targets have shifted the focus in HE and brought changes to how the processes of academic labour are discussed. An academic culture that once concentrated on: 'open intellectual enquiry and debate has been replaced with an institutional stress on performativity' (Olssen & Peters, 2005) at least, where academics are involved. Concerning students, there are further conclusions that I will allude to, about how marketisation has also altered how learners are widely perceived.

It is impossible to separate economic relations from social relations and both (due to inherent power relations) are encompassed by the political context (Hay, 2002: 3). For example, free markets do not naturally occur, but need to be forced on people (Anup, 2010). As these are deliberately engineered through neoliberal policy, they can disrupt socially-rooted markets that may have existed for centuries. I will come onto the ascendancy of neoliberalism in more detail, particularly through the 1980s and 1990s, but for now I would make the point that new forms of public management and discourse have emerged, based on new economic relations. Deliberately engineered policy changes in HE, based on economic interests alone, can disrupt the complex and deeply-rooted social practices of teaching and learning as individual choices and practice-led communities.

Foskett argues that markets have always been a familiar part of HE, and 'what has changed has been their character, modus operandi and impact. What we are seeing is not a process of marketisation, but a process of enhanced marketisation, with markets driving the world of universities in a way unprecedented in their history' (Foskett, 2011: 26). This topic will be discussed throughout the book, in relation to academic labour and the words of HE policy. However, to only offer critique, and not reflexively consider what might also be learned from economically driven policy discourse, would seem to miss the whole point of universities, in the acquisition, digestion and synthesis of knowledge. Therefore, alongside the textual analysis I present, I will also develop arguments related to the human activities of both production and consumption in learning and teaching, that take their inspiration from Marx, Weber and Ritzer, amongst others.

### *Buzz Phrases, Myths, Repetition and Fake News*

As mentioned earlier, HE policy texts frequently respond to rational arguments that seek to educationalise political, social and economic agendas relating to wider capitalist society. These agendas are labelled, packaged and delivered to universities for a response. Yet, as Apperley points out, in such policy directives there is: 'not only an insistence that such things as "the knowledge economy" or "the information age" have concrete existence', but that 'we must of necessity, develop policies that meet their demands' (Apperley, 2014: 732).

Few of us are strangers to the marketing of unnecessary products in modern consumer culture through persuasive language. These are the items that we did not know we needed, until a convincing campaign had us wondering how we ever functioned without such a commodity. It is possible for example to purchase 'Pet Sweep', which are dust boots that can be fitted to a dog's paws.

INTRODUCTION                                                                13

These are advertised as a way to put your dog to work in your home and avoid free-loading, lazy animals. I can almost hear the reaction as I write. Another example, is a necklace that acts as a form of sling for a wine glass, when in social situations people find themselves unable to balance the holding of a glass and a plate of nibbles, as they may also need to shake someone's hand. Of course, putting the wine glass down on to a table would be another option. These commodities and many others, manufactured for fabricated needs, are not so dissimilar to certain myths in HE policy language. Buzz phrases are also manufactured for our consumption. They often give a name to something we thought we already did to a good standard, such as providing pastoral as well as academic support to students. These activities have now been neatly absorbed into a handy phrase: 'the student experience', just as the labour of my hand holding a drink has been replaced with a handy sling. Buzz words and phrases persistently invade our busy lives, as forms of terminology requiring academic buy-in and response. I am not though convinced that they save us time or reduce our labour. In the case of products and commodities, we can refuse to purchase what we do not need, but it is a different matter when the direction of a university is being carved out through a similar marketing process, built around fabricated terminology, with policies and strategies generated to respond to this.

Often policy concerns important topics, rather than unnecessary items, but rarely are these brand new issues within education as Chapter 2 will illustrate. They are simply re-branded problems that are presented back to universities through government policy, in a shiny re-arranged combination of words. These are words that present rational arguments that suggest a general consensus of agreement around these topics. It is though hard to take a stance against common sense matters related to *student experience, engagement* and *employability*. It becomes more difficult still if endless repetition drowns out alternative forms of expression. There are parallels that might be drawn here with some dilemmas around 'fake news' and the issue of repetition. Pennycook, Cannon, and Rand (2018) suggest:

> Only a small degree of potential plausibility is sufficient for repetition to increase perceived accuracy. As a consequence, the scope and impact of repetition on beliefs is greater than previously assumed. (Pennycook, Cannon, & Rand, 2018)

Therefore, as people confront a sharp rise in misinformation and its possible effects, we all need to ask how well-equipped we are to separate quality information from false details or trivia, especially given high levels of repetition across many digital channels. Though fake news is often associated with political communication, in the press and across social media:

> Repetition may also play an important role in domains beyond politics, such as the formation of religious and paranormal beliefs where claims are difficult to either validate or reject empirically. (Pennycook, Cannon, & Rand, 2018)

Based on these arguments, HE policy would appear to be another suitable domain for forming beliefs through repetition. Yet, according to some research, the situation is more complex still. It seems personal ideology can impact people's assessment of news legitimacy and they may also apply a form of 'motivated reasoning' to accept a falsehood that supports their own predisposition or goals (Stecula, 2017). This is a situation that may also be paralleled in HE, where rational forms of misrepresentation, or fake news, could have their uses to certain groups and individuals. For example, systems such as lecture capture, attendance monitoring or learning analytics may have little effect in enhancing student engagement, but if a university has purchased these systems, they could be rolled out under the myth that students accessing these will be more engaged. In the same way that a consumer of news may choose to accept a false broadcast, senior managers, academics and students may simply adopt ideas or buzz words from policy, rather than resist or question them.

### *CDA to Examine McDonaldisation of HE Policy and a 'Therapeutic Turn'*

My textual analysis will reveal how universities appear to have generated surprisingly similarly structured institutional strategies, in response to a range of buzz phrases that have emerged from increasingly commercial policy narratives during the last two to three decades. As mentioned already, I have referred to this as a McDonaldisation of HE policy, applying the theory from George Ritzer (1993, 1997, 2008, 2018) concerning the global growth of fast food restaurants, to the duplication of repetitive statements concerning academic labour, in the written policies of universities. A similar logic to providing a cheese burger or a McMuffin that is a standard product, regardless of which global branch you visit, seems to have been adopted in student engagement and employability strategies, for example, regardless of which university you attend, work in, or visit.

My corpus-based Critical Discourse Analysis (CDA) of policy is fully explained in Chapter 3, but I then draw connections with Ritzer's theory, in terms of noticing how *efficiency, predictability, calculability,* and *control* are enacted and progressed via the discourse. This is not to say that such developments are isolated, but rather that together with many other political, economic and cultural factors, these rational linguistic structures in policy play their part in a wider rationalisation. McDonaldisation provides an accessible route for wider public understanding of the linguistic examples presented, because it 'connects the everyday world of the "twenty-something consumer" with sociological analysis' (Ritzer, 2008). Applied in HE, McDonaldisation theory is not without its critiques, but it helps to highlight neoliberal connections that cut across political, economic and cultural contexts. Therefore, my analysis through CDA highlights examples of a McDonaldisation of university policy, that might otherwise remain unseen. It also helps to pinpoint how McPolicy discourse may further 'a therapeutic turn'.

Dennis Hayes and Robin Wynyard (2002, 2016) argue that in HE there is 'an ineluctable connection between the forces leading to McDonaldization and the therapeutic turn'. They suggest that as university management have restructured universities as McBusinesses, these have at the same time become therapeutic universities, with academics failing to see or challenge a new 'student-centred culture' (Hayes & Wynyard, 2002, 2016). The growth of therapy culture in universities, side by side with marketisation, may be seen then, as distinctly divisive for students and academics. On the one hand, you may encounter the individual academic struggling to meet an enormous breadth of diverse demands on their time and measures of their performance. At the other extreme, their students are assumed to be fragile, in need of 'safe spaces' away from risky ideas (Jarvie, 2014), requiring a 'Disneyfication' of academic courses, and ultimately the preservation of 'the student experience' (Hayes, 2017: 106).

Furedi (2016: 9) suggests that these developments on campus are really a 'victimisation' of students, which is 'founded on a diminished view of human subjectivity, which regards individuals not as agents of change, but as potential victims of the circumstances they face'. Furedi argues that although this is a doctrine that is rarely expressed in a systematic form, it supports a paternalistic etiquette that now dominates campus life:

> This is often expressed through a language that its critics label as political correctness – in reality, despite its moralistic outlook, this prescriptive etiquette self-consciously avoids the language of morality and values. Outwardly, it presents itself as non-judgemental and open-minded, while in practice it promotes an intolerant approach towards forms of behaviour that violate its norms. Rhetorically, it preaches the value of diversity; in practice, it refuses to tolerate a diversity of opinions. (Furedi, 2016: 9)

I extend such concerns by providing examples of how the term: 'the student experience' literally takes on a life of its own, aided by the populist narrative that surrounds it. This terminology claims to represent the unified 'will of the student', taking on a form of populism (Molloy, 2018) that suggests to academics that if you are not enhancing 'the student experience' then you must be against it. Unfortunately, alternative viewpoints then cease to be given a platform. As a buzz phrase, 'the student experience' describes diverse student individuals as if they had come straight off a production line. Treated as clones, 'the student experience' attributes only one understanding, capability and knowledge to students, but it gets worse. In closer examination through CDA, 'the student experience' is positioned in policy documents in such as way that it proceeds to literally act on behalf of both students and academics alike.

Whilst the academic role has been subjected to a distinct form of rationalisation over decades, so has the student role in recent years. In separate ways, each group is portrayed as 'deficient'. In the end, as analysis will demonstrate, both forms of rational policy meet each other in the discourse, in an ultimate disempowerment of academics and students. Academics have been recast as performance-managed workhorses, with little time to explore the role of their bodies and emotions in self-reflexive teaching (Rowe, 2012; Shahjahan, 2015). Students are now branded as 'snowflakes' (Fox, 2016: 178), with their bodies cast into a distorted form of vulnerability and weakness in policy (Brooks, 2017). Furthermore, policy discourse such as narratives around 'learning gain' are now closely intermingled in the UK with mutually constitutive media discourse. Leach refers to a narrative that:

> Tells lecturers they must be motivated by boosting students' future earning power. And it tells students they need to be motivated by their own self-interest – constantly judging what they have gained. (Leach, 2018)

Whilst the work of government, policy makers and the media clearly play their part, the academics and students participating in this culture also uphold it. The irrationality of these forms of rationality need to be exposed across the many dimensions through which they are articulated. One powerful way to confront this divisive political discourse, is to draw from strategy texts themselves, the many irrational examples demonstrating exactly how the human academic labour (of students and staff) is perceived in McDonaldised HE policy.

### *Rationality and Irrationality*
Much has been written in relation to rationalising approaches in a neoliberal HE context (Shore & Wright, 1999; Ball, 2012). The relevance of the perhaps

over-used term of neoliberalism in relation to HE will be unpacked in the next two chapters in relation to forms of rationality. McDonaldisation offers a helpful lens through which to consider analogies with how HE policy is written, and a convergence of homogeneous institutional policies, which seem to be aimed at tackling an increasing number of social issues. These comparisons will not be stretched too far. I put them forward for further discussion and development, since despite the marketing claims of universities pointing out their distinctive qualities, their written policies appear to tell another tale. Ritzer's arguments concerning 'irrationality of rationality' are considered in practical terms in Chapters 4, 5 and 6 via a detailed analysis of the discourse around these buzz phrases: *Technology Enhanced Learning, Student Engagement* and *Employability* respectively. An increased homogeneity brings with it dehumanising elements (Ritzer, 2011: 169). Thus, in taking rational approaches to an extreme, humans may eventually encounter inefficiencies or less inclination to innovate. This is problematic when the issue of technological unemployment due to rapid automation is also an imminent concern (Aoun, 2017). I draw analogies with Ritzer's concepts of 'nothing' and 'something' in relation to policy discourse in a neoliberal HE context. As mentioned earlier, nothing involves (largely) empty forms lacking distinctive content, whereas something is defined as a form that is rich in distinctive human content (Ritzer, 2011: 172). Whilst Ritzer applies these ideas to organisational contexts, I have developed my analysis to explore his concepts in relation to HE policy language.

A close scrutiny of a large quantity of HE policies focused on student-centred topics revealed a proliferation of therapeutic terminology, but written in a manner that supports Ritzer's concerns over an irrationality of rationality. For example, if universities declare a student-centred culture across their websites, where is the evidence (through variety and distinctive content) that students now co-write institutional policy? Recently, Gwen van der Velden, referring to a government white paper from 2011 called "Students at the heart of the system" asked (seven years later) 'What if we were serious about students at the heart of the system?' (van der Velden, 2018). She expresses her concern at a potential removal of student engagement from the Quality Assurance Agency's (QAA) code of practice. She rightly points out that we need to think more, not less creatively, about student representation. Unfortunately, when 'student representation', just like 'student engagement', is simply treated as if it were a product with a shelf life, it leaves these concepts vulnerable to being 'discontinued' from the range, like any other consumer goods.

### *Higher Education Bodies and the Arguments They Propose*
How much the role of language matters to each individual, depends on context. On the one hand, I may be convinced by a misleading argument that promises

an outcome from a product. I could purchase the item based on this information, but then find it fails to deliver. Alternatively, misleading marketing of a health product may result in actual physical injury. For such circumstances, there are consumer laws designed to protect against these eventualities. Even in the case of university marketing, there have been instances where action has been taken against institutions that make misleading statements about their performance in university rankings. The Advertising Standards Authority (ASA) recently ruled that six UK universities made claims about their performance in university rankings, student satisfaction tables or government indicators, that were 'misleading', with the watchdog ruling that the adverts 'should not appear in the current form again' (Bothwell, 2017). Whether claiming to be the UK's 'number one creative university' or in the 'top five for student satisfaction', these assertions were brought under scrutiny on the basis of the data this was drawn from, how the data had been treated and whether claims could be substantiated. The universities concerned were instructed by the ASA to back up their claims, given the large financial commitment of would-be students who would be basing their choices on such information found on the university websites (Bothwell, 2017).

Once UK students have paid their fees and enrolled onto their courses they still have some consumer protection. The Competition and Markets Authority (CMA) in 2015 produced compliance advice for HE providers which applies to their relationship with prospective and current undergraduate students. It sets out minimum standards for an HE provider's dealings with students regarding information provision and complaint handling and the requirement of fairness for terms and conditions (CMA, 2015). Yet whilst students are protected from misleading marketing and language about their taught programmes, it is worth reflecting on what standards (if any) are, or could be, applied to scrutinise the language adopted within university and government HE policies. This often refers to the activities and circumstances of students and staff in a McDonaldised format. The discourse appears to value empty statements over substantive content. Currently, students are discussed in many educational policies as if they were any other type of consumer, simply purchasing a product with some instructions for the workplace, rather than benefitting from the creative transformative potential university education offers for the whole of life (Hayes, 2015).

Consumer products are marketed with human attributes that suggest they are 'alive' and can perform acts of human labour. Yet students are described in our HE policies as if they were static objects in comparison. References in many policies to 'the student experience' almost invite the facetious response, 'do we only have one student to worry about then?' Referring to students as a homogeneous group with one collective 'experience' may give the façade of efficiency, but it is unlikely to engage a diverse population of individual undergraduates. It detracts from the actual labour of those who are making a real difference to students' lives. Furthermore, some universities have been swift to recruit leaders whose job titles embody such buzz phrases, namely as a Director, Dean or Pro Vice Chancellor of The Student Experience. The problem arising from attributing titles like this, that are lacking distinctive content, to people who are required to enact these functions, is that the basis of their whole role has been built on 'nothing', rather than 'something' (Ritzer, 2011: 172).

It is interesting to observe common phrases such as 'the 'body' of the curriculum or 'the student body'. Referring to these as if they were fixed, unchanging entities is also misleading. It seems commonplace to refer to the agencies who write policies related to HE as 'bodies'. For example, 'new university regulatory body, Office for Students, launched' (Faruk, 2018). On the QAA's website it states: 'we are the Quality Assurance *Agency for Higher Education (QAA)*: the independent *body* entrusted with monitoring, and advising on, standards and quality in UK *higher education'*. The term body evokes the idea of a human presence within these organisations, though the policies that emerge do not always acknowledge the authors who have written them or the students and lecturers whose bodies enact learning.

### *Who Decides, or Defines, Best Practice?*

Returning to my issue with best practice, as a term it was never defined. Yet best practice was, and still is, liberally referred to in HE policy as something for academics to consult, aspire to and disseminate. In the example below, which is a fairly typical wording, it is not only assumed that best practice exists, it is believed that encouraging it enhances the student experience:

> Encourage, support, and celebrate innovations and best practice to enhance the student experience.

Working in UK HE through the years of the New Labour government (1997–2007) and beyond, it was in relation to the terms of 'e-learning', and later 'Technology Enhanced Learning' (TEL), that best practice seemed to be conceived and this is elaborated in Chapter 4. As a phrase, best practice was widely adopted in HE discourse, aimed at teachers and liberally applied without apparent critique. This links also with performance agendas and an audit culture in teaching, but there are other trends to be observed around the concept of learning too.

Over the years, many other so-called buzz phrases, such as 'employability', 'sustainabiliy' and 'student engagement' have joined 'the student experience' and 'best practice', as social constructions in policy discourse that academics should address to improve student learning. An educationalisation of social issues as problems for universities to solve, seems to be a defining feature of our times (Peters, Jandrić, & Hayes, 2018). The issues themselves may be ill-defined, but still they powerfully re-shape popular understandings of 'the student' and their role in HE. This reconceptualisation of students has been achieved in part through the 'therapeutic turn', which according to Apperley (2014) includes:

> Increased emphasis on the student experience, signaled in part by the rhetoric of student-centred education, but also by the forced emphasis on universities as "learning institutions" as opposed to teaching institutions. The idea that universities might be *educational* institutions involving *both* learning and teaching has increasingly been suppressed by these rhetorical strategies. (Apperley, 2014: 732)

So here a separation of the labour of teaching from the labour of learning appears to be one of the casualties of marketisation and another is the increased academic workload that accompanies an educationalisation of social issues. This involves a simple calculation really: the more social agendas we educationalise into HE policy, the more an academic's plate fills up. Then the latest 'managerial hobbyhorse inevitably pushes things over the edge' (Bothwell, 2018). In the *Times Higher Education*'s first major global survey of university staff, the views on work-life balance report that academics feel stressed and struggling to find time for personal relationships and family around their ever-growing workloads (Bothwell, 2018). However, these are curious expectations when, upon closer examination, the buzz words and phrases themselves within policy documents appear to be liberally credited with having already performed the tasks under discussion (Peters, Jandrić, & Hayes, 2018). In HE policy, the academic labour of human beings working and studying in universities receives little acknowledgement. So, before proceeding further, I would hereby like to dedicate this entire book to all of the humans who are the living and breathing 'body' of HE, and not to the hegemonic, linguistic social constructions which, as shown in later chapters, get routinely accredited with our academic labour.

### Student Prosumers

Applying the work of George Ritzer on 'prosumption' (Ritzer, 2015) to perceptions of the labour of students and staff in HE policy is also interesting. The term of prosumer (Toffler, 1980) has been developed by Ritzer to discuss prosumer capitalism, where humans now undertake both production and consumption, rather than focusing on either one (production) or the other (consumption). This is particularly apparent in user-generated content online, where control and exploitation take on a different character than in other historic forms of capitalism (Ritzer & Jurgenson, 2010). Suddenly as consumers we are also providing our unpaid labour to wealthy organisations online, through our additional voluntary activities such as generating our orders, providing feedback, sharing opinions and 'likes' that constitute valuable information within algorithmic frameworks. Facebook and Amazon are examples amongst many, where people produce pages and valuable demographic details about themselves and they consume the Facebook pages of others for no payment (Ritzer, 2010). In this respect, their labour becomes abundant rather than scarce. Ritzer suggests that, though rooted in the model of rationality that developed self-service fast food outlets in the world of bricks and mortar, a much broader form of prosumption in augmented contexts now exists. These are important observations at a time in history when automation threatens to remove work as we know it for many humans. Human creativity of the kind HE can develop, may prove in the very near future to be vital for human employability (Aoun, 2017: 148). I argue that in this context there may yet be valuable lessons to be learned in academia, from the very mechanisms of production and consumption rooted in capitalism.

Ritzer argues that 'anybody who is learning anything is consuming information from books and teachers. They are also producing their sense of that knowledge, for themselves'. On this basis 'good education is always prosumption' (Ritzer, 2010). In a model of pure consumption, 'students would just absorb what teachers tell them without producing anything of their own out of it. That would be a terrible education' (Ritzer, 2010). Therefore Ritzer advocates thinking in terms of a production-consumption continuum, which is helpful in imagining both student participation in their own education, but also in examining progress in encouraging student participation in HE policy making. If students can be prosumers, in proactively ordering from Amazon and contributing to Facebook, what would such engagement to produce look like, if they felt a similar commitment to be active in their university education and indeed in HE policy creation?

In this book I express concerns over an absence of student and staff representation in the linguistic construction of our HE policy discourse around the topic of student engagement. The topic itself is of course an important one and it is the policy wording that I critique and not the issue itself. I explore student engagement as one of a number of socially constructed terms that university practitioners have recently been urged, through policy, to respond to. However, it gets worse. A closer look at the discourse reveals that the policy response appears to present the very concept of student engagement itself, back to students. A gold-plated brand of student engagement appears to be what students now purchase. Can engagement really be bought in this way? In a recent university policy, 'student engagement' is discussed as an entity that can be 'packaged, marketed and communicated to applicants, current students and staff'. I will therefore show how such patterns of words around buzz phrases are every bit as significant as the labels themselves, in structuring what messages are communicated. Through a simple, but powerful form of analysis, it is my aim to expose a disingenuous misappropriation of academic labour within recent HE policy discourse. It is for precisely this reason that any choice of words in policy should always be questioned, because language, referred to as discourse in its many contexts of use, perpetually intersects with social, political and economic forms of power.

**Human Performance**

Human abilities to perform are finite. That is, when compared with the machines that are now automating so many functions that previously required human labour. It is true to say that automation has transformed our means to travel, communicate globally and for many, but not all, extended the length of human lives. Such examples provide good arguments for technological progress, despite the historical fears of machines putting people out of work. Yet, recently authors are questioning why technological advances have not actually led to people working less (Ford, 2015). Others are suggesting that rapidly advancing digital technologies are now finally starting to destroy more jobs than they create (Brynjolfsson & McAfee, 2011; Frey & Osborne, 2013, 2015). The human capacity to both produce and consume is being disrupted in new ways with authors raising concern over the disappearance of work for many of us in the very near future (Aoun, 2017; Hyacinth, 2017).

*Strategies with Ambitions of Their Own*
Despite the proliferation of such arguments coming forward from global experts, HE institutions seem to be particularly slow in responding, beyond the production of similarly worded employability policies that usually cover a period of several years.

> This strategy describes our ambitions in relation to the employability development of our students. (University of Gloucestershire, 2016–2020)

> The University of Stirling's Employability Strategy 2017–2021 is clear in its ambition to: develop aspirational students and graduates with life-long employability skills who can compete successfully in a competitive global economy. (University of Stirling, 2017–2021)

In these examples, of which there are many more, it is a strategy, not a person, that describes or is clear in its 'ambitions'. If, as discussed earlier, a Vauxhall Grandland X lacks ambition, it seems that university employability strategies do not! There appears to be a curious confidence that employability can be enhanced through what a strategy sets out:

> This Employability Strategy sets out, in broad terms, the means by which we intend to enhance the employability of our graduates. (University of Winchester, 2016–2020)

Yet in stark contrast to such expectations, in a recent report the World Economic Forum predicted that robotic automation will yield a net loss of more than 5 million jobs across 15 developed nations by 2020 (Hyacinth, 2017: 42). With researchers predicting 'a 50% chance that AI will outperform humans in all tasks in just 45 years (Hyacinth, 2017: 41) we may not need to wait that long before robots are writing our strategies for us. Certainly, some documents read as if this were already the case. Yet before this futuristic notion becomes a reality, I suggest there is a pressing opportunity for a more radical response. We can begin by reconsidering the labour of our words in HE policy.

### Moving from Regulation of Performance towards Human Agency to Perform

There seem to have been repeated attempts to 'fix' a range of societal issues (such as student engagement, employability, sustainability, digital capabilities) by 'educationalising' these into university strategies. This lacks careful consideration of societal changes, both in demographics across student populations, and in relation to predictions of impending technological unemployment in a digital age. We have tended to regulate performance in HE in recent decades rather than develop creative human agency to perform. Performativity has been discussed by Stephen Ball as a mode of state regulation that 'requires individual practitioners to organize themselves as a response to targets, indicators and evaluations' (Ball, 2003: 215). The implications are that in this approach:

> People must 'set aside personal beliefs and commitments and live an existence of calculation. The new performative worker is a promiscuous

self, an enterprising self, with a passion for excellence. For some, this is an opportunity to make a success of themselves, for others it portends inner conflicts, inauthenticity and resistance. (Ball, 2003: 215)

A further concern in relation to performativity is that it produces opacity in organisations rather than transparency. So professionals compete to 'realise their potential', but this approach also marginalises less instrumental routes to knowledge in higher education. Barnett, in raising the concept of 'supercomplexity' points to the problem of universities losing their way, as enormous amounts of data on performance are generated, but much of the language of 'excellence' has little real content (Barnett, 2000: 2). Value becomes focused on *only* the aspects of education believed to support certain aspirations. This links with points from Ritzer that this form of rationalising eventually moves humans towards irrationality, serving to limit and compromise their actions (Ritzer, 1998: 55). For example, students are now confronted with baffling quantities of data to make informed choices with regard to applying to university, but this assumes that all students are equally aware of this data and are rational and self-interested with regard to weighing up career paths (Coiffait, 2018).

The production of policy that targets generic, actively engaged students, assumes the dubious reality of high performing staff across the board. This may produce instead a detachment from policy, where lecturers and students fail to recognise themselves in it. If there are apparently only positive outcomes discussed as a means to an end in a neoliberal economy, then it would seem there is little left *for* people to debate. Yet debate is crucial to develop new creative dimensions in humans that are beyond what might be automated through machines.

### *What Role Does an Analysis of the Discourse Play?*

It is worth commenting here that my use of corpus linguistics for an initial analysis of policy documents is an automated technique which yields patterns of text. It could be argued that this is rather a rational method in itself to adopt, when researching rationality in policy texts. However, in order to interpret findings, I apply Critical Discourse Analysis (CDA), to go beyond the initial quantitative sorting of words by software. CDA requires human insights that I then link with other theoretical viewpoints. It therefore might also be argued that corpus-based CDA illustrates rather well an enmeshing of the capabilities of human and machine in research. The searches in software provide the data for a human to intervene and interpret, then to type up these insights into a publication. These are dialectical processes that reveal the 'mutually constitutive' nature of technology and humanity (Mackenzie & Wajcman, 1999). Buzz phrases like Technology Enhanced Learning (TEL) can disguise this relationship, hiding facets of human labour and the subjectivity of individuals (Mautner, 2005). The central focus in this book is therefore not so much the proliferation of certain words and phases alone, but the range of actions associated with these popular nouns that would usually be enacted by humans.

In the language of 'new capitalism', certain phrases tend to carry assumptions about what we are all said to 'know' and these can gain a 'universal status' (Fairclough, 2003: 45). Others have focused on the discourse of university mission statements (Sauntson & Morrish, 2011), pinpointing managerialist institutional narratives that universities use to construct themselves, their students and graduates in the desired corporate image:

> Students, but also knowledge, research and teaching/learning are all offered as products of the university. Students are somewhat ambiguously positioned as, simultaneously, consumers, units of profit and as products of the university'. (Sauntson & Morrish, 2011: 83)

The confrontation of linguistic examples in HE policy construction offers something concrete to support a broader movement against these inappropriate aspects of rationalisation in HE and a McDonaldisation of HE Policy. Rational emphasis on the individual and their achievements in neoliberalism, strays into irrationality when the policy language is brought under scrutiny. A corpus-based CDA of this discourse demonstrates that it does not seem to be about humans at all.

### *A Need to Practice and Not Just Preach Reflexivity*

Certain rational arguments have come to dominate many HE policy texts covering a range of recent agendas. These are often hot topics in terms of social issues, both covered by the media and discussed in government papers, but they make their way into university policy documents in a curious linguistic form. It is a form that reinforces a disturbing and repetitive ideological standpoint, when quite simply, there are other possibilities for how these important topics might be conveyed. At this point, in the name of critical reflexivity, I declare my own position open for scrutiny too, as the author of a book that also puts forward arguments and interpretations of written policy through a chosen form of corpus-based Critical Discourse Analysis (CDA) and a focus on the particular linguistic feature of nominalisation. My chosen approach is not the only route for analysis. I could have interviewed students, staff and politicians, held focus groups or undertaken surveys. However, none of these methods of inquiry would have enabled me to scrutinise such a large quantity of policy text to reveal so many similar patterns. I do though both expect, and invite, critique of this book by readers, because that is the way that a greater understanding is developed and disseminated.

### *The Chapters to Come*

In the chapters to come, I will explore all of the dimensions discussed so far as they play out through HE policy texts that sound plausible and legitimate, rather than coercive. Yet findings mirror a form of prosumer capitalism (Ritzer & Jurgenson, 2010; Ritzer, 2015) where, in a commercial context, people readily offer their labour for free, for example by creating orders on Amazon, writing reviews about these goods and answering surveys. Consumers now act as prosumers and I suggest that in universities we appear to have moved in a similar direction, with staff and students labouring on many unrecognised tasks. The contribution of this book is to reveal how McPolicy simply attributes our academic labour to a variety of non-human entities.

On top of teaching and research, students and staff now provide many forms of records, attendance logs, impact statements, personal development reviews and copious amounts of other data, yet in the policy discourse their academic labour fails to be acknowledged. Instead, what results is akin to Ritzer's writings on the globalisation of nothing (Ritzer, 2004). Applied to HE policy discourse, I suggest that nothing refers to documents that are centrally conceived and without distinctive content. Policy texts containing something would be distinctive to the university and the individuals concerned, fully acknowledging the identities of the staff and students who have contributed. Empty homogenous forms of policy are less likely to be questioned though as they travel through institutional committees and into people's inboxes. As I travel and meet with colleagues from other institutions, or read the postings people place on professional mailing lists, universities all appear to be offering the same topics on their policy 'menus'. Of specific interest for this book are the patterns of discourse in which these topics are structured, and the manner in which this represents (or fails to represent) the academic labour of both students and staff.

CHAPTER 1

# The Labour of Words and Academic Labour

## Academic Labour

*Ever-Present Academic Lives*
Throughout the introduction I discussed topics to come, as is the general convention. Of course, my writing of this book did not progress in such a neat chronological fashion. I moved perpetually between sections, theorists, analysis, ideas, and indeed my choice of words, as the text developed. I sat for longer hours than I should (changing posture and location), as I experienced excitement, frustration and fatigue throughout my body, in the act of writing. I left countless windows open on my laptops (yes, two laptops). It seems one computer isn't enough these days, and nearby I have a phone and an iPad, competing for space around me, with scribbled notes, empty mugs, books, toiletries, family photographs and post-it note reminders. Referred to by Melissa Gregg (2013) in her book *Work's Intimacy,* as 'presence bleed', firm boundaries between professional and personal identities no longer apply. Jessop refers to a 'restructuring' of the relations between the economic, political and social (Jessop, 2000), which have also flooded people's personal lives. Location and time become secondary to the ever-present 'to do' list. New affordable technologies, rather than reduce workloads, contribute to 'function creep', because additional tasks silently slip in unseen, to absorb human capacity when it is already overloaded (Gregg, 2013: 2). With such a volume of words at the disposal of human beings, it would be easy to miss pervasive changes in how academic labour is represented in the discourse of McPolicy. Therefore, in this chapter I draw attention to the marginalised activities of academic staff and students. I do so initially through my own lived experience.

Whilst writing this book I frequently paused to respond to the many distinct tasks, people and things that an academic role entails, yet are frequently hidden from public view: my appointments with students, phone calls, Skype meetings with colleagues, preparation of teaching, upload of materials to the virtual learning environment, marking, recruitment of new staff, managing and mentoring of colleagues, disciplinary meetings, writing of references, reviews and feedback, external commitments, projects, reports, reflection on module feedback, annual monitoring reports, responding to email requests. These are just some aspects of academic labour, the topic that this chapter explores in relation to policy discourse. Such accountabilities for work no longer reside in my office. The increasingly digital nature of these tasks also leaves scope for further intrusions. As I am writing, email prompts me with messages awaiting a response. I am sent electronic receipts for purchases, that I have made from Argos, with survey requests for me to rate these items and the service that I received, so that others can benefit (or not, since their task load swells too!).

A key dimension of McDonaldisation is the 'iron cage' of control, via rationalisation, that was once contained within physical sites of bricks and mortar. The bureaucratic forms of regulation of labour discussed by Weber were within workplaces. Increasingly now, we encounter a 'velvet cage' (Ritzer, 2011) that takes us seamlessly back and forth between digital and physical sites of production and consumption, at the hands of non-human technologies, that threaten human labour and autonomy. Ritzer (2015) refers to 'prosumer capitalism', where the focus of capitalism has shifted from exploiting producers, as discussed by Marx, to exploiting consumers even more, during the post-World War Two era. Now he suggests capitalism is increasingly focused on manipulating prosumers (Toffler, 1980), where consumers are put to work as producers too (Ritzer, 1992). In Ritzer's example of McDonald's, con(pro)sumers do unpaid work to carry their own food and clear their own tables, but since the digital era, this takes place in augmented settings too. As prosumers, humans now produce for Facebook or Amazon.com for example, free of charge, even collecting their own parcels from local depositories. Companies grow very wealthy from an abundance of financially unrewarded labour yielding rich information, as a broader self-servicing pattern of human labour emerges across global digital society.

*Academic Prosumers*

In the McUniversity, academics maintain countless profiles. From university web pages to research repository records, from Orcid identifiers to Google Scholar citation records. As I write, LinkedIn networking requests arrive in my Inbox, alongside prompts to improve my online profile and impact, to connect with others and endorse them. I receive messages from Research Gate to tell me who has read or cited my papers, or requests from Academia.edu from those who wish to receive copies. Academic tasks such as marking and meetings that now straddle home and workplace are joined by countless tasks involving the self-evaluation of my academic performance and my endorsement of the performance of peers. At the same time, the intimacy of *presence bleed* is enacted as I reply to emails on family holidays and keep my phone ever-present beside the bed. Personal Facebook and Amazon messages compete for space in my inbox alongside requests from students. University directives for 'best practice' to increase 'student engagement' and 'employability' are extended further, by regular invitations to events across the HE sector, where university colleagues now train or mentor each other, in methods to measure their academic performance, in respect of these buzz topics.

Beneath the broad term of academic labour, I deliberately include student labour alongside that of staff. This is in defiance of policy rhetoric that persists in dividing these groups. Academics and students are positioned in different ways in McPolicy, but there are shared concerns that my analysis will reveal. Firstly, students are widely perceived as consumers (Molesworth, Nixon, & Scullion, 2011) and the 'therapeutic university' around them as providing a 'cotton wool' campus to protect and nurture 'the student experience' (Hayes, 2017: 11). Such narratives ignore diverse student groups (Czerniewicz & Rother, 2018) and simply legitimise (without questioning) contemporary reforms (Brooks, 2017: 15). Secondly, academics provide emotional accounts of the joy and pain of a brimming role that knows no bounds, citing injury and anxiety that has replaced their former enthusiasm, commitment and indeed love, of their work with their students (Berg, Huijbens, & Larsen, 2016; Hall & Bowles, 2016; Hayes, 2018b). I refer to these accounts in this chapter in order to draw attention to the real people that McPolicy surrounds, restricts, constitutes, but rarely praises, and as we shall see, frequently fails to acknowledge, or attribute (Gill, 2010, 2014; Bartholomew & Hayes, 2015; Hayes & Bartholomew, 2015; Hayes, 2016; Allmer, 2018).

I note too, the growth of a body of literature that demonstrates that the fierce intensity surrounding academic labour in HE cannot be separated from the struggles against capitalism (Callinicos, 2006: 7; Gulli, 2009; Winn, 2015), neoliberalisation of the academy (Berg, Huijbens, & Larsen, 2016; Smyth, 2017; Hayes, 2018b) and the McDonaldisation of HE (Hayes & Wynyard, 2002; Hayes, 2017). Leach refers to a growth of HE, accelerated by the very 'geopolitical phenomena that have come under attack across the West – globalisation, conglomeration, monopolisation, massification, digitisation, internationalisation, corporatisation, and the free movement of goods, finance, capital and above all: people' (Leach, 2018). As a result, rather than making society better, universities have come to be seen in a very public criticism as 'the symptom of a failed political philosophy' (Leach, 2018). This is a state of affairs which impacts considerably in shaping perceptions of the labour of academics and students, through policy discourse and the media.

### *The Labour of Words*

A demand on academics to be flexible in their work patterns is accompanied by a treatment of language as a commodity, just like any other. It is against this background that I assert that HE policy discourse, even when ignored, is not a thing that stands apart from humans. The buzzwords and the linguistic structures that surround these, are intertwined with how every minute of our labour is perceived and enacted. So, it is worth reflecting on the labour of words themselves. Words do not tire or share the frailties or emotions of humans. Words can be structured and restructured in unlimited ways, with their messages transmitted both on and offline, to reinforce and serve political and economic contexts. Consider, if you will, the performativity of a 'noun'. Connect it with any goal, via a verb, and it will enact that challenge:

> The Legacy Cream Kettle embraces the latest technology
> The Freedom Cordless Iron glides through even stubborn creases

From kettles that 'embrace' the latest technology, to irons that 'glide' through creases, these products take on the characteristics of human labour, via words from advertisements that neglect to mention who is operating the appliance. These technological actors won't go on strike either, or argue that their context is being misunderstood. They will do the task they were created for, whatever the hour of the day. Yet all words remain subject to exploitation across many cultural and political contexts. Those words that are applied to describe the capabilities of a commercial product will also be applied to explain what a strategy, framework, performance management system or student dashboard will achieve in HE. The discourse from the policy may also be adopted in committee papers, emails and reports. It will mingle with other material influences in our academic lives. McPolicy cannot be taken at face value alone, because words can, and are, engineered to serve someone's purpose.

### *Noticing*

Before discussing how the academic labour of students and staff has been debated and examined by others, it is worth considering the importance of the simple act of 'noticing'. By noticing, I mean paying attention (in a world full of technological distractions) (Crawford, 2015) to what forces surround the academic labour of students and staff in HE. Noticing broader connections within global consumer capitalism is a powerful antithesis to McPolicy. It builds a clearer understanding of why some economically-based agendas seem to separate people from their own labour and from each other. It can help in recognising more localised instances of rationality within universities and connecting these with a much larger neoliberal project of rationalisation. Let me borrow a more general example to illustrate the relevance of making cultural and historical connections with how human labour becomes economically rationalised and controlled. Matthew Crawford, at the start of his

2015 book: *The world beyond your head: On becoming an individual in an age of distraction* opens with a simple but powerful observation which he claims strengthened his motivation to write:

> One day when I swiped my bank card to pay for groceries. I watched the screen intently, waiting for it to prompt me to do the next step. During the following seconds, it became clear that some genius had realized that a person in this situation is a captive-audience. During those intervals between swiping my card, confirming the amount, and entering my PIN, I was shown advertisements. The intervals themselves, which I had previously assumed were a mere artifact of the communication technology, now seemed to be something more deliberately calibrated. These baitings now served somebody's interest. Such intrusions are everywhere. (Crawford, 2015: 3)

Asking that simple question can be revealing, *whose interests does this serve*? The same question can be raised in relation to how McPolicy is written. The adverts fed through the checkout screen are a form of cultural text that shape the experience of the person who is paying for their shopping. So, in a sense, these words and images have a job to do. They labour to maintain our attention (in a personal space which would otherwise have been our own). The decision to impose these words and images on people through a screen that they are obliged to use is also a cultural and economic change within capitalism. There used to be a human being where the payment screen now sits. As a customer, you would choose whether to converse with them or not. Now you scan the goods that you selected yourself and you receive uninvited advertisements, through an automated system that you cannot turn off. Someone's rational choices created this system, as such, these intrusions now control the spaces we occupy.

So, it is with HE policy discourse, as a social practice. It is now written in a manner that serves an interest and expressed via the language of new capitalism. However, just like the screen in the store it is here to stay, and we find ourselves using it. Along with other factors, these dominant linguistic constructions describing our human labour have a place in shaping what academics and students become. This is not to assume direct or obvious links between policy statements and academic practice, but rather to indicate where repeated textual patterns have a multitude of effects, as they link with other expectations within the HE sector, in a context of 'academic capitalism' (Rhoades & Slaughter, 2004). Whilst marketised representations of labour can of course be resisted, this is no longer a simple case of avoiding use of the term 'best practice' as an academic. A complex and multi-layered change process has now been effected across decades in HE, leading to new conceptions of the roles of academic staff and students. Flexible terminology has been applied in policy to the functions of learning and teaching, as if these were detached products, rather than intimate, interconnected acts of human labour. Continually reinforced, via a cumulative 'technologisation of discourse' (Fairclough, 1992), these representations have their place in supporting ongoing economic agendas, and consequently the HE sector itself, has changed.

### *The Rational Shaping of Student and Academic Roles*

Two distinct, but also interrelated forms of rationality are now explored, concerning the shaping of academic labour through policy rhetoric. Firstly, I consider how student labour is now shaped by policy and the media. This is linked to a wider consumer culture of self-care, where products and services are now marketed to humans in general, as if they were forever deficient in some way. I then point to how students have come to be positioned in HE policy discourse as customers too, but with vulnerabilities that situate them as weak, rather than empowered, consumers (Brooks, 2017). Whilst terms like 'learning gain' suggest a strong student focus, branding of this kind risks reducing and not increasing student participation. Secondly, as student labour becomes marginalised, through their representation as a group of grumbling customers not gaining enough value for money, the academic labour of staff in turn, becomes cast within an aura of under-performance. Lecturers are unfortunately shaped as deficient in McPolicy, because as Dennis Hayes has pointed out, and my own analysis of policy demonstrates, the discourse repeatedly suggests they are never doing enough to improve 'the student experience' (Hayes, 2017, 2018a).

The deeply intertwined academic labours of teaching and learning then become separated, as academics and students are constructed along different rational routes. An isolated emphasis on 'learning' pushes the practice of 'teaching' into the background (Apperley, 2014). With students constructed as consumers, new policies introducing a Teaching Excellence Framework (TEF) and an Office for Students (OfS) can be legitimised as 'stemming from student demands' (Brooks, 2017: 15). As mentioned in the introduction, a form of populism might then be observed that alienates those academics who cannot sufficiently measure their contributions towards their students' learning gain and future earning power. If the performance of academics cannot be shown to be enhancing 'the student experience', then it may even be assumed they are against it. Efforts to reconnect the labour of students and academics towards shared goals could be aided though, if these rational forms of policy and media discourse are challenged by *both* groups. I suggest that if students and academics nurture an ongoing 'sociological imagination' (Mills, 1959) this aids a step towards collective resistance, because it helps people to notice and contest divisive rhetoric.

I will place this rationalisation of human activity against the historical background to political order and theories of rational domination that precede Ritzer's McDonaldisation theory. This will help to contextualise the emergence of McPolicy as a discourse which alienates people from their own labour. Drawing on Ritzer's famous theory, which has been discussed already in relation to HE more generally (Hayes & Wynyard, 2002; Hayes, 2017), I will then apply McDonaldisation to the specific realms of HE policy discourse. In so doing, I will prepare the ground for a later analysis of policy data, through a corpus-based Critical Discourse Analysis (CDA). This provides many concrete linguistic examples to inform further discussions concerning the part that rational forms of policy discourse play, in shaping HE in the form of the McUniversity. Therefore, to contextualise this debate, I will review how theorists have discussed the rationalising of human productivity and how Ritzer's theory has taken such ideas forward, to acknowledge broader changes across consumer culture. This leads into how academic performance has been measured and audited in UK policy as forever deficient and I will then draw on some accounts of the injuries experienced by academics as a result. Finally, I will question (at a time of HE review in the UK and formation of the OfS) where exactly is the public office that will regulate the quality assurance and enhancement of HE policy discourse?

### *Investing in Our Ever-Diminished Selves with the Aid of Algorithms*

This is a milieu where humans are now, through countless cultural prompts, encouraged to anxiously work on themselves, as if their human bodies were an ongoing, always-deficient, project. Picking up a magazine near to me as I write, I notice a section entitled 'be selfish'. The text below declares that 'self-care is the buzzword for 2018, and just ten minutes each day can keep you energetically topped'. This approach may seem reasonable, but it is accompanied by endless products that underline our deficits as humans, such as shampoos, conditioners and moisturisers that always imply people have 'damaged' hair, or 'ageing' skin. In response to the natural human reactions of anger, sadness and anxiety, people are invited to undertake an 'emotional detox' to minimise the effects on their skin. In seeking solutions for their shortfalls, people now provide endless hours of free labour, ordering and reviewing self-improvement products online.

This is a setting too where, as prosumers, people are at the mercy of algorithmic culture. Algorithms work tirelessly to direct the labour of words and images to influence our choices. Therefore, algorithms can now be thought of as ubiquitous actors in the global economy, as well as in our personal social and material worlds (Jandrić, Knox, Macleod, & Sinclair, 2017). Complex relations are at play between humans and non-humans through algorithmic culture and these have flooded academia to also help drive efficiencies. Where once the remit of teaching and research sat firmly with the academic concerned, there has been a significant shift where software and coding have now pervaded this work. How algorithms intersect with learning, teaching and research is an important area of ongoing research.

As I will come on to discuss, political, economic and social trends much bigger than HE are connected with a movement from bureaucratic and hierarchical forms of the audit of human activity, to self-improvement and self-audit of personal appearance and performance. As academic prosumers, we labour to develop a presence and profile on numerous research indexing sites (such as Research Gate, Google Scholar and Academia.edu), we collect forms of professional accreditation (for example progressing through the levels of the UK Professional Standards Framework) and we complete logs of how our weekly hours are spent using a system that tracks the tasks on which we focus. As such, I draw attention to the way that McDonaldised academic lives are now structured, not so much bureaucratically, but in new forms of flexible self-regulation. How I choose to spend my time as an academic is still my choice, but I have multiple masters to satisfy, and not all of these are human.

Yet HE policy discourse has failed to reflect these significant social changes. As my analysis will show, policy texts are still structured as centralised, McDonaldised directives. Yet at the same time, these statements accredit non-humans with academic work Across a wide range of universities McPolicy continues to offer the same predictability of content as any menu for a burger or a latte. They do not invite the participation of the academic prosumer to disrupt the language in which they are written, either online or offline. Indeed, HE bodies and agencies convene meetings and events marketed with homogenous agendas bearing the same buzzwords. The same speakers appear with regularity, to re-emphasise, borrowing Ritzer's term, a policy of 'nothing'. However, our ignoring of the latest policy directives hardly matters to senior management, or government bodies, if we are already self-directing our labour in new forms of compliance anyway: ones that we may scarcely even notice.

Some years ago, I taught Sociology to undergraduates. On my courses about popular culture, technology and social theory, I would encourage my students, in the spirit of C. Wright Mills (1959), to use their 'sociological imagination'. I would set them tasks to build connections from their daily lives with classical and contemporary theory. Their assessments required them to link classical sociological theory with topics of their choice in popular culture, such as tattoos, music or reality TV, to observe how far Marx or Weber for example, could take them in understanding aspects of modern culture (Matthewman, 2011; Barron, 2013; Hayes, 2015c). Students learned to form their own original observations by noticing how a classical sociological theory might be applied in a contemporary situation. They also learned where it might fall short, and perhaps need input from new contemporary theorists, to aid understanding. Key to this approach is being able to notice and theorise about human labour in capitalist society and to understand how individuals might become ruled by certain powerful abstractions that can alter over time. Students made connections between the design of shopping malls, that encourage consumers to walk in some places, but keep them out of others. They recognised how reality TV and tattoos are cultural communications with layers of meaning in a capitalist context. Another topic my students and I discussed was the self-help industry that has arisen in recent years around people, covering everything from self-medication, exercise and nurture, to personal betterment and wellbeing, as the welfare state has declined.

Furedi refers to a 'deficit' model that underpins this form of therapeutic culture, where the self is portrayed as 'diminished' and individuals require 'the continuous intervention of therapeutic expertise' (Furedi, 2004: 21). Apperley suggests that against this background, 'public policy – including that of education – must be redirected towards shoring up the emotional deficit of the individual' (Apperley, 2014: 734). Apperley develops these arguments to suggest that, as governments implement policies to meet the perceived needs of capital, education policy is written to fit individuals for their roles as 'flexible' and 'adaptable' workers. Citing work by McGee, the destabilising of the self can be seen as a potential goal of the education system itself, with a 'therapeutic turn' in education policy a part of this project (McGee, 2005; Apperley, 2014: 739). An analysis by Brooks (2017) of the ways in which students are constructed in contemporary English HE policy supports these concerns. Whilst students may be assumed to be 'empowered consumers' in today's commercially driven universities, their vulnerability is emphasised in policy by both government and student unions (Brooks, 2017: 1). This then feeds into broader government narratives, legitimising contemporary reforms and excusing apparent failures of previous policies (Brooks, 2017: 1).

### *Choosing to Place Learning in the Context of 'Gain'*
Topics that have always been of interest to students and academics are now given new titles in marketised forms of policy discourse. For example, a

dedicated lecturer with a passion for their profession will no doubt be interested in what their students are 'gaining' as they learn. The quality of personal gain has recently been re-badged in HE policy as something with an independent 'exchange value' (Marx, 1867) that institutions might measure, entitled 'learning gain' (Millward, 2015). Perceptions of 'value' are, though essentially a function of language (Graham, 2001: 764) and language is a systematic resource for exchanging meaning in context (Halliday, 1994). Unfortunately, as language is enacted as discourse, it can then spread powerful and dominant economically-based viewpoints which can appear to be legitimate, yet are also limiting for human practice. What students gain from university is without doubt a topic of importance, so it cannot be argued with. This is partly because students pay so much to study for a degree and they need to secure future employment, often discussed in terms of 'graduate attributes'. However, it is also important for other factors, such as the increased confidence and resilience that participation in HE opens to people throughout life.

A recent national conference on Learning Gain (HEFCE, 2018) and subsequent articles concerning the work undertaken nationally on this topic, indicate that this term has been both adopted in HE, but also critically examined (Kernohan, 2018). Many universities now have policies on, or connected to, learning gain. However, whether this is really a measurable entity is a complex consideration. It could also serve to distract from a more human contact with students, instead placing quantitative measures in this space. It is important to be clear though, from the very outset, that in applying the concept of learning gain, or any other socially constructed label to student learning within education policy, a choice has been made. Someone chose to present learning within the context of 'gain', therefore how 'gain' is understood, and how involved, or not, students were in the creation of this term, ought to be made transparent and fully explained.

It is important to question too, who in fact really gains from this form of terminology? A critically reflexive form of learning may not only concern gain, but also loss. The loss could involve shedding some previous narrow assumptions a student held, that would have hindered their development, in order to take on board new approaches. In shopping for a new outfit, sometimes it is necessary to let go of some existing items. If student fees are simply spent on purchasing a fashionable label, such as learning gain, how much is it tailored to fit them personally, enabling them to display individual flair in augmenting any learning already acquired? I suggest that the term of learning gain frames learning in such a way that the complex dimensions of interactions between students and teachers become marginalised, in a form of 'branding' process.

### Branding Academic Labour

In his book, *Culture of the New Capitalism* (2006), Richard Sennett described a process of 'gold-plating' a basic manufactured item to make it into branded goods. Here, the label has a potency and 'the brand must seem to the consumer more than the thing itself' (Sennett, 2006: 147). Branded labels of fashion designers or luxury models of cars would fit into this approach. I propose that a similar process can be observed in the design of labels ascribed linguistically to academic functions in policy. Terms like learning gain, employability, student engagement and many other buzz phrases now come to reside in the headlines of our university policies and to structure the arguments within. The diverse human labour of students and staff within universities becomes packaged under a linguistic form of gold-plating through these labels. This generates a form of potency or power that enables arguments concerning effectiveness to be more quickly and easily exchanged to support wider economic goals in capitalist society. Students and academics now 'wear' these linguistic labels in university life, whether they like it or not. Unlike the brands we might contemplate purchasing, the designer labels in HE have been chosen for us.

Gold-plating opens up interesting territory however, between the marketing of goods, and the reactions of consumers. Sennett refers to the role of 'participation' that a consumer plays in passing 'from what marketing intends, to why consumers respond'. In the process of buying, a consumer does something to the item purchased that is linked to their perception of self. Referred to by Goffman (1979) as 'half finished frames' these then invite consumer participation. If consumer participation in the act of branding commercial goods is so important, and it is the gold-plating that matters more than the platform (Sennett, 2006: 149), then this is worth some reflection, in a day and age where universities seek to brand their offerings to attract students, and brand staff to meet the demands that this then engineers. Loath though I am to consider students as customers alone, the reality that they pay fees for their time spent at university (at least in the UK) needs to be acknowledged. Yet this purchase of an education is far from a simple transaction. Those universities that structure themselves largely as commercial enterprises, offering branded goods for students to buy, need to be mindful of their returns policy when disputes occur.

The recent cases of Pok Wong and Faiz Siddiqui attest to this. In separate litigation claims against universities they attended, they refer to a 'Mickey Mouse' degree, and 'inadequate teaching', respectively (Polianskay, 2018). So it may not follow that if universities advertise a gold-plated education, it will lead to student satisfaction. If students are treated in the same narrow vein as customers though, a similar complaints procedure may well follow. This rational sentiment was voiced recently by student Robert Liow, when organising a petition during strikes in February 2018 by staff at 64 UK universities over pensions. Students were calling for money back, given that they pay fees and were missing tuition and on the basis that if universities refused refunds they would be profiting from the dispute, as they do not pay lecturers on the strike days:

> I believe education is a public good and not a service to be sold – but we are being treated as consumers. If we are going to be treated as consumers we are going to ask for our money back if we don't get the service we paid for. (Burns, 2018)

The logic may make sense under the circumstances, but it illustrates how the rationality of marketising education can actually change who both students and staff *are*. George Ritzer refers to today's universities as 'cathedrals of consumption', which rather like fast food outlets or supermarkets, can cause people to consume in a largely unthinking kind of way (Ritzer, 2010). Ritzer argues that as 'people wander through a supermarket, they and their kids often pick up products in a random sort of way' (Ritzer, Jandrić, & Hayes, 2018). I suggest that we should consider whether our university branded goods, packaged under the designer labels within McPolicy, risk reducing or eliminating a self-awareness and self-criticism in our students in a similar manner. This would link with the concerns raised about 'therapy culture' (Hayes & Wyngard, 2002).

Furthermore, Ritzer's arguments on product placement are relevant here too. He comments: 'customers are most likely to pick up things found on the endcaps of supermarket rows, and producers pay dearly to place their products in these spots'. Shopping on the endcaps provides people with products that a store wants to sell, but are these always what people want, or need to buy, in terms of an investment that will last? These products are in easy reach, but more valuable goods may require a commitment to invest time, as well as money. So it is with learning in a university. McPolicy may be supporting universities to become cathedrals of consumption, offering only short term 'learning gain' packages, easily picked up from the endcaps. If institutions simply present students with a finished product to consume, they risk losing rich student participation. Students in turn miss an opportunity to develop an education that is embodied in their perception of self. Such an education lasts. Drawing once more on Goffman, we need to provide students with half-finished frames in the form of learning processes to work with (not mass-produced finished products), during their time at university.

### Re-Connecting the Disconnected Labours of Teaching and Learning

A therapeutic turn has now made HE students as much of a focus for the national press as staff. This is to the extent that the increasing measurement of students through learning analytics and learning gain are now strong policy agendas for political point-scoring, along with mental health and wellbeing (Hughes, Panjwani, Tulcidas, & Byrom, 2017). Given that HE is now measured by the numbers of students it attracts and subsequently places into well-paid jobs, an intense pressure on time has led to methods where the learning experiences of students are broken down into discrete modules. Whilst this provides consistency for curriculum design processes, students can come to view their learning processes in rather a fragmented way, within the modular system. Topics are presented chronologically, week-by-week and students simply complete a set of tasks to eventually 'have a degree', rather than to 'be learners' (Molesworth, Nixon, & Scullion, 2009: 277) in relation to their own past, present and future.

In the next chapter, the route through UK policy towards these changes is uncovered in more detail. Practicing personal techniques for noticing is still the focus of this chapter. Noticing is one way for both students and academics to reflexively understand the ways that neoliberal forms of HE encourage individualistic routes of progression and self-improvement, within a wider therapeutic culture. However, as was noted in the introduction to this book, this is a culture that *separates*. It separates humans from their own labour and it separates the labour of teaching from the labour of learning. Thus, as the rhetorical strategies of McPolicy emphasise 'the student experience' and various student-centred approaches in a therapeutic culture, a connection is lost. Universities have moved towards becoming *learning*, rather than *teaching* institutions, but remaining *educational* institutions would help maintain the mutually constitutive nature of learning and teaching (Apperley, 2014: 732).

Much has been written about the route to becoming a teacher or a researcher in HE and indeed developing as a professional (Weller, 2016). Emphasis is placed on the responsibility of those who are teaching and learning to regularly reflect on their progress and development. Such texts are valuable in introducing new academics to models, debates and skills that experts suggest make a difference to academic practice. However, alongside such advice, it is important for HE professionals of all roles and status to be watchful of political, economic and cultural factors. How these play out institutionally and globally can continually shape universities and their activities therein. The contested nature of HE should always invite interrogation of the evidence that supports various claims, particularly those concerning how aspects of academic practice relate to learning and teaching (Lea, 2015).

Noticing is a form of contemplation that I distinguish from therapy culture, which exploits separation and emphasises weakness. I suggest that noticing instead supports making key connections. Treated with critical reflexivity, noticing can help with connecting the elements of our personal and professional experiences and identities that neoliberal HE policy excludes. I interpret noticing as nurturing an ongoing 'sociological imagination' (Mills, 1959) as an academic and as a student. The ideas that Mills expounds are powerful in their simplicity and they are applicable to all of us, not just those training to become Sociologists.

Mills advises that successful scholars do not split their work from the rest of their lives, but treat scholarship as a choice of how to *live*, as well as a choice of career. The idea of *living research* (Hayes, 2015) is my own adaptation of the approach suggested by C. Wright Mills (1959) to students in The Sociological Imagination. In *living* research, an academic commits to a personal, critically reflexive and on-going development as a researcher of the context around them, where all surrounding influences are acknowledged. Later in this book I will return to debate about how an academic might re-draw the boundaries of personal practice and take ownership of what is important in academic life. For now, it is worth examining the theories of rational domination that precede Ritzer's McDonaldisation theory before applying it to McPolicy.

### Rationalising Human Activity

#### *A Justification for Rationality*

Rationality brings positive as well as negative effects. The nature of the labour that academics undertake is being rationalised through government and institutional reform, where multiple complex factors alter academic identities too. It is helpful therefore to reflect on connections across the work of theorists such as Marx, Weber and Ritzer: Marx, because humans define themselves through their tools and their work; Weber, because our human labour has become something that we increasingly invest in; Ritzer, because we are now subject to new forms of augmented rationality leading to presence bleed, through McDonaldisation and prosumer capitalism. The McDonaldisation thesis developed by Ritzer (1993/2018) and building on the work of Weber is critically examined throughout this book, as it provides an accessible route into noticing connections between the rational labour of words in HE policy, and political, economic and cultural changes in wider society.

Therefore, to introduce the concept of 'rationality' itself, I draw briefly on the governance of human labour wrought by modernity, which concerns social and political relations associated with the structural rise of capitalism. Centuries ago Hobbes (1651) provided a model of political order as a product of the rational self-interested actions of individuals (Scott, 2012: 2). A commitment to these liberal 'rights' amongst humans highlighted a role and justification for government. A shift from 'traditional' to 'modern' society, from feudal to capitalist forms of production is understood, through the concept of modernity, to have affected most areas of human life. A commitment to the freedom and capacity of human beings to 'reason' is traced back to The Declaration of the Rights of Man and of the Citizen (1793). As an early policy, this is an application of the rational principles of modernity, in terms of 'individual and collective self-determination and in the expectation of ever-increasing mastery of nature and ever more reasonable interaction between human beings' (Wagner, 2012: 4). In seeing such principles as 'universal', there is an assumption that these are normative claims that will be endorsed by all of humanity. However, from the mid-nineteenth century to the mid-twentieth century, early sociologists undertook major critical inquiries into the dynamics of modernity (Wagner, 2012: 17).

*Critique of Political Economy*
The critique of political economy, as developed by Karl Marx was the first of these. For Karl Marx, the central issue of modernity was the capitalist structure and its domination over human labour. Marx first brought to light the concern that in economies based on market exchange and the forced sale of labour power, relations between human beings would change into relations between things, as they were mediated by commodities. Markets would transform phenomena with a 'use value' for human existence, into commodities where their main emphasis would become the monetary value for which they might be exchanged for profit (Wagner, 2012: 17). Marx described the need to sell human labour under capitalism as an 'activity of alienation' (Marx, 1970: 72). Richard Hall has recently looked at 'academic alienation' in this light to consider what the re-engineering of HE actually means in academic lives that are frequently structured around a 'labour of love' (Hall, 2018).

New forms of organisation of production can unfortunately mean that labour no longer acts as a basis of human self-definition. Instead labour becomes something external to workers and therefore alienated from them. Human labour becomes discussed as if it were a marketable item and people referred to as if they were objects, not subjects, through 'reification' (Lukács, 1971). This can be noticed in policy discourse where buzz phrases, rather than people are said to achieve things, independently of humans. It can be observed in the way that products are marketed with human qualities we might respond to, such as a Marks and Spencer coat, where we might 'love it for less'.

The starting point for a Marxist analysis through political economy concerns people and their social relations in specific historic periods (Scott, 2012: 13). At around 1800 in the UK, the majority of people were based in rural areas and living off the land. As a consequence of the Industrial Revolution, by 1900, large towns and cities had been developed and much of the population had moved to live in overcrowded and unsanitary conditions to work in the new industries. This removed control of the immediate production process from those who had once been direct producers, where workers had once been in charge of tools, machines now took charge of them (Matthewman, 2011: 29).

Previously a craft worker had seen through an entire labour process of an article subjectively, from start to finish. New manufacturing techniques now meant both a shift from subjective to objective technologies and the ability for machines to transcend human limitations (Marx, 1990: 506). For Marx, these objective machines helped to reproduce a social order that benefited the ruling class (those with control over the means of production) by exploiting the working class. More specifically, it was the capitalistic employment of machinery (to make profit for private owners) that maintained worker domination (Sweezy, 1968: 115). Marx saw economic processes as entrenched within the wider social context. In any time period, the fundamental social relations are the relations of production through which humans secure their means to survive. As people secure their basic needs, this ultimately leads to new needs. It is the creation of new needs which necessitates systems of production and distinct divisions of labour to satisfy these (Barron, 2013: 11). New needs take the shape of 'commodities' which are things that satisfy human want and which I discuss below in terms of different forms of 'value' related to human labour. Firstly, I link the role of ideology into this process, where people come to believe they actually have new needs that particular commodities might satisfy. In an HE context this has a parallel with a creation of commodified terminology – such as 'the student experience' and 'learning gain' – these are social constructions, but academics are obliged to respond to them through the powerful discourse of HE policy.

### *Ideology and False Consciousness*

In a Marxist analysis, it is conflict between the owners of the means of production and those with labour to sell, that is a prime mover of social change. As modern capitalist society has developed from previous feudal society, such tensions have simply taken on a new form. This raises the question of why the proletariat (or general populace) at any point in history would tolerate enslavement to a system where the bourgeoisie (ruling class) are controlling production and trade. Marx analysed this in terms of an ideology which creates a 'false consciousness' amongst the proletariat. In *A Contribution to the Critique of Political Economy* (1859) Marx provides an explanation that the propertied class can translate their economic power into control over the political, cultural and social institutions, such as education, law and policy and then use these institutions of the 'superstructure' to naturalise the nature of the economic 'base' of society (Barron, 2013: 13). By this account, it is possible to see how capitalism presents itself as an endlessly perpetuating natural order (Williams, 1977: 93). This situation is maintained materially, to benefit a ruling class, for example through structures such as palaces, schools and prisons (Williams, 1977: 93). It is also a state of affairs that is maintained discursively, through rational forms of political discourse, the narratives that promote particular ideologies about capitalist and neoliberal forms of organisation, within particular periods of history. Capitalism has a central purpose to make profit, but inequalities are legitimised when labourers appear to be working for themselves. This illusion is maintained in a capitalist structure where labour is actually generating wealth for capitalist owners. In neoliberal forms of capitalism, the emphasis on individual forms of gain becomes even more relevant. The language of learning gain fits with such a context, along with changes in how performativity has altered from an external expectation, to embodied forms of academic self-improvement.

### *Labour Power as Use Value, Exchange Value and Surplus Value*

Social relations of production are an important premise in the sociological study of modern capitalist society, discourse about human labour and indeed, related knowledge. In Capital Volume 1, Marx draws attention to a distortion of technological development under capitalism, impelled by the logics of profit and domination (Matthewman, 2011: 38). Marx suggests that to direct rage against instruments of production themselves is misguided however. The way in which machinery is utilised is determined through the relations of our economic system (Marx, 1990: 554–555). Marx drew on the fundamental priority of 'use value' from any technology that helps people to secure their subsistence through productive labour (Scott, 2012: 13).

Marx described people's capacity to work as 'labour-power' (Marx, 1867). Under capitalism people have moved beyond the generation of personal use value from their labour power. They now need to sell their labour to earn money to live, but along with it, they sell also their intimate and personal creative strengths. People sell themselves as 'objects' which generate a 'surplus value', or profit, beyond what they can earn. This surplus value is 'capital', and it is freely available then for those managing it, to re-invest it, and repeat the process. Labour is the source of all value, but a strange metamorphosis takes place through the stages of the capitalist process. Labour power produces products, which, depending on the labour time needed to make these, are ascribed a rate of value. This value bears no relationship to a subjective human material use value, for personal subsistence. This rate of value, known as exchange value, is a quantitative and objective measure that relates simply to the necessary labour time needed to produce an object. It is through this rational and calculating judgment of time and costs that the object becomes 'commodified', and at the same time, the human labour does too. Both assume the qualities that this form of labour (exchange value) has given them, as if they actually contained them in the first place (Matthewman, 2011: 36). It now becomes possible to draw an important analogy. The rational calculations that commodify human engagement with our own labour is expressed as an exchange value said to yield an enhancement (a surplus in the form of profit). This is a process that can be applied to any form of labour. It is one that is worth noticing, as it is mirrored in rational forms of HE policy discourse, in relation to commodification and enhancement of human academic labour.

### Human Reinvestment

For Max Weber, an increasing rationalisation of society, politics (and by implication, related policy) was an issue unique to contemporary society. Weber thus sought to explain the origins of capitalism through cultural factors, as well as economic, in *The Protestant Ethic and the Spirit of Capitalism* (Weber, 1905). This highlighted the necessity of human reinvestment, rather than merely consumption, to further capitalism. Weber suggested religious beliefs through Protestantism provided a motivation for this, the ethic of working hard, to gain an assurance of salvation (Edgar & Sedgwick, 2002: 236). However, what started out as a religious ethic of ordering one's life rationally to serve God became, according to Weber, the 'spirit of capitalism'. Weber discussed the dehumanising effect of bureaucratic decision making (Weber, 1905). This is a rationality that transcends other forms of human action, because it is based on an impersonal application of the systemic principles of modernity. If results are not influenced by personal beliefs, but by administrative structures, these are more 'efficient' in achieving collective political ends to further the greater good, so to speak. This is a form of logic that places emphasis on finding the 'best' means to a given end. Perhaps it is not so surprising then, that 'best practice' remains a popular rhetoric. Rationalisation offers a route into understanding modern capitalist society and its effects on individuals. There can be many benefits from rationalisation that improve our lives. These include scientific advances in healthcare and inventions that save us time, but equally there can be pitfalls. The human motivations for social action that were once ethical, can be replaced by a detached reasoning aimed at greater efficiency. Cultural values once connected with humans are instead abstract notions that aid impartial decision making. This results in alienating colleagues from each other in the HE context, which can hamper, rather than further, institutional goals (Hayes, 2018b). Irrationality follows however, as the very system put in place by people themselves comes to exert dominance over them: 'rational domination suppresses individual freedom and spontaneity, and threatens to enclose society within an iron cage' (Edgar & Sedgwick, 2002: 224).

### McDonaldisation

Taking forward ideas from the Weberian theory of rationalization (1864–1920), Ritzer has since described a continuation and even acceleration of this process, which he termed the 'McDonaldization' of society (Ritzer, 1998: 42; 2015). Ritzer explained that the fast food restaurant represents the components of rationalisation such as efficiency, predictability, quantification and control, through the substitution of non-human for human technology (Ritzer, 1998: 46). Efficiency is concerned with seeking the best means to an end, but equally following these rules can become an end in itself, where those involved lose sight of the real end objectives. In an HE example, the hiring of many temporary lecturers to save money may result in a loss of consistency for student learning. This could hinder the objective of getting students through assessments. In this way, there is scope for efficiency to function in unpredictable ways. Predictability is about ensuring consistency across different settings. Whether hotel chains, high street stores, or the online versions of these, consumers encounter a predictable experience. I argue that in university policy topics, this is mirrored through a predictable pattern of discourse, somewhat consistent with the bureaucratic model described by Weber. The busy daily lives of academics and students as prosumers does not seem to reach into the domain of McPolicy, which appears to require little intervention or human investment.

Quantification refers to a calculability, that in HE might be noticed in measures of academic productivity, across research and teaching. The recent introduction of the Teaching Excellence Framework (TEF) alongside the Research Excellence Framework (REF) and a new framework for Knowledge Exchange with industry (KEF) provide routes to measure academic work. Control concerns the routes to managing uncertainty, which may be applied to workers of many different kinds, as well as consumers. Moving towards automation brings even greater levels of control. Using these categories, Ritzer discussed disparate phenomena, where packaged and assembly line forms of life have sprung up to bring extraordinary forms of change. Making an important distinction, Ritzer referred to rationalisation as the historical process, and rationality as the end result. I therefore describe an ongoing project of rationalisation in HE spanning decades. This is interspersed with a variety of forms of rationality, one of which is the focus of this book: a particular form of HE policy wording I call McPolicy. Whilst the various agendas of rationality expressed through policy discourse occupy our attention with educationalised social issues, such as lifelong learning, these are mere distractions from a much larger progressive form of ongoing rationalisation of HE globally.

Despite the economies that may be achieved through rationalisation, ultimately a form of irrationality emerges (Ritzer, 1998: 54). The division of society from any of its tools and outputs becomes a major obstacle for its future advancement. To apply these arguments in the context of HE, extreme rationality within policy discourse starts to create a restricted context of practice where lecturers and students eventually perceive themselves as less able to innovate. Given the aspirations of a globalised society, which requires individuals to adopt neoliberal values such as entrepreneurism and innovation, this becomes ultimately self- defeating. When I discuss the role of rational policy discourse in relation to Technology Enhanced Learning (TEL), I link the concerns of replacing people with nonhuman technologies with recent works on an impending threat to humanity from technological unemployment (Hyacinth, 2017; Aoun, 2017; Peters, Jandrić, & Hayes, 2018). What may once have appeared to be a rational policy to engage the use of technology to enhance learning can be understood to exercise a form of control that actually restricts creativity. Therefore, there are risks in introducing expensive technologies into universities, if humans are sidelined in the ways in which these are discussed in McPolicy. Without the realisation in policy that technology-based solutions to emergent challenges require human agency to be actioned, investments in technology-enhanced learning systems may not yield the hoped-for solutions (Hayes & Bartholomew, 2015).

Ultimately though, we are faced with a dilemma. Just as a return to home cooking would threaten fast food outlets, in the HE sector, human individuality and diversity present a significant threat to rational forms of policy statements about academic labour. Therefore, academics who are committed to developing creative and critical pedagogies with their students (that are difficult to quantify), may be simply acting on a form of goodwill, that both increases their workload, but remains unacknowledged institutionally, in McDonaldised policy discourse.

## A Deficit Model Ignores Human Strengths

*Constituting Academic Labour in an Audit Culture*
In 1930, John Maynard Keynes suggested we would all be working 30 hours a week by 2030. Our problem would then be *too much* free time (Falkner, 2017). As this is now not much more than a decade away, this prediction is interesting to reflect on. So far, we seem to have witnessed the opposite situation. During the 1980s, working harder, for longer, somehow became desirable, and even demandable too by employers (Falkner, 2017). Focusing now on the second form of rationality discussed at the start of this chapter, in relation to academic staff, I reflect on a culture of audit and performativity that has grown up in HE since the 1980's. This has developed in a wider economic context, where overwork has been interpreted as commitment, rather than inefficiency, with judgments freely made about those who work less hours.

To briefly chart what had gone before this situation in the UK, from the end of the nineteenth century until the early 1970s, effective systems of regulation were through Fordism. This is where mass produced and standardised products were based on large economies of scale in the car manufacturing plants of Henry Ford (Barron, 2013: 74). This led to a 'golden age' of high production and consumption (Cohen & Kennedy, 2013) with significant technological progress and strong productivity growth making workers more, rather than less, valuable (Ford, 2015: 51). Then in the 1970s, productivity fell, as the economy received a major shock from the oil crisis and entered an unprecedented period of high unemployment combined with high inflation and a lower rate of innovation. Whilst the 1980s saw increased innovation, particularly in the information technology sector, this brought different impacts for human labour. For those with the right skill sets, computers increased their value, just as the innovations in the post second world war era had done for nearly everyone (Ford, 2015: 51). For others though, it meant their jobs were destroyed or deskilled, making these workers less valuable, until they were able to retrain (Ford, 2015: 52). The 1990s saw IT innovation accelerate, with the Internet taking off widely in the second half of the decade. Chapter 2 will pick up this story, in relation to changes in HE and policy in the run up to the New Labour government taking office, the Dearing Report (1997) and new forms of discourse that emerged in relation to academic labour. Though I make no assumptions about how policy transfers into HE practice, Ball argues that policy is communicated 'both to achieve material effects and to manufacture support for these effects' (Ball, 2007: 41). The policy statements themselves therefore do not actually need a particularly close alignment to the material effects that follow. The popularity of buzz phrases can be found in the space that they leave for interpretation. If support for a particular performance management of how staff should enhance 'the student experience' is forthcoming, then the policy principles will have served someone's rational choice and judgements.

In this way policy discourse governs and regulates the space around students and academics. Policies reshape understandings as they are introduced (Shore & Wright, 2011). Shore and Wright (2015: 24) describe audit culture as 'the process by which the principles and techniques of accountancy and financial management are applied to the governance of people and organisations' and indeed the related cultural consequences of this. They point to the way that audits and rankings are a form of rationality that often relies on human complicity and agency (Shore & Wright, 2015: 27). As such, the academic prosumer in an audit culture participates in a form of self-measurement and governance of their own labour and performativity. This comes to constitute their very being, leading to new professional subjectivities (Ball, 1997: 263).

### *Questioning the Form That a Discourse of 'Quality' Takes*

As universities have come under pressure to deliver better value for money in recent decades, given the economic context sketched out above, new forms of control have been exercised over academic work. Some of these changes under the auspices of 'quality' have improved clarity for students, but other rational audits have accompanied these. In the absence of a clear definition of what is meant by quality, it can become a signifier for improved performance around almost any academic activity. Thus, Worthington and Hodgson (2005) suggest that quality assurance has both intensified workloads under the guise of improving service provision, but 'in reality it is a subtle form of panoptic power, control and surveillance over the academic labour process' (Worthington & Hodgson, 2005: 96).

Quality assurance in HE encourages the forms of self-regulation and self-development that will best sustain and support the wider global economic society that graduates will enter. The role of policy discourse in investing quality with forms of morality that academics cannot ignore is discussed by Moreley (2003), who points to the terms of 'enhancement', 'development' and improvement' as key examples. However, the power dynamics around quality continue to change to reflect wider political, economic and social struggles. The audit of quality as a managerial exercise has changed to encourage academics instead to organise and evaluate themselves and their performance. These advanced forms of liberal governance produce a performative worker in the form of 'a promiscuous self, an enterprising self, with a passion for excellence' (Ball, 2003: 215).

### The Measure of an Academic Is Always within a Field of Judgement

At the start of the chapter, I drew attention to a culture of self-care, where humans monitor their 'deficiencies'. As prosumers, people purchase and assess products to improve their appearance and performance. Fitbits, Fit-flops, fitness apps, healthcare plans and countless other items are marketed to encourage us all to take responsibility for our health, fitness and well being, augmenting the role of a diminished welfare state. In the realms of consumer culture, there are many products people may buy to meet perceived 'needs' that are generated by advertisers. In HE there has been a movement too, towards academics taking responsibility for the audit of their own performance, via time-consuming monitoring reports, tracking of how their hours are spent and many other self-defining measures. Yet as Ball points out, 'individuals and organizations take ever greater care in the construction and maintenance of fabrications' (Ball, 2003: 215). Recalling Matthew Crawford's checkout screen at the start of this chapter, the infomercials that flashed across the display trapped his attention and disrupted his experience. Academic labour is subject to equally distorting forms of regulation and disruption through 'performativity' processes that we now administer for ourselves. Just as we might collect cash from an ATM, or pay for our groceries through a screen, we assume the role of academic prosumers. We may not always be trapped by a screen displaying adverts, but we are contained within a field of judgement. The challenge we each face is to understand who controls this:

> The performances (of individual subjects or organizations) serve as measures of productivity or output, or displays of 'quality', or 'moments' of promotion or inspection. As such they stand for, encapsulate or represent the worth, quality or value of an individual or organization within a field of judgement. The issue of who controls the field of judgement is crucial. (Ball, 2003: 216)

Ball (2003) discusses such 'performativity' with reference to an article by Boyle from 2001 concerning an increasingly dominant role of numbers and statistics in modern society:

> We take our collective pulse 24 hours a day with the use of statistics. We understand life that way, though somehow the more figures we use, the more the great truths seem to slip through our fingers. Despite all that numerical control, we feel as ignorant of the answers to the big questions as ever. (Boyle, 2001; Ball, 2003: 215)

And so it is with TEF nearly two decades on from 2001. Not only have such observations on university reform and the audit of academic staff stood the test of time we have the recent experience of institutional ranking through TEF to reflect upon, alongside critical analysis of the launch of OfS. The TEF was included in the 2017 Higher Education and Research Act (HERA) in Section 25 which permits the Office for Students (OfS) to:

> Make arrangements for a scheme to give ratings to English higher education providers regarding the quality of, and the standards applied to, higher education that they provide. (UUK, 2017: 5)

At the time of writing the Subject Level TEF is now about to be implemented, causing analysts to reflect on the policy effects of TEF that bear little resemblance to the measures:

> Initial feedback from the sector suggests that the TEF isn't measuring what it originally set out to measure, probably isn't delivering against stated aims, but is influencing institutional culture surrounding teaching and learning, though not always in a positive way. (Harris, 2018)

Ball, however, makes an observation that is significant when examining academic labour:

> The novelty of this epidemic of reform is that it does not simply change what people, as educators, scholars and researchers do, it changes who they are. (Ball, 2003: 215)

This observation is made too by each living, breathing cohort of academics I find myself teaching, as they choose to progress through a self-enrolled Masters in Education (MEd), where they negotiate research projects for personal transformation. They struggle to bring their fragmented identities together as a coherent self, whose role they can critically and reflexively develop, because their academic and personal values are challenged, to their very soul. Ball refers to the 'terrors of performativity' (Ball, 2003: 216), the measures and judgments of academics, that alongside policy technologies of reform have changed the relations between lecturers and students.

In a chapter called 'Introducing the concept of "a corresponding curriculum" to transform academic identity and practice', that I wrote for a book called *Learning-Centred Curriculum Design in Higher Education* (2017), I share details of the contemplative techniques that we explore on the MEd. These are adopted by colleagues alongside the formal curriculum. A co-construction of knowledge acts as a powerful antidote to their lives within daily audit culture. We have learned together on the MEd that curriculum does not need to be seen as a 'product' to deliver to students, and 'engagement' is not always observable or measurable, when is it personally transformative (Hayes, 2017a: 246).

Once more I point to the two streams of rational HE policy discourse that divide, rather than connect academics with their students. If lecturers are now alienated from their own labour and from their colleagues, via many measures of performativity, they are also reminded to constantly enhance 'the student experience' of their customers, rather than a diverse groups of individual learners. As discussed earlier, Dennis Hayes (2017) argues for the importance of 'therapy culture' to be included, as part of an application of the McDonaldisation thesis to HE, to help understand why the 'McExperience' goes unchallenged (Hayes, 2017: 10). There are considerable risks though for both academics and students to make a stance against the formulaic quality approaches that now surround teaching and academic labour. Yet, if they don't, HE moves ever closer towards Ritzer's model of 'nothing', rather than 'something'.

Dennis Hayes suggests a Socratic turn is necessary to argue and critique everything (2017: 112). I would add that if students and academics nurture an ongoing 'sociological imagination' (Mills, 1959) this supports such arguments and aids resistance to divisive rhetoric. It is this form of critical imagination that enables crucial connections to be made across society and not just in HE. Words in consumer culture regularly urge us to 'express ourselves' in fashion statements and choices of how to live. Students can choose any amount of 'signature trainers' or lifestyle-tailored jackets, yet free speech in UK universities has never been more under threat. At the same time as Prevent (2011) is rationally enacted to close down routes for debate in HE, human outrage over trivialities seems to be increasingly played out over social media and in the national press (Furedi, 2016).

Global digital developments have made many more forms of measurement, calculation and judgment possible, in terms of augmented forms of rationality enabled by algorithmic culture. Ritzer has revisited his McDonaldisation thesis to incorporate new forms of efficiency, control etc, that digital society has now normalised. These changes do not stand alone. They are intermingled with the reform of HE. Reform is enacted through McPolicy which contributes to how in turn academic labour is shaped and perceived. Through rational arguments, people are persuaded to buy into the new values of the McUniversity, just as they are persuaded to purchase and rate commodities that promise fabrications for self-improvement.

### *Which Buzz Phrase Is Conducting Your Performance Review?*

The language of HE policy is therefore deeply implicated in maintaining a particular organisation of academic labour. As human attributes become discussed objectively in strategy documents, in terms of exchange value, this risks alienating people from their more tacit understandings (or use values) in terms of what they do. Though academics are increasingly self-monitoring individuals, performativity measures can enter the realms of punishment rather than self-realisation, reflecting a more general Western notion of labour power that has grown up since the Industrial Revolution. Even at a professorial level, ever-increasing performance targets stand in the way of people ever actually 'becoming' (Morrish, 2015). Under the discourse of 'best practice' or enhancing 'the student experience', any amount of measures of an academic might be layered into regular performance development reviews (PDRs). At best, these would be written down in formal criteria that it is actually possible to meet. At worst, the measures of an academic are not communicated clearly to individuals until it is too late to attempt to match these slippery targets. The larger project of rationalisation of HE is therefore furthered via reasoned measures of performativity, played out therefore through PDRs, promotion processes, forms of accreditation, responses to REF and TEF, which are partly constituted by actions and partly by words.

Such measures, that often stand between academic labour and promotion and progression, are precarious for institutions though, as well as for their staff. Eventually these processes risk irrationality. Forever instilling insecurity in a culture where academics are 'always starting over' (Sennett, 1998) disrupts and destroys forms of creativity and innovation that rely on individual and institutional memory. Universities badly need these qualities, if they are to compete in the global and increasingly automated marketplace. HE policy discourse cannot be analysed in isolation from these changes, and whilst I now provide some accounts from academic staff, it is important to keep student labour in mind too, whilst reading these. Students, as mentioned earlier, are being cast as fragile beings, whilst academics are expected to suppress all emotion. There is no space in a punishing academic's schedule to consider the role of their body, alongside their mind. For students, it would seem their emotions and stress on their bodies has become a chief concern, when 'the student experience', rather than their learning processes, is now of paramount concern.

As Morrish (2015) points out (in stark contrast to the political construction of students as 'snowflakes') there are new mechanisms in the PDR discourse that are specifically designed to take academics out of their comfort zones. This discourse wrongly assumes that comfort zones (and indeed panic zones) are experienced equally by all, as it refers to 'stretching objectives' (Morrish, 2015). If 'stretching objectives' are now the actors who direct our PDR processes, then there seems little room for the personal circumstances that statistically will exist in most academics' lives, such as domestic commitments, children and elderly parents, illness, bereavement or indeed the acknowledgement that teaching and research may already be accompanied by high levels of stress for some people (Morrish, 2015). The practice of noticing how McDonaldised HE policy has contributed to the ongoing rationalisation of academic lives, requires a conscious effort to pause and take stock. Walker draws attention to the challenges this presents, when academic work appears to have intensified causing people to internalise the managing of time in a 'demonstrably efficient manner' (Walker, 2009: 284). Referring to academic capitalism (Rhoades & Slaughter, 2004), Walker suggests faculty and students are not only justifying their use of time but 'seeking to outsmart it' (Walker, 2009: 285).

### *Marginalisation of the Human Body in Higher Education*

I am not alone, though in questioning where the sense of pressure and guilt academics carry alongside this race against the clock, is permitted to surface. The literature on academic injury, dubbed by some as 'quit lit' has grown significantly in recent years. It is not easy to measure time spent with an anxious student, or a demoralised staff member, or for these meetings to be logged even, when they are often confidential matters. However, an urge to rationally take the measurements of the varied dimensions of academic labour in HE, in a culture of audit and performativity, has persisted nevertheless.

Furthermore, academic work is perceived as occupying the mind within a cognitive approach, but 'often at the expense of an attention to bodily sensations' (Spelman, 1989: 170) including emotion. As a form of labour, in my experience, academic roles are multifaceted and frequently full of passion and excitement. This observation is based on years of teaching students and in recent years, nurturing the development of other academics. Through our emotions, boundaries are made and unmade, as we respond to both objects and others (Ahmed, 2014: 10). Thus, we shape the nature of our academic work and it shapes us, within mutually constitutive cultural, political and economic contexts. However, many academics now point to how our society's economic organisation under neoliberal forms of capitalism have come to alienate them from their own vocation and indeed their bodies and emotions in HE (Gill, 2010; Morrish, 2015; Hall & Bowles, 2016; Hall, 2018). How these accounts contribute to a form of 'emotional contagion' (Gibbs, 2001) has some relevance, though Ahmed suggests this concerns 'the objects of emotion that circulate' (Ahmed, 2014: 11), rather than the same emotions transferring from one body to another. We cannot be sure of what others are feeling or how they interpret policy. We can, though notice and scrutinise rational forms of discourse and understand these as potential objects of emotion in the lives of staff and students, despite a portrayal of humans in McPolicy, in a highly objective and non-human form.

In considering this further, I turn to analysis by Hall and Bowles (2016) who argue that these changes in HE need to be understood within broader transformations of labour and capital, in particular through the concept of subsumption. They reflect on the extent to which HE is now designed to 'function robotically through the sequencing of managed tasks, as a machine whose primary purpose is its own continuously accelerating navigation through an uncertain world' (Hall & Bowles, 2016: 33). They suggest that HE 'like other knowledge work industries, especially in technology and software development—has exploited and normalised anxiety-driven overwork' (Hall & Bowles, 2016: 33) and that this has become 'a culturally-acceptable self-harming activity' (Turp, 2001). Additionally, the labour functions of students and staff are detached and re-branded in policy discourse and so they become marketable in a similar way to any other consumer goods. How well universities then perform in this market place, is another matter though. Institutions continually restructure their campuses and staff, rebranding people as if they were companies offering new products, but when examined alongside giants like Google, Microsoft and Amazon, they are not well structured to compete in this commercial environment. It is time to consider whether HE now reflects the need, capacities and long term interests of global society (Winn, Hall, & Erskine, 2017). Alongside humans functioning robotically in their roles in HE, institutions also appear to ignore concerns about computers rapidly becoming adept at human capabilities (Ford, 2015). Thus, as rational policy directives continue to 'educationalise' social issues under 'the student experience' and swell the academic workload in the process, we miss a much more fundamental point.

In HE we may be laboring under a false dichotomy now, concerning the nature of academic work and study. A key debate persists concerning whether a university education is either about a practical route into employability, or is a more critical learning pathway for life. Aoun argues that this debate itself is now redundant. Rapid automation means that we can discard the former belief that a 'remunerative career is predicated on the study of an applied practical subject' (Aoun, 2017: 147). He argues that jobs of the future will now rely on the very creativity and higher order skills that rational HE policy discourse has for so long displaced in academics and students.

### *Where Is the Quality Assurance and Enhancement of the McPolicy Process?*

This brings me to the final section of this chapter and indeed a key question posed by this book. Amongst the many quality measures applied to audit academic performance to enhance 'the student experience' in universities, where is the Office for the Scrutiny and Regulation of HE Policy Discourse? Not exactly translatable into a slick acronym, but still a valid proposition, given our regulatory climate, where questions are being asked about the role of OfS in relation to policy. If policy discourse, in conjunction with the media, constructs how students and lecturers are widely perceived, then how do we propose to regulate the quality of the very words that shape (even replace) our academic labour and voice in HE?

Universities have quality procedures that require those who teach to be qualified, to monitor and respond to their student feedback and continue their professional development and reflection. Students are required to complete surveys on the quality of their taught experience. In observing the range of tasks related to the monitoring of teaching that lecturers and students are expected to participate in, I question how and when, in HE institutions and government offices, do we scrutinise and reflect upon the way in which we create and write policy documents? I refer here to the process of conceiving, discussing and writing policies and strategies for HE (rather than examining the textual content within these documents, which I undertake later). Policy writing practices appear to follow a universally accepted format that does not command a lot of scrutiny. Odd though, when other processes such as curriculum design are examined for alignment of outcomes with assessment and inclusion of stakeholders.

As an issue arises which seems to be important for universities to address, a document is constructed by someone with an overview of the topic and some points to be actioned. This may well become a strategy in time, but the colleague(s) who have written it will rarely be identified. Accountability for McPolicy has slipped through the audit net it would seem and a general trend of educationalising any amount of social issues has ensued. The process itself of constructing these texts, who is involved, how these are written and upheld is opaque and seemingly outside of regulatory quality processes. Why? Incongruous indeed, when most other HE practices are routinely and regularly audited.

### *Silent Actors That Silence Humans*

Corbett argues 'we are the university' and 'as citizens of the university, the way forward is to fully engage with the committee structures, with other governance activities at all levels, and with our unions' (Corbett, 2018: 4). Indeed, if the policy and strategy documents discussed in this book are articulated anywhere, then such governance committees would seem a good place to start. Yet despite university committee structures, the strategies I discuss in later chapters concerning student learning do not declare if students or staff were consulted or involved in their construction. In most cases no names are present on the policy document to identify authorship. It is therefore unlikely to be at all clear to teaching staff, let alone students, how university policy and strategy documents actually come into being at all, and who is charged with writing communications which direct what people should do in relation to their practice (Bartholomew & Hayes, 2015: 22). Given an increasing number of short-term and casual staff employed by universities globally, those on fixed contracts may find understanding these processes even harder. Thus, people may simply react to policy, rather than actively seeking routes where they might input into it. Yet, if policy does not bear the accounts of practitioners and students, then what are the elements of human practice that are present to inform it (Bartholomew & Hayes, 2015: 23)?

I will return to these questions, to reflect further on how policy and practice may either feed, or restrict each other. For now, it is worth considering who benefits from authorless strategies that speak, think and act on our behalf, yet apparently require no input or scrutiny from us. Nick Couldry (2010) draws attention to the dangers of losing the capacity as humans, to narrate things about ourselves. Smyth (2017: 30) picks this point up, to argue that such silences are useful in the reform of HE to fit with basic neoliberal principles. These are based on a 'peculiar form of reason that configures all aspects of existence in economic terms' (Brown, 2015: 17).

In the next chapter I proceed to reflect on how neoliberal values have come to define and organise university policy and practices (and therefore academic labour) in what Brown refers to as the 'governmental and social rationality' of *homo oeconomicus* that 'extends market principles to every reach of human life' (Brown, 2011: 118). To avoid ending this chapter on too sober a note though, it is worth reflecting also on a point raised by Davies (2015):

> Maybe the spread of economics into all walks of life is not a sign of capitalism's dominance, but rather of its growing weakness. Maybe the ideal of *homo oeconomicus* needs propping up to the extent that it does, out of a deep political fear of how little humans are really 'economic' by nature. And while it may be little comfort to the English literature student staring down the barrel of £45,000 of debt, maybe universities are the target of so much auditing, tinkering and ranking precisely because they retain a powerful ideal of how they might be otherwise.

CHAPTER 2

# The Words of Labour

### Progressing Rationalisation via Rational Policy Discourse

*Self-Actualisation or Self-Preservation?*

In Chapter 1, perceptions of the intensity of academic labour, through accounts of lived experience by staff, were the key focus. Some authors described personal injury from the pressure of rational metrics and systems, that irrationally separate them from their students and colleagues. With the ascendancy of neoliberalism through the 1980s and 1990s, new forms of public management and discourse have emerged. Strong emphasis on benchmarks, regular audits, greater entrepreneurial skills and measures to enhance output and achieve targets have shifted the focus in HE and also brought changes to academic language. This is a culture that breeds anxiety too, as people attempt to adapt, retrain and repair themselves, in response to changes in the economy, as these are played out in their institutions, via McPolicy. Alongside an apparent culture of flexibility and self-care, quality frameworks for auditing the performance of staff have been developed and applied in HE across recent decades. As academics have responded to rational judgements of isolated aspects of their practice, this begins to alter who they are, and how they relate to their students. So, is academic labour a self-directed project, or a carefully governed endeavour? With the quotation from Davies that ended Chapter 1 in mind, perhaps it is both, and we have quite a struggle on our hands in universities.

### *Banking Our Attributes*

Staff and students now labour upon their own bodies, as if these were ongoing, but ever-deficient projects, in a wider therapeutic culture. This conception fits with a rationale that suggests people need to be flexible and enterprising in uncertain economic times, developing and 'banking' skills, attributes and impact. Whilst this is a different kind of 'banking' to Freire's concept of education, it is still potentially an instrument of oppression. In Freire's banking concept, it is presupposed that the instructor or teacher owns the knowledge and 'deposits' it into passive students who attend the class (Freire, 1972). However, to deposit only one version of 'how things are' negates education and knowledge as processes of inquiry and critique (Freire, 1972: 72). Whilst people may now be actively depositing skills for themselves, rather than passively absorbing knowledge bestowed by a teacher, this new 'enterprising self' does not seem to be any more empowered.

Though academics are increasingly self-monitoring individuals, performativity measures can enter the realms of punishment rather than self-realisation. As mentioned earlier, this reflects a more general Western notion of labour power, that has grown up since the Industrial Revolution. I will return to this point in Chapter 6, in relation to the buzz phrase of 'employability' and predictions many authors are now making, concerning fundamental changes to work through the Fourth Industrial Revolution. Employability emerged as a central concept of so-called 'Third Way' policies, part of the New Labour approach to economic and social policy in the UK (1997–2005). Alongside employability, the rational ideas that education should serve the interests of the economy, and that learning should be lifelong, were both at the heart of the Dearing Report in 1997.

So, this chapter considers how these, and other related concepts, have influenced the way that academic labour appears to be rationalised in McPolicy. Firstly, I discuss some different perspectives on the general purposes of policy. I then ask whether humans manage the words of policy, or whether these words are now managing us. These are important considerations, given the New Labour policy background that encouraged a wide belief in an autonomous and enterprising self. Yet the written HE policy texts which I scrutinised, appear to suggest quite the opposite! So, I question what kind of efficiency has been assigned to the words of policy that communicate my labour on my behalf and I ask why this situation seems to be tolerated, as if this is 'just how things are'. Yet what is omitted from policy texts is, in a sense, as problematic as what is said, because it leaves room for flexible interpretations. As I focus on the lead up to the New Labour government taking office in the UK in 1997, I consider what neoliberalism has 'taught' us in HE. I make some distinctions between the interconnected labels of neoliberalism, globalisation and McDonaldisation and I ask: *when did so many societal challenges become university responsibilities?* These issues have taken the form of a range of strategies across HE that are now shaped to address these.

### *Is Policy a Process or a Means to Solve Problems?*

Policy is often linked to a notion of 'a problem' and the strategies that are needed to solve it (Harman, 1984). This would certainly appear to be the case with the university strategies examined in the coming chapters. Yet taken to extremes, a rational 'problem-solving' approach towards policy may yield positivist ideals and objective world views (Shulock, 1999). Whilst problem solving is important, as a way to recognise issues, it can tend firstly, towards a static model in policy, where a document provides a guide for all principles, actions and routines and a belief that, when strictly followed, this will bring about desired change (Trowler, 1998). In applying such principles to the fluid and dynamic field of education this is bound to encounter some difficulties, particularly if the document itself sits apart from the processes that actually do effect institutional change.

Secondly a problem-solving approach neglects the 'socio-cultural dynamism of policy processes' (Nudzor, 2009: 503). These are not constituted in isolation but comprised through many factors, for example, institutional and global change, the personal context around individuals and commentary in the media. Yet to consider on the other hand a 'process-based' definition of policy, which focuses on what policy actors do in response to policy formulation, articulation and interpretation may, in analysing the micro, risk forgetting 'it is the macro level actors who often set the ground rules for negotiations involved in the policy process' (Nudzor, 2009: 508). Therefore, understanding how policy is shaped more broadly, globally even, within the confines of dominant discourse about economic agendas is also needed. Nudzor concludes that policy is neither a problem-solving tool, nor a process, but both (Nudzor, 2009), citing Olssen et al. (2004) who describe policy as fundamentally an exercise of power and language used to legitimate the process (Olssen, Codd, & O'Neill, 2004).

### *Do We Manage the Words of Policy, or Do These Words Manage Us?*

As noted before, policy and strategies are communicated 'both to achieve material effects and to manufacture support for these effects' (Ball, 2007: 41). Therefore, this chapter explores a form of rhetoric that emerged from the policy making of the New Labour government since 1997. The policy discourse of New Labour is considered worthy of focus as a particular form of rationality, within the longer project of rationalisation of HE. I would like to think that Chapter 1 opened a context around HE policy discourse to show that these texts require attention. Whilst what I point out in this book concerning nominalisation is nothing new, my hope is to raise awareness that, at a time when HE is under more media scrutiny than ever before, policy and strategy documents themselves cannot sit outside of any proposed reforms. I make no direct links between written policy and academic practice, but still these communications define, not only what can be said and thought about policy problems, but also who can speak, where, when and with what authority (Ball, 1993).

As chapters 3–6 will show, it is very often non-human entities who are said to be acting, thinking and speaking for people, in the many cross-institutional documents I analysed. Although these are policy documents produced in the

UK, they shine a light on a continuity of a global language of 'new capitalism' (Fairclough, 2003; Simpson & Mayr, 2010: 38), as it continues to be constructed from within universities. Discussed sometimes as the language of the free market, because of the adoption in European HE of a corporate-business discourse, this results in the academy being discussed 'in terms of a 'knowledge industry' or 'revenue generator', where intellectual resources are 'leveraged', and knowledge is a 'commodity' (Webster, 2003: 85). Thus, knowledge and also language, become considered as simply products to be 'managed'. Some obvious examples are the straplines and marketing slogans that universities use on their websites and in their brochures. Less obvious elements are the statements that reside within strategies, where human labour processes are discussed as if these were products to be managed. I suggest these move us closer towards the question of whether we are managing the words of McPolicy, or they are managing us.

### *A Partial View of the Production and Consumption of Learning*

In the substitution of non-human technology for human labour, workers may experience only small detached elements of a whole *production* process. In terms of consumption, people may eat fast food, but not experience the process of preparation and cooking of this food, which is out of their sight. In the McUniversity, there are analogies to these examples, in the way that a lecturer may teach a class or a course in the modular system, but not see or understand how the other parts of a taught programme come together. Equally, a student has their semester broken down into weekly sessions and chunks that make it hard to get a sense of the whole degree they are enrolled on. As we rationally separate and package learning and teaching in HE in order to be efficient, McPolicy is written describing the way in which these detached processes lead to success for institutions. Separation seems to be a constant within neoliberal organisations. Whether it takes the form of disconnected learning materials, or disconnected people, coherence and a sense of community seem to be scarce (Hayes, 2018b).

Just as automation of a payment process means that a machine now 'discusses' my bank balance, payment and withdrawal of cash with me, a similar rational and impersonal process is enacted, when a university strategy handles my labour of teaching on my behalf. The labour of a cashier has been reassigned to a machine in the first example. The machine defines what can be said and asked in relation to my bank account. I am restricted to what the words on the screen will permit me to do. There is no space for conversation that might deviate from the parameters that have been set through the software, that route has been removed. In the case of the university strategy, my labour has been reassigned to textual constructions and buzz phrases that now communicate what I, and my students, do. Like the cashier who once was, I am no longer a participant in these transactions, simply an onlooker. The cashier was replaced by a machine, with the goal of efficiency in mind. So, what kind of efficiency has been assigned to the words that communicate my academic labour, on my behalf, in McPolicy?

### 'It Is What it Is'

In reply to this question, a form of sham freedom could be said to be surrounding peoples' sense of personal autonomy within neoliberal universities, where rationality based on market values goes largely unquestioned, as if this is 'just how things are'. For example, how many times are conversations halted by the comment: 'it is what it is'. In a sense, the origin of this popular phrase doesn't matter. It signifies (as it is sometimes voiced alongside a shrug of resignation) acceptance of a situation that people believe they cannot change. However, Couldry suggests that the notion of freedom underlying neoliberalism is abstracted from the social processes that underpin 'voice'. He argues that 'neoliberal rationality is reinforced not just by explicit discourse but through the multiple ways in which that discourse and its workings get *embedded* in daily life and social organization' (Couldry, 2010: 12). Therefore, as these norms and values, such as the value of entrepreneurial 'freedom' are internalised by groups and institutions they become 'culture'. Over time, neoliberalism crowds out other rationalities and ways of organising labour. As neoliberal rationality becomes institutionalised culture, it shapes the *organisation of space*. This means that some types of spaces become prioritised and others fall out of use. One example is that few universities can these days boast staff common rooms, yet colleagues can still be heard reminiscing about the days when they had both space (and time) to meet with each other to collaborate (Hayes, 2018b). The human voices related to these shared spaces that once existed just stop being heard. Therefore, neoliberalism 'literally changes where we can and cannot speak and be heard' (Couldry, 2010: 12).

### *Space for Interpretation*

The 'embedding' of neoliberal rationality that Couldry refers to can be clearly observed in the textual examples to come. Frequently references are made in university strategies to the idea that 'technology enhanced learning', 'student engagement' and 'employability' are entities that can be 'embedded'. Some key features of discourses in new capitalism are their decontextualised and universalised nature that suggest all of the changes of managerial politics are inevitable in a global economy. This is a language full of 'empty and ideologically contested buzzwords' (Simpson & Mayr, 2010: 38). Webster argues that adoption of this discourse within the academy 'has important implications for the future of European higher education' (Webster, 2003: 85).

Therefore, I will now reflect on how such discourse has developed within UK universities over the last two decades, as a part of contemporary transformations of capitalism. What is omitted is, in a sense, as problematic as what is said, because it leaves room for flexible interpretations of the meaning of 'student engagement' or 'employability'. A fait accompli has even been embedded in phrases like 'technology enhanced learning', expressing the assumption that learning will *always* be enhanced by technology (Hayes & Jandrić, 2014; Bayne, 2014). So, whilst these discourses of 'new public management' can easily be ignored, there is still the question of what is being replaced by buzz phrases, such as, for example, a 'traditional professional culture of open intellectual enquiry and debate' (Olssen & Peters, 2005: 313).

### *Rationalisation of Academic Labour Encounters a 'Post Truth' Era*

Rationalisation is understood as an ongoing historical process that meets with points of rationality in history that might be examined in more detail in relation to theory. As previously discussed, for the purposes of this book, I have drawn on theory from Marx to shed light on how humans define themselves through their tools and the process of creating something from start to finish. I have pointed to Weber's theory regarding a detached reasoning within capitalism, devoid of cultural values, that seeks the 'best' route towards efficiency. Ritzer's arguments then pick up Weber's standpoint to demonstrate how new cultural norms emerge, as rationality is enacted through *efficiency, predictability, quantification* and *control.*

The interconnected ideas from these theorists are helpful in appreciating both historical forms of rationalisation, that have led into our present context, and a rationality shaping academic labour currently, through HE McPolicy. McPolicy though does not sit outside of wider cultural change, which is why McDonaldisation offers a helpful contemporary overview, through which patterns of rationality can be noticed, as they gain a more universal status. In HE discourse, it is important to consider the cumulative effects, not only from the words of McPolicy, but those of the media and government. These are discourses that are dialectically related to populist arguments about value for money in HE, as discussed in the Introduction. Furthermore, on a global basis, increased debate on the issue of 'post truth' led recently to Oxford Dictionaries declaring this phrase to be its international word of the year (Flood, 2016). If what shapes public opinion about the value of HE is based on emotional appeals and unfounded universal judgments discussed as 'truths', then these need closer scrutiny. The rational language of HE policy is deeply implicated in maintaining understandings of how academic labour is organised. As later analysis demonstrates, the lived reality of students and staff can be packaged into 'post truth' in policy, just as easily as it can be presented in a newspaper article.

In recent decades, numerous social problems, have become educationalised and portrayed in HE policy, as if these were issues to be solved by universities. This has coincided with a perceived demise of the welfare state and a recognition of the global economic importance of HE. Connecting a country's economic viability with the production of skills through HE to achieve this, has led to an auditing and accounting of academic performance to achieve targets, but also a rhetoric that supports the flexible self improvement ideals discussed above.

### Reflecting on What Neoliberalism Has Taught Us

#### *New Habits*

It is worth reflecting on what the pervasive culture of neoliberalism has actually been 'teaching' us as practitioners in HE in recent decades. As a society, it would seem that we have learned new habits, brought to us, for example, by McDonalds, Starbucks and Amazon. These companies have changed how we structure our days around fast food, coffee and shopping. This is not necessarily pessimistic, after all we are not all bound to participate in these commercial enterprises. We can choose to sit in a different environment and take time over a meal if we wish, or not shop online, but browse instead in physical stores. However, when the same logic of McDonaldisation brings neoliberal values to bear on HE, we can simply adjust, or we can instead resist, as Dennis Hayes points out:

> There is a lesson for lecturers here. McDonaldization only gathers momentum when what is on offer is discredited or not defended. With good reason, lecturers bemoan poor pay and conditions but have put little effort into defending the education and training at the heart of the curriculum. (Hayes, 2005)

As the economic importance of HE in a global economy has been recognised, and structures have changed around academic labour, it has sometimes been easier to change with them, and simply bemoan these changes, whilst participating in them. This point links back to the case for 'noticing', discussed in the previous chapter, and also whether noticing is enough motivation to effect change. People may resist and subvert discourse, using dominant narratives strategically, without necessarily believing in them (Trowler, 2001). So, whilst is true that the ascendancy of neoliberalism and associated discourse during the 1980s and 1990s has produced 'a fundamental shift in the way universities and other institutions of higher education have defined and justified their institutional existence' (Olssen & Peters, 2005: 313), the related discourse may still be negotiated, displaced and resisted. Or people may simply acquiesce.

Complex processes surround academic labour and the discourse that shapes it. Many authors have discussed a strong institutional stress on performativity, evidenced by an increasing emphasis on measured outputs, strategic planning, performance indicators, quality assurance measures and academic audits (Slaughter & Leslie, 1997; Shore & Wright, 1999; Ball, 2003; Olssen & Peters, 2005). University strategy discourse does though provide a window at least, on the rational arguments that support these measures. It is also a means to notice when these move towards irrationality.

### *Neoliberalism, Globalisation and McDonaldisation*

Whilst links can be made between the overlapping labels of Neoliberalism, Globalisation and McDonaldisation, there are important distinctions to be made. Globalisation refers to the broad changes in technology and science that have brought many parts of the world closer together as they have influenced how we communicate and treat information and how we travel. Ritzer suggests that McDonaldisation is an aspect of the larger process of globalisation, which might be partially understood as:

> A transplanetary process or set of processes involving increasing liquidity and the growing multidirectional flows of people, objects, places and information as well as the structures they encounter and create that are barriers to, or expedite those flows. (Ritzer, 2015: 186; O'Byrne & Hensby, 2011)

McDonaldisation has come to be seen as at least a part of these global changes. However, globalisation is more complex than this, with multiple often conflicting outcomes (Ritzer, 2015: 188). Olssen and Peters argue that neoliberalism is independent of the forms of globalisation described above. They suggest 'the advent of neoliberalism would not have prevented this process from occurring, and thus, it must not be confused with globalization as such' (Olssen & Peters, 2005: 314):

> Neoliberalism is a specific economic discourse or philosophy which has become dominant and effective in world economic relations as a consequence of super-power sponsorship. (Olssen & Peters, 2005: 314)

At the economic level, neoliberalism is linked to globalisation, but: 'it is a particular element of globalization, in that it constitutes the form through which domestic and global economic relations are structured' (Olssen & Peters, 2005: 314). It should therefore be understood as 'a politically imposed discourse, which is to say that it constitutes the hegemonic discourse of western nation states' (Olssen & Peters, 2005: 314). As mentioned earlier, some authors discuss an aspect of neoliberalism as the global language of 'new capitalism' (Fairclough, 2003; Simpson & Mayr, 2010: 38). This term is helpful in the word 'new' because it demonstrates that significant changes have taken place in our language, in order to accommodate new corporate policies within UK HE. These have been accompanied by much physical expansion of universities too, since the New Labour government declared it the right of those who have potential, to go to university. However, at the same time, important goals of social justice have been shaped by priorities linked to the needs of big business. Major reconstruction in HE has meant scholarly institutions have been changed into profit centres in which universities, departments and individual academics are encouraged to compete with each other (Callinicos, 2006) as enterprising individuals. So, this is an entrepreneurial 'freedom' which becomes internalised and so comes to constitute our 'culture'. Alternative values are hushed along with other ways of organising academic labour (Couldry, 2010: 12).

### *New Labour and the 'Enterprising Self'*

Returning then to where this book began, with the buzz phrases that first caught my attention during my early years in HE, I will briefly reflect on the run up to the Dearing Report of the National Committee of Inquiry into Higher Education (1997) and to Labour's 'Third Way discourse' (Fairclough, 2000). Apperley argues that the ambition of the Dearing inquiry committee to construct a learning society characterised by lifelong learning, has had its part in bringing about the therapeutic turn in HE in the UK, by exhorting people to embark upon a lifetime of labouring upon the self. Costea, Crump, and Amiridis (2007) refer to *therapeutic habitus* which they describe as a new mechanism of governance which makes employees the focus of a quasi-therapeutic encounter. This approach to management draws on the central themes which fuel modernity itself:

> The centrality of the self, expressive individualism framed in endless horizons of self-affirmation, the centrality of ordinary life as the ultimate source of meaning and reality of the self, and the cultural centrality of the 'economy'. (Costea, Crump, & Amiridis, 2007: 16)

Therefore, the two broad agendas for education of, on the one hand creating the lifelong learning society, and on the other constructing the post-welfare state, are closely interrelated. Education now plays a significant role in an integrated social policy aimed at supporting the economy and reducing the welfare burden on the government (Mulderrig, 2003).

In the late 1990s New Labour were able to take forward neoliberal arguments about enterprise and competition from the previous Thatcher-Major years (1979–1997) of authoritative government and development of a free economy. The Thatcher years had sought to restore wealth to the UK through conviction politics that a free enterprise economy is the only secure basis for individual freedom. During eighteen years of the Conservative Party in office many changes in the mode of regulation of public and private sectors had taken place. Political discourse had been gradually re-shaped to implicate ordinary people within nationalistic agendas. These included anti-union, pro-family, pro-property ownership in which articulation of such political elements led to novel restructurings of Thatcherite discourse (Fairclough, 1989: 177). This shaping of new 'professional' subjectivities (Ball, 1997: 263), for example, where new 'self-appraising individuals' were urged to notice where they might improve their performativity, was developed further under Tony Blair, as 'new' Labour took office.

Blair then propagated the view that Britain should be 'repackaged' as a society with deep roots in history and culture but that was also economically dynamic and forward thinking (McCormick, 2012: 28). A strong emphasis on the role of education in support of economic competitiveness meant people needed to commit themselves passionately to continuous learning and use of information technology to deliver the right skills. This may however be ultimately 'self-defeating'. Stephen Ball suggests these goals are based on an 'impoverished view of learning' that in the long run will simply fail to meet the needs of a 'high skills' economy (Ball, 1999). As such, Ball cites three 'untouched and unquestioned' principles that were carried across from Conservative to New Labour policy and from 2008, have remained in the coalition and subsequent government agendas:

1. Choice and competition. The commodification and consumerisation of education.
2. Autonomy and performativity. Managerialisation/commercialisation of education.
3. Centralisation and prescription. The imposition of centrally determined methods. (Ball, 1999)

Though emphasis on this mix of hierarchical and neoliberal values varies at different points in time, the general 'make over' of education itself into a commodity form is a continuous theme which is 'framed and reframed' (Ball, 1999). Competing and contradictory discourses are 'stitched together' in the new policies (Taylor & Rizvi, 1997: 9). Though contested through different theories, this is often described as a 'new capitalist' development of discourse (Fairclough, 2001, 2004; Sennett, 2006).

Whilst New Labour retained some key elements of the Thatcher programme, these were also combined with much more material claims than had previously been stated: 'claims about the importance of information and communication technologies, the information economy, the culture industries, the knowledge base, and human capital, as the crucial foundations for competitiveness, in an irreversibly globalizing economy' (Jessop, 2000). This perspective on new global communications has important implications for how technologies (the topic of Chapter 4) are now perceived, both in broader society, and within universities to support learning. Neil Selwyn refers to a sustained agenda of policy-making throughout the 1998 to 2007 period of New Labour government, where education was 'just one of many segments of the public sector which were subject to so-called 'information age' policymaking' (Selwyn, 2008: 702). This included 'e-government' services, health, welfare, and social security, to name just a few. Policy makers sought to transform (or modernise) existing services through perceived positive effects from the use of technology. Selwyn suggests from the outset that the economic, rather than pedagogic significance of new technologies, was driving its implementation in education. The constraining nature of our current experience of 'educational technology' has resulted from the New Labour ICT agenda (Selwyn, 2008: 708). If this is the case, revealing what New Labour policy discourse has structured and transferred into university policy discourse is key to questioning how it might be otherwise.

Stephen Ball has argued that the 'policy continuities' we have witnessed in the UK in recent decades between the Conservatives and Labour should also be viewed as a manifestation of 'global policy paradigms' (Ball, 1999). Peters suggests that a profound shift away from the welfare state to a cultural restructuring based upon the neoliberal model of the 'entrepreneurial self' moved people from a 'culture of dependency' to one of 'self-reliance' (Peters, 2001). With the promotion of a new relationship between government and knowledge, 'government at a distance' could be developed, to include new forms of social accounting embodying an actuarial rationality (Peters, 2001: 69).

### Stakeholder Society

Mulderrig (2003) points out that in Blair's 'stakeholder society', emphasis was placed on individual endeavour and responsibility, in which the government was cast as an 'enabler' rather than a guarantor of citizens' rights. Economic metaphors of 'stakeholding' and 'investment' illustrate the instrumental, exchange-value logic that underpinned the mechanisms to achieve New Labour's goal of social justice (Mulderrig, 2003: 103). These observations are upheld in the examples of strategy discourse. What had once been 'education policy' now became part of a wider social policy aimed at creating the 'learning society', in which education and training become subsumed under 'learning' which is 'lifelong'. Though New Labour took office over twenty years ago, the changes described here underpin an educationalising of social agendas into HE that has continued, as discussed below. As Mulderrig points out, an 'ongoing accumulation, credentialising and upgrading of skills' was constructed as one of the key objectives for both students and staff in New Labour education policy, supporting the progressive development of the 'knowledge economy' and its managerial infrastructure (Mulderrig, 2003: 103).

Mulderrig argues that textual representations of educational roles and relations in policy discourse that link success (and by implication, failure) with individual commitment and aspirations, potentially act as a powerful form of social control. This takes place through self-regulation in which the individual is responsible for and invests, through learning, in his or her own success. The coercive force comes not from the government, which is constructed as a facilitator, but from the implicit laws of the market (Mulderrig, 2003: 104). Furthermore, this situation can be discussed as a 'response' to instability in the labour market and the demands of the economy for a highly skilled, motivated and adaptive learning society. However, rather than being a 'response' to the globalised economic system, Mulderrig argues that this learning policy constitutes a key ideological mechanism in actively constructing and legitimising globalisation and these human roles within it (Mulderrig, 2003: 104).

### When Did So Many Societal Challenges become University Responsibilities?

With this background in mind it becomes easier to see how a series of societal challenges, such as widening participation, lifelong learning, sustainability and mental health, have all found their way into HE policies, comprised of rational arguments. These topics are important demographically and ethically, as well as economically, for universities. Considerable staff labour supports students from diverse backgrounds, to encourage their participation, retention and success in completion (Pope, Ladwa, & Hayes, 2017). I mentioned at the opening of this book, my personal connections with such agendas, as both a first generation university student of the 1980s, then a returner to HE in the late 1990s.

However, complex societal issues are often referred to in HE policy statements in rational arguments, as if these challenges were easily solved. Furthermore, the newspaper and media accounts that report on issues such as student mental health give the impression that this is a new problem. At the time of writing, a 'best practice' charter is being drawn up by the OfS in the UK, in collaboration with charitable bodies and student unions. Positive steps towards supporting students should however not give the impression that this is work that is only just beginning. If it does, then the pastoral work that has always been a part of academic labour is dismissed as if it never existed. It is the insistence that social agendas are easily solved by more education that has led to increased support needs for students. Therefore, the mental health and wellbeing of students cannot be isolated from government initiatives.

The idea that more education can resolve the major problems of our times, particularly the impending challenge of technological unemployment, is a political construction which has largely failed to deliver its promise (Peters, Jandrić, & Hayes, 2018). Watts suggests that the framing of social problems as educational problems simply moves these into a form of 'simulacrum' (Watts, 2008). In other words, by writing these into HE policies, this transports social challenges into the model of something that does not exist, 'making it impossible to return to the source to interrogate an event, a character, a discourse about its degree of original reality' (Baudrillard, 1993). Watts asks therefore 'if higher education is the answer, what is the question?', observing that whilst there has been a significant increase in the number of young people entering university in the last 20 years, participation rates of those from lower socio-economic groups remain low (Watts, 2008: 142). Furthermore, the number of poor students who drop out of university before finishing their degree is now at its highest for five years (Pope, Ladwa, & Hayes, 2017).

Given that the drive to widen participation is framed by economic and social justice issues, there is firstly the argument that a knowledge-based economy requires greater numbers of graduates (Watts, 2008). Regarding social justice, this concerns making available the opportunities that HE offers to all those who have the potential to benefit from them, regardless of their background. Elsewhere I have argued that universities now have so strong a student focus that staff who are also students may get overlooked (Hayes, 2018b). Watts argues that 'the rhetoric has replaced the reason for it and taken on a life of its own so that as long as something is being seen to be done it does not matter what is actually done' (Watts, 2008: 142).

Picking up on the notion from Watts that social challenges are being placed into a model of something that does not exist, my analysis will pinpoint some particular irrationalities emerging from what appear to be rational HE policies. To be clear, this is in no way intended to detract from the importance of tackling societal injustice, or the role that HE might play in this. Instead I question why HE policy is constructed in its current form, when faced with perhaps the biggest societal challenge we have seen in centuries. This is the prospect of technological unemployment due to automation and the global crisis that could follow. As authors are calling for an urgency to develop the creative capacity and social 'presence' of human beings (Aoun, 2017), it would seem that HE policy has already, rationally and efficiently, written humans out.

CHAPTER 3

# The Labour and Delivery of Buzz Phrases

## Packaged Consumption

### *Constructing the 'Iron Cage' of 'the Student Experience'*

Giving birth to buzz phrases, as the title of this chapter suggests, involves the human labour of writing, as well as the chosen means for textual delivery. I suspect many colleagues to whom the task of writing policy falls, are not aware that, in drawing on statements from existing university strategies to inform what they write, they are simply expanding the issues that this book raises. So, whilst it is the means of delivery (in form of many university policy texts) that have provided the main data for my analysis, I want to draw attention also, to a need to reform the human practices of actually writing policy. This is because the repetition of buzz phrases within nominalised arguments is not the only option open to us all. It is simply a convenient one. Indeed, it is the apparent lack of scrutiny of these texts that suggests a general detachment from written policy may have developed across universities. If this is the case, it is dangerous to assume that what is silently written into a policy text won't at some point have a material effect in our working lives.

In Chapters 1 and 2, the neoliberal context around academic labour, and an educationalisation of social issues channelled into university policy, was explored. Given that university students have been increasingly defined as 'customers' by the UK government, since the introduction of tuition fees (Dearing, 1997; Browne, 2010), ways to demonstrate 'value for money' have moved high up the policy agenda (Dickinson, 2018). These developments have tended to emphasise the role of a degree as a consumer 'product', purchased to secure future employment (Peters, Jandrić, & Hayes, 2018), rather than as an experiential learning 'process' that continues well beyond student life (Hayes, 2015: 130). With these considerations in mind, over the next few chapters I will focus firstly, on how certain buzz phrases might support these neoliberal ideologies, in terms of an emphasis on 'exchange value' (Marx, 1867) from these concepts. Secondly, I will consider what mechanisms for this are revealed, by examining closely, the structure of the discourse. Thirdly, I will explain how these observations are relevant to a McDonaldisation of HE policy, that I have called McPolicy. So following some introductory sections, in this chapter, I will explain in some detail the approach I took to collect and analyse 'student experience' strategy texts, thus setting up the framework too, for Chapters 4–6, which each closely examines a particular phrase in context. In labelling the university strategies I collected as McPolicy, I propose that these texts provide valuable sources through which to examine how academic labour is perceived, in the contemporary McUniversity.

Just as a reminder, this is not a book about linguistics as such. It is a wider commentary on the culture we appear to be shaping in UK universities, observed through the lens of HE policy discourse. The linguistic analysis that I have undertaken is just one way to move beyond theorising alone, with regard to the effects of marketisation of universities, in shaping how academic labour comes to be understood. After initially sketching out my understanding of McPolicy below, I will then introduce the first buzz phrase chosen for close scrutiny: 'the student experience'. Buzz phrases are socially constructed entities, therefore I will comment on what this means in relation to the language in use, in the form of discourse. This is a strong rhetoric that emphasises 'the student experience' as a package, including leisure, well-being, future employment and other 'extras'. On the one hand, this could be perceived to be a positive step, where all elements of student life are acknowledged and a student takes an active, autonomous part in their personal process of experiential learning. Or alternatively, policy discourse concerning 'the student experience' could be critiqued as a concept that now transcends the notion of a degree as a utilitarian product. Instead, a more disturbing impression is generated, where universities are now delivering a packaged experience of consumption itself, to students (Argenton, 2015: 921). If a rationalised experience is constructed on behalf of students, then universities as 'cathedrals of consumption' (Ritzer, 2010) align themselves with any other provider of consumer experiences, where the thinking has all been taken care of. In such a discourse, students are not necessarily conceptualised as empowered consumers either (Brooks, 2017) but trapped instead within an 'iron cage', even before they set foot in the workplace.

### *McPolicy: The McDonaldisation of HE Policy*

A fast food restaurant is not only about food. The experience of eating takes place within a context that carries certain social and economic values. In the same way, HE policy discourse is not only about written words. It also concerns the surrounding social and economic context in which policy texts for universities are developed and consumed, and indeed how this discourse is experienced by students and staff. Around the concept of 'fast food' there are expectations from both the producers and consumers that are reinforced in all sorts of ways. Whilst a large number of people can participate in fast food restaurants (just as they can in HE, if they are eligible), these people are expected to eat efficiently, even to the point of this being enforced. For example, aimed at customers, there are 'no loitering' signs above the service counter in some US McDonalds restaurants, indicating a 30 minute time limit for consumption of whatever is purchased (Ritzer, 2015: 145). Consistent menus across branches speed this process up, enabling value for money to be easily calculated. In the *McDonaldisation of Society* (2015), Ritzer discusses a 'scripting' that staff adhere to, creating a predictable interaction between workers and customers (Ritzer, 2015: 116). I will demonstrate where I perceive there to be certain similarities with this approach in the production of UK HE policy in recent years. These texts seem to rationally script how the academic labour of students and staff should be structured, for efficient outcomes. I suggest that, just as divisions between customers and workers in a fast food chain are mapped out, increasingly the role of students is rationally predicted, and also distanced from the role of academics, via HE policy.

The discourse of 'best practice', for example, suggests there is an optimum way of academic working that might be universally applied. Such a concept can be connected with the idea of 'scientific management', as established by Taylor in the late 19th and early 20th centuries, where principles designed to rationalise work were established. Ritzer argues that McDonalds could be said to have built on these early bureaucratic approaches and the idea of the assembly line, adopted later by Henry Ford (Ritzer, 2015: 36). Furthermore, the managers of chain restaurants often do little conceptualising of their own, as they work to a 'centrally conceived' model, which Ritzer discusses as 'devoid of distinctive substantive content' (Ritzer, 2015: 188). Considering how such a model might apply to whole policies or certain buzz phrases in McPolicy, best practice could be said to be a linguistic version of this concept. As such it lacks distinctive content and encourages replication. Equally, 'the student experience' provides a centrally conceived concept of students, as this chapter will illustrate. Therefore, how such terms and the linguistic structures surrounding them, might further McDonaldised practices in HE through McPolicy discourse, is a central concern of this book.

The analogies that I make with the work of Ritzer mean that, rather than an isolated analysis, the linguistic patterns that I have noticed can be placed into a wider cultural context that has already been extensively theorised. Building on the work of Weber, Ritzer used fast food chains as an accessible metaphor for a set of trends that he observed as increasingly characterising society. He discussed a wide-ranging rationalisation where *efficiency, predictability, calculability,* and *control* are the key dimensions emphasised. Ritzer provides many diverse examples of organisations, to underpin his assertion that McDonaldisation is now a wide ranging process dominating more and more sectors of global society. His focus includes rational systems involved in the running of hotels, restaurants, supermarkets, hospitals and universities and also the McJobs of a wide array of related staff. As mentioned earlier, McDonaldisation of HE has already been discussed in terms of the McUniversity, with authors arguing that even HE can become dominated by similar principles to the fast-food restaurant, in terms of the 'fetish' of efficiency (Ritzer, 2015: 103). However here I will develop the argument that such analysis might be extended further still, by examining a large quantity of written HE policy, that I refer to as McPolicy. Ritzer's principles of McDonaldisation in the McUniversity often appear to be reinforced around certain buzz phrases in HE policy. In the illustration that I have chosen for this chapter, 'the student experience', it is worth noting that this generic concept of what the life of students should entail has been developed to the extent that McJobs with this title are now routinely advertised in the form of a 'Student Experience Officer', 'Director of the Student Experience', 'Dean of the Student Experience', and so on. This is interesting, as a buzz phrase becomes 'buzz work' in order to enact the policy, yet the policy discourse continues to attribute *words*, not people, with the credit for undertaking this labour.

### The McStudent Experience

The buzz phrase 'the student experience' is the first of several examples I will analyse in the coming chapters. University policy texts often read as though 'the student experience' is a benefit that can be served up to students, with the same ease as delivering a pizza to order.

> The purpose of this Student Experience Strategy is to deliver the student experience ambitions of the University as set out in Strategy 2020.

There is an assumption here that students should merely receive 'the student experience ambitions of the University'. This does not empower students with much part in shaping their own experiences if these are the 'ambitions of the University'. Furthermore, just as many toppings can be added to a take away pizza, 'the student experience' is a phrase with capacity to absorb endless social issues. In critiquing 'the student experience', I do not suggest that the social issues that afflict students are not the concern of universities. Far from it: academics have always supported the pastoral side of student learning and have always been concerned with the experiences of their cohorts of students. My critique relates to the manner in which the diverse experiences of individual students are commodified within this terminology, as if these were one product, not a deeply personal, experiential process. There is a curiously assumed 'exchange value' that 'the student experience' is expected to yield. This can be noticed again in the analysis of 'technology enhanced learning', 'student engagement' and 'employability' in the chapters following this one. Many overly simplistic claims tend to be made under the umbrella of these phrases. This linguistic treatment provides opportunities for manipulating the concept to accommodate limitless expectations on staff labour, as well as the potential disempowerment of students.

> It is vital that every member of staff fully understands their contribution, and that of their colleagues in delivering the Student Experience.

This statement implies that staff simply deliver an experience as if responding to a fast food order. To suggest that students have no collaborative part in shaping their experiences with staff at university directly conflicts with other strategies and pedagogies for student-staff partnerships. Students are a very varied population, one that includes many staff too who are undertaking further qualifications (2018b). In the UK at the time of writing, the recently established Office for Students (OfS) has released their first strategy which features important concerns for students. Yet, in addressing these via the new regulatory framework, considering the experiences of staff are surely necessary too. Unless the mutually constitutive relations of students and staff are fully appreciated, before we know it, we could be greeting our students with their new course outline to ask the equivalent of: 'do you want fries with that?' (Ritzer, 2015: 116).

There have been critiques of Ritzer's theory in the context of HE that also need to be taken into account. In Dennis Hayes and Robin Wynyard's book: *The McDonaldization of Higher Education* (2002) the consequences of the process of McDonaldisation to the university were considered. The concept of the "therapeutic university", already touched on, was put forward to in part explain an acquiescence of academics and students to the bureaucratising aspects of McDonaldisation. In *Beyond McDonaldization: Visions of Higher Education* (Hayes, 2017), Dennis Hayes describes a cultural climate in universities where today's students are viewed as emotionally vulnerable and incapable of coping with challenging ideas (Hayes, 2017). By examining 'the student experience' in more detail, this is one buzz phrase through which to consider both McDonaldising qualities and therapeutic ones at a textual level. I look at how the process of nominalisation, discussed earlier, commodifies the diverse experiences of students into one homogenised McStudent experience that can be referred to, expanded on and then simply delivered back to students.

### *The Social Life of a Buzz Phrase*

As I proceed to explain the framework for examining how 'academic labour' appears to be undertaken by certain buzz phrases within McPolicy, I jest of course when I say that every hard-working buzz phrase also needs a social life. Yet there is no denying that buzz phrases do get around a bit! So it is important to explain from the outset how I understand the analysis of such discourse, within social life and in relation to social theory, before taking a stance towards analysing actual written policy texts. Following the work of Fairclough, I understand language as 'an irreducible part of social life, dialectically interconnected with other elements' (Fairclough, 2003: 2). As mentioned earlier, when language is played out in different social, political and cultural environments, I am describing this as discourse. To suggest that discourse is 'dialectically interconnected' refers to a conception of social relations as partly discoursal in nature, and discourse as partly social relations (Harvey, 1996; Fairclough, 2003: 25). Fairclough suggests that although 'the discourse element of a social practice is not the same as for example its social relations, each in a sense contains or internalizes the other' (Fairclough, 2003: 25).

So, using the example of an academic, and their perceived identity in relation to buzz phrases, this could not be considered purely 'textual'. Elements of a person's identity may be socially constructed via discourse, but that person has their own agency and positioning in relation to language. People also have an embodied and practical engagement with the world which begins before they even learn languages, a form of self-consciousness and identification that continues throughout life (Fairclough, 2003: 160). Whilst 'buzzwords get their "buzz" from being in-words, words that define what is in vogue' (Cornwall & Eade, 2010: 3), this is only part of the story. Any presentation of these words as being natural, normal or neutral within policy discourse is problematic, as different linguistic formations surround buzz phrases, and these are ideologically invested. So, I take the position that all written texts are neither neutral or disinterested, but are shaped by political beliefs and socio-cultural practices (Simpson & Mayr, 2010: 4). A close linguistic analysis can help reveal ideologies embedded in discourse, enabling a better understanding of how these are sustained, via textual repetitions, in HE policy.

### Increasing Consciousness of the Labour of Words

#### *Corpus-Based Critical Discourse Analysis*

Whilst it is necessary to refer to some linguistic terminology now, to discuss the steps undertaken in a corpus-based CDA, this will be kept to a minimum and fully explained. In so doing, it is my intention to open up these techniques to a larger audience than linguists, should other interdisciplinary researchers wish to adopt a similar process of corpus-based CDA. A corpus-based Critical Discourse Analysis (CDA), CDA hereafter, helps to reveal where there are manipulative functions within discourse that might otherwise remain hidden. By gathering a large number of policy texts into a corpus, the patterns that can be noticed quantitatively across these documents can be more closely interpreted via CDA, to suggest possible effects. The motivation for exposing these mechanisms is 'to help increase consciousness of how language contributes to the domination of some people by others, because consciousness is the first step towards emancipation' (Fairclough, 1989: 1). It is therefore always worth asking why arguments are presented in one way, and not another, and whose interests are represented by the form and structure that discourse takes. Whilst this book focuses on HE policy discourse, I do not view this in isolation from wider society and culture. Discourse is shaped by people's values, and as such, it may constrain or empower what people believe that they may say, and how they interpret meaning.

*Corpus Linguistics*

A corpus can be understood as a collection of naturally occurring language, in this case the HE policy texts that were gathered and which are freely available in the public domain, through university websites. Corpus linguistics (Baker, 2006) offers structured ways to search a large bank of text files and examine constructions of language in use, or discourse. The initial quantitative findings are in the form of word lists and frequencies of words. These can be explored through searches on particular words to reveal common patterns of grammatical structures. Whilst these initial quantitative findings do not prove much, beyond pointing to repetition of certain patterns, a more qualitative approach through CDA, can then be used to examine more closely grammatical structures in relation to critical theory.

*Critical Discourse Analysis (CDA) to Reveal What Might Otherwise Remain Hidden*

As already mentioned, CDA is an approach through which the social, ideological and political dimensions of discourse might be examined. This is important because discourse is a dynamic feature of our daily lives that actively shapes our understandings and interpretations of reality. Therefore, "when we speak or write, we always take a particular perspective on what the world is like" (Gee, 1999: 2). So how power is exercised in the way that texts are produced, may then alter what options people believe are open to them.

Fairclough's three-dimensional model for the analysis of discourse conceives of any discursive 'event' as a simultaneous and three-dimensional phenomenon (Fairclough, 1992: 73). So, a policy would be a written or spoken text, an instance of discourse practice and an instance of social practice (Simpson & Mayr, 2010: 53). The discourse practice element concerns the production, distribution and consumption of the text in society. The social practice element relates to the dimensions that might be socially analysed in terms of power relations and ideological struggle (Simpson & Mayr, 2010: 54). There are different frameworks for conducting CDA, but the form of analysis that I have adopted throughout this book is drawn from the work of Michael Halliday on 'systemic functional linguistics' and more specifically, as discussed below, concerns transitivity analysis (Halliday, 1994). I have found transitivity analysis to be particularly helpful in demonstrating the effects of 'nominalisation', which I discuss further below, after explaining my approach for gathering university 'student experience' strategies for analysis.

### *Collecting University 'Student Experience' Strategies for Analysis Using Wordsmith*

In this first example, during April 2018 I collected as many UK university 'student experience' strategies as I could find, using a general web search for 'university student experience strategy'. This yielded 20 strategy documents of this nature, which I converted into text files. I then examined these documents through software called *Wordsmith* to observe which quantitative patterns emerged through corpus linguistics (Scott, 1997). Initially the software revealed that there were a total of 54,200 words in this corpus. Whilst not a particularly large corpus, compared to the one discussed in Chapter 4, these strategies, like the 'student engagement' strategies discussed in Chapter 5, have only emerged over the last 5 years. Moreover, only some UK universities have separate strategies for 'student experience'. However, whilst it is important not to read too much into the examples provided below, they do provide illustrative content to explore alongside theory. More significantly, the patterns of grammatical structures present in these strategies are frequently repeated in very similar ways across the other collections of strategies that I have chosen to analyse: 'technology enhanced learning', 'student engagement' and 'employability' strategies. Each corpus was examined initially through *Wordsmith,* which supports corpus linguistic analysis through *keywords*. Keywords are words that are statistically significant when measured against a comparison corpus, in this case, the British National Corpus (BNC). The British National Corpus was chosen as it contains 100 million words of written and spoken English from a wide range of sources for comparison purposes. A large corpus of words is 'net-like' (Hoey, 1991) and reveals the values of those producing these policy texts, whether they are aware of these or not. However, whilst this does not explain why particular patterns occur, these searches do provide significant empirical content to examine and discuss.

Table 3.1 shows some of the keywords highlighted by the software and how often these appeared in the corpus. These keywords are not unexpected, given the topic of these strategies, but it is the patterns around these words that are of real interest.

TABLE 3.1  Example keywords in the 'student experience' corpus

| Keyword | Number of instances |
| --- | --- |
| Students | 874 |
| Student | 826 |
| Will | 612 |
| For | 584 |
| University | 488 |
| Experience | 450 |

To see how these keywords are positioned regularly in the statements of the strategies, *concordance* lines are produced. Each concordance line shows how words and phrases are ordered alongside each other in their actual context of use. The numbers at the side of these lines are provided through the searches in Wordsmith so that these examples are easily retrieved. So, it then becomes possible to see what patterns emerge across all 20 university student experience strategies, as in the concordance lines in Figure 3.1, where a selection of statements from the corpus are shown.

### *Identifying Who Is 'Acting' to Achieve Something*

The order in which words are placed alters meaning. In Figure 3.1, an emphasis is often placed on textual constructions or entities (rather than people) who are enacting academic practices. To demonstrate this further, I have broken down what is happening in each concordance line. I have highlighted firstly (in bold text) who/what is 'acting' to achieve something in each line of text e.g., in the first corpus line (18) where the student experience was actually mentioned, the entity enacting something is: learning technology and its contribution. Secondly, I have underlined the verb, which in this case is: makes. Finally, I have placed in italics the goal, or achievement from this action, which in line 18 is: *the student experience.* Such patterns are not easy to spot when simply reading through a strategy document. They are

18 **Review the contribution our learning technology** <u>makes</u> *to the student experience*
24 **This Student Experience Strategy** <u>delivers</u> *the student experience ambitions of the University*
28 **The student experience is interpreted holistically** <u>as embracing</u> *the student learning experience*
32 **The Teaching, Learning and Student Experience Strategy 2013–2020** <u>will drive</u> *our success*
43 **World-class research and engaging teaching approaches** <u>provide</u> *an excellent learning experience*
77 **The Student Experience Strategy** <u>sets out</u> *the priorities for the student experience*
78 **Deliver an excellent student experience** <u>that is</u> *an exemplar of good practice*
86 **This Strategy** <u>ensures</u> *that considerations of the student experience are central to all that we do*
154 **Encourage and celebrate innovations and best practice** <u>in enhancing</u> *the student experience*
165 **This strategy** <u>outlines</u> *initiatives aimed at bringing significant and measurable enhancement in the experience of our students*
168 **The strategy** <u>sets out</u> *our vision for an unrivalled student experience*
189 **Operate effective quality assurance and enhancement mechanisms** <u>that drive</u> *enhancement of the student learning experience*
286 **Ensure the Student Experience** <u>is</u> *integral to recruitment, selection, induction and staff performance*
334 **Develop the distinctiveness of the University student experience and** <u>ensure</u> *this is embedded in the culture and work of students and staff.*
335 **Ensure that the experience of joining the University** <u>enables</u> *students to transition effectively and maximises their opportunities to succeed and excel.*
370 **The University will offer innovative and outstanding student support** <u>that understands deeply</u> *the student learning experience of today's students.*
371 **The University's infrastructure and services** will be <u>focused on</u> *supporting the quality and effectiveness of learning, teaching and research, and enhancing the total experience of students.*
391 **The university operates effective quality assurance and enhancement mechanisms** that <u>drive</u> *enhancement of the student learning experience*
445 **Encourage, support, and celebrate innovations and best practice** <u>in enhancing</u> *the student experience.*

FIGURE 3.1   Concordance lines from the student experience corpus

easily ignored even when identified, as it could be argued that this is simply the manner in which formal documents like strategies are written. However, after observing these patterns via corpus linguistics across many different types of strategies, it is worth questioning the effects of this form of discourse. Who does it benefit to write in this way? What do these statements prioritise and in turn marginalise? Furthermore, at a time when many questions are being asked about fairness and equality for students, should these strategies be closely scrutinised to assess the manner in which students are portrayed?

### Transitivity Analysis

What I have demonstrated in the highlighting of the concordance lines above, is a very simplified form of *transitivity* analysis (Halliday, 1994). Transitivity is a way to look in detail at how grammatical processes are described in language. Grammar, though a structural foundation for human expression, does not stand alone. It cannot be divorced from its relationship with meaning (semantics), or from its effects when used in real situations (pragmatics) (Crystal, 2004: 27). Each grammatical construction has a meaning that is applied in a social and political context, and this is governed by human choices, of even the order in which something is said. Semantic categories are groupings of vocabulary within a language which organise words that are interrelated. 'To do a transitivity analysis it is necessary to identify every verb and its associated process. It is then necessary to identify patterns in the use of these processes' (Janks, 1997). This involves breaking down a sentence, which is a grammatical unit (a clause) stating some form of proposition. The proposition describes a process happening in the world around us that is being undertaken by a subject or actor. These components of a clause can be labelled as follows:

> **The participant:** who is doing what to whom (the person or entity 'acting')
> **The process:** the participant's actions realised by verbs (e.g. to drive, ensure)
> **The circumstances:** concerns the time or place, related to the process/participants

The concepts of process, participant and circumstance are semantic categories that explain how these phenomena of the real world are represented as linguistic structure (Halliday, 1994: 109). By looking at a statement in this way, it allows an analyst to distinguish and identify different kinds of 'goings-on' (Thompson, 2013: 94). Halliday provides a breakdown of *process types*, which includes:

> *Material* processes: 'doing' something, for example: to create, to drive, develop
> *Mental* processes: 'experiencing' or 'sensing', for example: to see, hear, know,
> *Verbal* processes: 'saying' something, for example: to communicate or ask
> *Relational* processes: about 'being' or 'becoming', for example: 'is', 'to be'.

In summary, the basic concept of transitivity is simple, in that a small number of process types can be identified. Each of these has their own types of participants, and so the labels attached to these 'actors' varies. Whatever the process type, the same decisions are involved in categorising what is happening in the clause. A little later in this chapter I will present examples of how to label a clause with some of these process types, using statements from the 'student experience' corpus. However, in later chapters I won't mark up each and every textual example in this way. I will simply explain which process type is involved in each example. I will then discuss possible wider effects in how meaning may be construed from the structure of the wording. For those who are interested in reading a more detailed explanation of transitivity analysis, with all of the process types, and some useful examples, Geoff Thompson's *Introducing Functional Grammar* (2013) is an excellent source.

### 'Fossilised Labour' through Nominalisation

The generic example below is not taken from the 'student experience' corpus, but it is helpful to show, as a first step, how transitivity analysis works in practice. It also illustrates *nominalisation*. Two different ways of describing a situation are detailed below:

**Example 1**

| A lecturer | provides | feedback | to a student to improve their experience |
|---|---|---|---|
| (Participant) | (Process) | (Goal) | (Circumstance) |

In example 1, the reader can be quite clear about the participant or actor (a lecturer) who is undertaking the process (provides) towards a goal (feedback), in certain circumstances (to a student to improve their experience). In Example 2 below, these different elements of the clause are not so apparent:

**Example 2**

| The provision of feedback | improves | the student experience |
|---|---|---|
| (Participant) | (Process) | (Goal) |

In example 2, the participant (the provision of feedback) is now detached from human labour. The nominalised way in which the second statement is worded means that the individuals involved (the lecturer and the student) have been moved out of sight of a reader's view. The active verbal process (provides), that was previously attributed to a human in example 1, has now been absorbed into the new participant. It has been 'thingified' by being expressed as a noun (Thompson, 2013: 246). What may appear to be a small change, has in fact considerably altered the emphasis of this statement. If this was a statement in a strategy or policy, it could be argued that the ideological standpoint has also changed. The second example means that 'the provision of feedback' is no longer a process attached to a lecturer. The staff labour involved in providing feedback to a student is no longer acknowledged. Indeed 'the provision of feedback' has been linguistically 'freed' to be referred to, and credited with, the way in which 'it' (not a person) improves 'the student experience'. Meanwhile, from the point of view of the student labour involved in a feedback process, the circumstances (to a student to improve their experience) in example 1, have now changed in example 2. Instead of referring to the individual interaction of a student with their lecturer, a further 'thing', a goal called 'the student experience' has been introduced. Any student labour that may have been involved in responding to the feedback process has now been absorbed into 'the student experience'. This is another free entity. A buzz phrase that can be manipulated, referred to and called upon in numerous ways within policy documents, as I will proceed to demonstrate. Lastly, in example 2, these linguistic changes have also separated the lecturer and student from each other, through two faceless statements linked by 'improves'. The humans are no longer present: the labour of words is alive and well.

Nominalisation appears to be in harmony with scientific writing and with the aim of establishing generic truths and detached processes, rather than tied to specific people (Thompson, 2013: 246). To link nominalised ways of writing policy back to the wide-ranging process of McDonaldisation described by Ritzer, analogies can be noticed in a rationalisation of language, where *efficiency, predictability, calculability,* and *control* are key dimensions. If in the McUniversity *efficiency* entails getting more and more students into and through HE, then Example 2 is an *efficient* way of writing. It takes longer in example 1 to detail exactly who is involved in this academic process of giving feedback. If *Calculability* concerns the range of comparison tables between universities, such as the National Student Survey (NSS) in the UK which measures student satisfaction then *calculation* of staff performance is made much easier, if *predictable* entities like 'the student experience' are referred to, enabling a greater *control* to be exercised. However, nominalisation also leads to 'fossilised' processes (Thompson, 2013: 246) of human labour, which has implications for individuals when academic performance is being measured and audited in HE. It has further implications in relation to the issue of technological unemployment, which I discuss in Chapter 6.

### *The Work of a Buzz Phrase: 'The Student Experience'*

Looking now in more detail at some of the 'student experience' corpus examples, these can be broken down further, via transitivity analysis, to consider the *type* of processes that 'the student experience' as a buzz phrase engages with. Taking the second concordance line (24), this statement can be labelled as below to demonstrate a *material* process. In a material process the participant is called an *actor* who undertakes the process to achieve a *goal*:

| This Student Experience Strategy | delivers | *the student experience ambitions of the University* |
|---|---|---|
| (Actor) | (Material process) | (Goal) |

Despite the people that are usually involved in both working on a strategy and enacting it, it is **This Student Experience Strategy** that we are told, through a material process, <u>delivers</u> the goal of *the student experience ambitions of the University*. Spot the human if you can.

Below, in concordance lines 32 and 391, similar patterns can be noticed. It is a **strategy** and **effective quality assurance and enhancement mechanisms** that each enact the material process <u>drive</u>:

| The Teaching, Learning and Student Experience Strategy 2013–2020 | will drive | *our success* |
|---|---|---|
| (Actor) | (Material process) | (Goal) |

| The university operates effective quality assurance and enhancement mechanisms that | drive | *enhancement of the student learning experience* |
|---|---|---|
| (Actor) | (Material process) | (Goal) |

In concordance line 43 below, the same pattern is repeated, but **world class research and engaging teaching approaches** (rather than engaging teachers and researchers), via a material process, <u>provide</u> the goal of *an excellent learning experience*. In concordance line 445, it is **innovations and best practice**

THE LABOUR AND DELIVERY OF BUZZ PHRASES                                85

that are to be supported and celebrated, via a material process, <u>in enhancing</u> the goal of *'the student experience'*.

| **World-class research and engaging teaching approaches** | <u>provide</u> | *an excellent learning experience* |
|---|---|---|
| (Actor) | (Material process) | (Goal) |

| **Support, and celebrate innovations and best practice** | <u>in enhancing</u> | *the student experience* |
|---|---|---|
| (Actor) | (Material process) | (Goal) |

In the next two examples (77) and (168), verbal processes are demonstrated, as each **strategy** (referred to as the 'sayer') <u>sets out</u> (as a form of communication through a verbal process) goals of *the priorities for the student experience* and *our vision for an unrivalled student experience*.

| **The Student Experience Strategy** | <u>sets out</u> | *the priorities for the student experience* |
|---|---|---|
| (Sayer) | (Verbal process) | (Goal) |

| **The strategy** | <u>sets out</u> | *our vision for an unrivalled student experience* |
|---|---|---|
| (Sayer) | (Verbal process) | (Goal) |

In line 371 below, a mental process is enacted by The University's infrastructure and services. The actor of a mental process is referred to as a 'senser'. This senser will, via a mental process, be <u>focused on</u> the 'phenomenon' of *supporting the quality and effectiveness of learning, teaching and research, and, in general, on enhancing the total experience of students.*

| **The University's infrastructure and services** will be | <u>focused on</u> | supporting the quality and effectiveness of learning, teaching and research and on enhancing the experience of students. |
|---|---|---|
| (Senser) | (Mental process) | (Phenomenon) |

If the university's infrastructure and services can do our thinking for us on supporting all of these elements, then what do we need people for? Finally, below in concordance line 286, a relational process is illustrated. This is where a relationship is set up between two concepts, in this case through the word is. Here the more general category is labelled as the 'value' and the specific embodiment is categorised as the 'token' (Thompson, 2013: 98).

| The Student Experience | is | integral to recruitment, selection, induction and staff performance |
|---|---|---|
| (Value) | (relational process) | (Token) |

In this example, the Student Experience is understood, via the relational process is, to be equal to *recruitment, selection, induction and staff performance*. Whilst on face value this is a valid proposition, where students would experience all of these interactions in a positive manner, the addition of *staff performance* at the end skews the relationship between students and staff once more. This choice of wording once again moves understanding further away from a student-staff partnership approach, which is often emphasised in other strategies and pedagogies.

### *A Populist Narrative*

In these examples, the populist narrative discussed earlier in this book as surrounding the buzz phrase of 'the student experience' can be noticed. In a similar way to the concept of value for money, it is implicit, rather than explicit, that if you are not *for* 'the student experience' then you must be *against it*. Things are not that simple though. As a socially constructed 'container', any amount of agendas can be placed under the banner of 'the student experience' and indeed 'value for money'. As a socially constructed object, 'the student experience' can be referred to, and also placed anywhere in policy, as an actor.

These examples help to linguistically confront concerns raised by educators, such as Peter Scott. Writing in *The Guardian* (2014), Scott voiced alarm that the complexity of the experiences of students: 'becomes reduced to a one-size-fits-all definition, in the term: the student experience'. As an academic, Scott points out that this current buzz phrase over-emphasises: 'short-term satisfaction as measured in instrumental and transactional terms' (Scott, 2014). He adds:

> But like most market-speak labels, it conceals more than it reveals. What is the 'student experience'? Does it focus on the process of being

a student – and, if so, is good teaching more (or less) important than facilities like accommodation, bars, swimming pools, night life? Or is the 'student experience' about the product, winning a place at a 'top' university, getting a good job or being able to sport a high-status 'brand'? (Scott, 2014)

The texts that I have discussed, seem to rationally script how the academic labour of students and staff should be structured concerning 'the student experience', for efficient outcomes. At the same time, in delivering a predictable 'experience' to students, this discourse also contains a presupposition that students will experience events evenly, and in equal measures. Yet society is not equal, and therefore these tacit assumptions in policy are problematic. When reference is made to 'the student experience' this could be said to be representing the 'will of the student', but unfortunately it is a phrase that overlooks diversity, attributing only one unified (McDonaldised) persona to the student population. Furthermore, it seems to be treated as a consumer package to be delivered to students, not as a shared endeavour between university staff and students. It serves too as a disciplinary measure for staff whenever they do not appear to meet its movable criteria.

When participating in a fast food restaurant as an 'experience', customers may be largely unaware of the limitations placed around their visit, or they may be specifically seeking out these features. At this point it is worth distinguishing universities from other McDonaldised systems to reflect about their potential for civic engagement in the wider community. Such an approach could widen the perception of what 'student experience' might mean, in terms of academic labour, by demonstrating the value of a public role to students. However, this may not be deemed to offer the same 'value added' as other more instrumental extras. Relph argues that there are rewards for institutions in being creative in building the identity of their 'offer' in close connection with local organisations and networks (Relph, 2016). Universities have the creative and imaginative culture needed to do this well, but it would require a shift away from mainstream policy discourse which currently narrows, rather than widens these opportunities.

In the three chapters to follow, I will provide detailed analysis of HE policy documents written on the topics of: Technology Enhanced Learning (TEL), Student Engagement and Employability. These phrases share a number of qualities. Firstly, it has proved easy to 'transport' these concepts as general abstractions, and as such, many institutions have written related policies. Secondly, in the text around these words a similar form of exchange value can be noticed, where these terms or their strategies are said to enact processes that would usually be attributed to humans. Thirdly, each of these terms has a related social agenda or issue that might be educationalised. Technology Enhanced Learning concerns digital capabilities and perceived efficiencies from online learning: Student Engagement concerns admission and retention rates: Employability is linked to value for money from universities in supplying industry with a workforce. Finally, these policies all concern the environment around staff who are teaching and students who are learning. They portray the labour of students and staff in a particular, rational manner. In the introductory section for each chapter, I will explain why the topic has been chosen and the context for exploring it. I will demonstrate why attention should be paid to how written HE policy is structured, when repeated patterns indicate that the embodied nature of student learning and teaching practice has been replaced with a sinister rationality that fails to acknowledge human labour. Out in the augmented world of consumer culture the role of humans as prosumers is exploited, as companies reap the benefits of free labour from their clients (Ritzer & Jurgenson, 2010). In the UK, HE students pay for their education, but are denied their place in written policy concerning their labour. Inviting students to be at the heart of the system, including as central voice in the recently formed UK Office for Students, means nothing, if we proceed to write regulatory documents in a tone that denies the presence of both students and staff.

CHAPTER 4

# Technology Enhanced Learning McPolicy

## The Value of Technology Enhanced Learning

### Why Technology Enhanced Learning?

At the beginning of Chapter 1, I drew attention to the example observed by Crawford concerning the advertisements on the payment screen. Crawford later comments that 'turning unavoidable public surfaces into sites of marketing isn't inherently 'digital' (Crawford, 2015: 4). To this I could reply, well *what is*? At a time when authors are exploring what it means to be post-digital (Jandrić, Knox, Besley, Ryberg, Suoranta, & Hayes, 2018), Crawford's comment is a reminder that the choices to develop technologies to distract and proposition humans, in this manner are made by people, not digital devices. People are now administered in their daily lives in ways that they are largely unaware of. Whether this administration concerns the placement of products in a local supermarket, or involves nudges to act in some other way via Amazon or Argos, Crawford refers to 'choice architectures' that are installed in public places through the 'darker precincts of capitalism' (Crawford, 2015: 87). Could there be some parallels to be drawn then, in the 'choice architectures' deployed in the construction of written policy documents concerning technology and learning in HE? For example, how does the attention of a lecturer become channeled towards what learning technologies *are*, and what they *do*, through HE policy?

Over many decades, politicians have emphasised the promise of technology for education, but education is not inherently digital either. We now have decades of experience to vouch for this because 'despite generations of technological onslaught, education systems have not changed fundamentally, and the university as an institution appears remarkably resilient' (Flavin, 2017: 1). So why in HE policy are direct links made between introducing 'the use of technology' into course design and an assumed enhancement of student learning? Some strategy documents even suggest *"a paradigm shift where technology transforms* what *we learn and* how *we learn it"* (European Commission, 2009). To address these considerations, my CDA of UK educational technology policy texts since 1997 is an examination of those assumptions surrounding 'the use of technology'. Given a strong global focus on Technology Enhanced Learning (TEL) in recent years, the way that claims are structured will be analysed. There are two initial points that influenced my choice to look closely

© KONINKLIJKE BRILL NV, LEIDEN, 2019 | DOI:10.1163/9789004395374_005 at this particular buzz phrase in the context of HE policy. Firstly, Technology Enhanced Learning, referred to as TEL from hereon, is worthy of close inspection due to an inherent pre-supposition. This is namely a choice to include a deterministic assumption in the ordering of these three words: that *technology* itself *has* enhanced learning. Essentially then, an economic calculation is embodied within TEL:

*in exchange for the use of technology, there will be enhanced forms of learning*

> This is quite a presupposition given that technology means different things to different people in different situations and cannot simply be assumed to have inherent positive qualities where learning is always enhanced. (Hayes & Jandrić, 2014: 198)

TEL is a rational choice of phrase that suggests an inbuilt exchange value accompanies the use of technology as an enhancement of learning. This assumed value provides a vehicle for neoliberal agendas to make simplified claims politically in the name of technology, which unfortunately can disfigure and pervert the values of human learning communities. Statements like: 'the use of technology will enhance the student learning experience' are commonly found in university and government policy documents. Such a discourse divides technology from society, removing humans from their material practice with technological objects and from their relationships with others. A sense of closure to alternative conceptual routes follows.

Secondly, TEL has a linguistic structure that conceals any credit for the humans involved in the processes of learning through technology, as I will later illustrate. Human beings design and undertake learning, not technology. If technology has already enhanced learning, then where is the academic labour of students and lecturers acknowledged in the policy? Others too have expressed concerns over an apparent general acceptance of TEL as a discourse. In 2010, Price and Kirkwood argued that TEL is:

> The latest in an assortment of terms that have been used to describe the application of information and communication technologies (ICT) to learning and teaching. Unlike other terms such as e-Learning or online learning, technology enhanced learning implies a value judgment: the word "enhancement" suggests an improvement or betterment in some way. (Price & Kirkwood, 2010: 772)

Price and Kirkwood also questioned what learning is actually being enhanced, in what ways, and whether there is in fact any generally accepted view of what constitutes learning in HE or how it may be enhanced by technology (Price & Kirkwood, 2010: 772). Bayne later argued:

> 'TEL', has become a widely-accepted term in the UK and Europe for describing the interface between digital technology and higher education teaching, to a large extent taking the place of other recently-popular terminologies such as 'e-learning', 'learning technology' and 'computer-based learning'. Yet there has been little critique in the literature of the assumptions embedded within the terminology of TEL. (Bayne, 2014: 5)

These are important concerns to raise, particularly when Technology Enhanced Learning is frequently referred to under the acronym of TEL, thus concealing from view the full linguistic construction of the term. However, in this chapter these critiques are taken further. A detailed textual analysis reveals why paying attention to the words that *surround* TEL, in HE policy, can be even more illuminating than the buzz phrase itself. Elsewhere I have drawn attention to the 'social nature of even (seemingly static) written policy texts in being able to reinforce and perpetuate myths about what technology can achieve on our behalf' (Hayes & Jandrić, 2014: 198; Hayes & Bartholomew, 2015). Fairclough discussed a 'technologisation of discourse' with reference to the way that 'new knowledges are constantly produced, circulated and consumed as discourses (economic, organisational, managerial, political or educational)' (Fairclough, 1992; Simpson & Mayr, 2010: 39). Bayne adds that:

> TEL has been adopted as an apparently useful, inoffensive and descriptive shorthand for what is in fact a complex and often problematic constellation of social, technological and educational change. (Bayne, 2014: 5)

It is a 'shorthand' that conceals decades of critical theory about technology itself, from Science and Technology Studies, STS hereafter. STS has its origins in a belief that the content and direction of technological innovation are amenable to sociological analysis and explanation' (Wajcman, 2002: 351). STS scholars therefore suggest that technology is not only isolated objects (actual or virtual) but is also activities, knowledge, material structures and modes of organisation which take the form of 'sociotechnical systems' (Matthewman, 2011: 12). Like language, these varied technologies are never neutral or external to humans, but have powerful implications for people that are unpredictable. If technology is considered to be 'a constitutive part of human labour, inseparable from politics and culture' (Winner, 1980; Travers, 2001), then how technology is discussed in relation to learning, cannot be isolated from these debates.

### *How Does TEL McPolicy Support a Neoliberal Ideology?*

Yet TEL effectively achieves just this. TEL 'packages' a particular rationality concerning 'the use of technology' *as enhancement,* extinguishing other more critical understandings. For many decades, theorists have argued that technology is not isolated from human politics and values, but in TEL the space for these debates is gone. Technology *enhances* learning. TEL has spoken. This approach is useful though, for governments and universities because statements about *embedding* TEL into neoliberal organisations cannot be reasoned with. As noted in Chapter 2, people will shrug and concede that 'it is what it is', but what if it isn't?

These forms of rational separation are a given, within neoliberal institutions but as the norms and values of technology as a simple *enhancement* are internalised, this shapes the culture in which student learning is designed and enacted. As someone who has taught sociology students critical social theory about technology, I know how hard it is to swim against this tide, because neoliberal rationality is reinforced in multiple ways, and discourse is only one of these. McPolicy is very good though at describing detached economically-based processes concerning technology that lead to success for institutions. In Chapter 5, I will show how this applies to 'student engagement' too, as benefits to the university are flagged up. It seems that students' own engagement, just like enhancement from technology, can be packaged up and irrationally marketed back to students, in statements that flag up the paybacks for universities.

The trouble-free discourse of TEL may serve the purposes of perpetual accumulation required to maintain neoliberal organisations, but it does not serve humans to build new critical and creative forms of knowledge in the face of technological unemployment. The Joint Information Systems Committee (Jisc) recently published key themes from its response to the UK parliamentary inquiry into the implications of the Fourth Industrial Revolution. Whilst important data on student opinion is shared, there are still statements such as the one below that imply that 'technology', rather than people, can achieve the outcomes stated:

> Technology such as AI has the potential to both enhance and accelerate the education experience for students, as well as streamlining organisational processes. (Feldman, 2018)

Just as the widespread availability of 'take away' solutions to eating and drinking alter our cultural norms, a persistent emphasis on a 'quick fix' from technology to solve a multitude of complex issues in universities changes institutional expectations of what can be achieved (Selwyn, Gorard, & Williams, 2001). The problem is that the human labour required for this 'potential' from technology such as AI to 'enhance and accelerate', is missing from the calculation. Both time and academic labour are required to achieve these goals.

Using the example of shopping malls and chain stores around the world, Ritzer describes a growing convergence of these forms of 'nothing' that are a feature of globalisation (Ritzer, 2004). These are the easily replicated outlets that sell the same items regardless of the locale. They are staffed by 'non-people' because these employees have become absorbed into scripted parts within businesses offering 'non services' (Ritzer, 2011: 173), Ritzer contrasts these with 'something', where humans provide a distinctive content. This is a phenomenon that I observe in a textual form in HE McPolicy. Statements of 'nothing' are continually made concerning the buzz phrases examined in this book. Often the 'non-people' are not even mentioned. Just like the branded goods that Ritzer refers to, as largely devoid of distinctive content (Ritzer, 2011: 172), so our university policy discourse for student learning is now flooded with 'non services' due to an absence of distinctive content. The repetition of this form of discourse across universities will become more apparent than ever in this chapter, as 'the use of technology', just like a branch of Primark or Ikea, turns out duplicate statements that are devoid of human content. I therefore contrast this form of 'trouble free' policy discourse consisting of 'nothing' with ideas concerning 'troublesome knowledge' (Mezirow, 1991; Meyer & Land, 2006). I perceive this to be about building a critical conceptual space for personal, distinctive knowledge, via more transparent interactions with technology, as a 'prosumer'. These would acknowledge human labour along the 'production-consumption continuum'. The challenge is for this to become 'something' in our written policies.

In the sections to come, I will firstly elaborate on the economic calculation that I perceive to be inherent in the structuring of the words: technology enhanced learning. I will explain why theory from Marx is helpful in recognising the framework of exchange value that surrounds TEL. Yet despite the framing of students as consumers, education is about production, as well as consumption. Ritzer has pointed out the role of 'prosumer' that so many of us now undertake and that entrepreneurial companies rely heavily on (Ritzer & Jurgenson, 2010). So it is worth considering how the complexities of such interactions are mirrored in universities but also masked by the basic discourse of TEL McPolicy. I will then explore a little recent history to examine how TEL has come to replace other popular terminology. The background I provide here intersects with the narrative in Chapter 2: *The Words of Labour*. However, here I explore the lead up to the New Labour government and beyond, through specific policy discourse circulated in the UK, with regard to educational technology. Following a theoretical analysis of some persistent assumptions about the nature of technology itself, in relation to the human labour of learning and teaching, I will provide linguistic examples to illustrate these points. Whilst the focus is on UK policy data, the patterns that I demonstrate may be observed more globally too. However, no detailed analysis of policy beyond the UK has as yet been undertaken. That may well be the topic of a later book!

### TEL *is Based on Exchange Value*

In the policy language surrounding TEL what becomes repeatedly reinforced, as examples in this chapter will show, is the simple economic calculation: *in exchange for the use of technology there will be enhanced forms of learning*. Yet such a discourse, which is based only on a simple 'exchange value' (Marx, 1867) then inhibits questions being raised about the diverse ways students and their instructors really experience technology. In other words, the distinctive elements that Ritzer refers to as missing from McDonaldised instituitions. As such, TEL distorts the values of human learning communities in HE (Greener & Perriton, 2005; Hayes & Bartholomew, 2015: 113). To illustrate how this happens, technology, like any commodity, has 'value' which also represents a quantity of human labour. Marx distinguished between 'use value' and 'exchange value'. 'Use value' relates to human social necessities, which in this context might be applied to the teaching or learning aspects that a technology might fulfil in conjunction with the labour of the student or teacher involved. On the other hand, 'exchange value' is a value that takes the human labour involved for granted to realise a direct profit in an economic market. Exchange value seems to be reflected in TEL in the form of a guarantee that 'the use of technology' will (without doubt) enhance learning and yield a profit. This is illustrated in a simple calculation based on what technology enhanced learning implies:

*(learning context)* + *(introduction of technology)* = *enhancement of learning*

However, by structuring arguments within this narrow perception, where educational technology provides an economic 'fix' for perceived issues in HE, a multitude of important assumptions are concealed (Hayes & Bartholomew, 2015: 114). The discourse of TEL confines learning with technology within the frame of exchange value, where other forms of human reasoning, that relate to personal use values, are omitted. Another analogy would be that TEL, rather like 'the student experience' as discussed in Chapter 3, serves as a form of 'iron cage' (Weber, 1905). It offers a rationality and efficiency intended to produce the most gain, leaving people themselves as expendable. In this vision, students consume enhanced learning through a McDonaldised (Ritzer, 1993/2018) interpretation of educational technology. Any elements of distinctive practice are reduced to an argument of automatic enhancement focused on students as consumers. Linguistically, there is little room left for negotiating alternative understandings.

### *Educational Technology as Prosumption*

Yet education is (and always has been) about production, as well as consumption. In a recent interview, George Ritzer describes a 'production-consumption continuum' in education, that involves teaching which leads students to produce their own ideas and perspectives, 'so good education is always prosumption'. Equally a good teacher will 'consume body postures, expressions, to say nothing of the questions and ideas, that the students pose' (Ritzer, Jandrić, & Hayes, 2018). The concept of prosumption (Toffler, 1980) has been developed by Ritzer, in terms of prosumer capitalism, pointing out the degree to which people, as prosumers, are now exploited for their free labour in online and augmented settings. Ritzer argues that 'when we give Amazon.com the information on what products we want, we are consciously producing for them. However, the most serious aspect of all of this is the unconscious provision of information'. Ritzer refers to this as 'the exploitation of the con(pro)sumer', where human activities in terms of information provision are tracked through algorithms. Thus when we serve ourselves online as consumers of McDonaldised commodities, we also produce valuable information used by Amazon.com, Facebook and many other entrepreneurial companies who are growing fabulously wealthy on this unpaid human labour (Ritzer, Jandrić, & Hayes, 2018).

Not to push a point too far, but there are some parallels that might be drawn in universities, which Ritzer includes under his label 'cathedrals of consumption' (Ritzer, 2010; Ritzer, Jandrić, & Hayes, 2018). HE takes on some of the traits of shopping malls and supermarkets as argued above. These draw people into forms of mindless consumption (both online and offline) and are designed to attract and service large numbers of customers and rationalise operations (Ritzer, 2010). Ritzer argues that in the McUniversity 'students are increasingly seen, and see themselves, as consumers of education who are there to get their money's worth'. As such, experiences are required to be instant with technology automatically delivering enhanced learning. Such expectations however can limit human self-awareness and opportunities to be self-critical for the purposes of learning. Such skills may not be included in the top 10 that it is assumed future employers seek. However, future employers may be becoming scarce, as Chapter 6 will explore, therefore students may need a stronger understanding of how their mental skills can serve them across life and not simply for the next job (Aoun, 2017: 75).

In the McUniversity there are also hidden forms of labour performed by con(pro)sumers. For staff, this may come in the form of the additional, unacknowledged academic labour that is involved in the setting up and maintaining of online and distance learning courses, or the recording of research and teaching activities to generate metrics for the measurement of research and teaching excellence. For students, there is both the endless completion of evaluation surveys to rate courses, providing metrics for institutions and regulatory bodies and also learning analytics data built from student activities. These complexities, and others, remain hidden in the trouble free discourse of TEL which suggests a simple one-way consumption, omitting the labour of production. Yet, as discussed in the Preface, a displacement of human labour has not always been articulated in educational policy, other voices have been present alongside deterministic rhetoric about technology, as the next few sections will illustrate.

### *What Is the Background to Technology Enhanced Learning Policy?*

During the 1960s and 1970s, computer systems were largely considered deterministic entities (Luppicini, 2005: 106). The famous speech given in 1963 by Harold Wilson at the Labour Party conference included a warning that Britain was experiencing a period of unprecedented technological change. Wilson's predictions of a 'new Britain' in the 'white heat' of a 'scientific revolution', though discussed by David Edgerton (1996) as something of an illusion, offer a point of reference for the later political narratives by Tony Benn during the 1970s, and then Tony Blair and New Labour government in the late 1990s and beyond. These policy narratives around the theme of technological change provide continuity across the decades, sharing the general premise that technology is a distinct force, separate from people, and able to 'act' independently of other social processes.

Yet in contrast to such rhetoric, as early as June 1973, scholars were carefully considering the use of computers in education as more than simply machines that we might use to extract economic value. In 1973, in memo (no: 298), from the Artificial Intelligence Laboratory of the Massachusetts Institute of Technology, entitled Uses of Technology to Enhance Education, it says:

> It is not sufficient merely to have a computer. It is necessary to develop contexts in which the computer can be used by a child to serve real personal purposes. Such a context needs to be both material and conceptual. (Papert, 1973)

So here is an early reference to a personalised use of a computer to support someone learning in an individual context, where both material and conceptual factors are acknowledged. There is no presumed enhancement from simply introducing a computer into a learning space. Instead the reasoning in this memo is more akin to the work of Illich and 'fashioning the computer into a convivial tool' (Illich, 1973; Papert, 1973: 10) which is also hospitable. Technology, in this vision, is a welcoming place for people to inhabit. In Tools for Conviviality (1973), Ivan Illich draws a contrast between a 'convivial' approach and the previous hundred years of human technological development which has tried to fashion machines to simply work for us, and to 'school' us in their service (Illich, 1973: 16). Illich suggests we discard the hypothesis that machines can replace slaves, because the result from this model in fact enslaves people. This point is thought provoking with regard to the forms of technological employment that now seem to be imminent globally, which I return to in Chapter 6. Changing the mindset from a resignation that people will simply be replaced by machines, would enable more creative thought about how universities should respond. However, before this can happen, it is necessary for politicians and university leaders to notice and agree that technology never stands alone. Below, Illich considers the broader context of schooling around technology as a structure implicated in repeating a misuse of technology that has gone before. Enframing machines in a maximum-yield conception turns people into consumers which conceals alternative uses:

> As the power of machines increases, the role of persons more and more decreases to that of mere consumers. (Illich, 1973: 17)

Illich provides here a visionary concept for technology which in many ways now seems prophetic. His ideas that people 'need their tools to move and to dwell' (Illich, 1973: 17) seems to apply more than ever in modern society, where our lives are increasingly mobile and people now sleep with their phones. Illich coined the term 'conviviality' to designate the opposite of the use of technology for increasing industrial productivity alone. Now, more than ever, in the light of technological unemployment as a reality it is worth examining Illich's ideas with critical posthuman visions of technology.

A 'conviviality' with our tools as humans, is representative of individual freedom, and personal interdependence that are important considerations in the context of learning. If 'conviviality is reduced below a certain level, no amount of industrial productivity can effectively satisfy the needs it creates among society's members' (Illich, 1973: 18). This vision of humans starved of creativity, on a treadmill to improve surplus value, yet never satisfied by the endless consumption it provides does not sound like a promising route to build a framework for educational technology research. Now, nearly a half century on from Illich's observations, if our current educational technology policy discourse is used as the measure, it seems we have not progressed far in realising conviviality in educational technology. Papert follows Dewey, to emphasise that 'knowing' is provisional. It must be founded on experience, not fixed absolutes (Dewey, 1938: 361). Educational technology was recognised by the AECT Definition Committee in 1972 to be about facilitating human learning:

> Educational Technology is a field involved in the facilitation of human learning through the systematic identification, development, organization, and utilization of learning resources and through the management of these processes. (Luppicini, 2005: 106)

Just a few years later it was acknowledged that serious conceptual work was needed in order to advance research, as demonstrated in the 1977 AECT Definition of Educational Technology publication quotation below:

> I firmly believe that the future of Educational Technology is now in the hands of the thinkers. What is needed is a handful of experienced people who have thought widely and deeply, and who are literally obsessed by the problems posed. These people must have the ability to analyze and synthesize, and, in effect, to invent whole new conceptual frameworks. If they do not have this latter ability, they will soon be reduced merely to improving what is. (Luppicini, 2005: 103)

Here is a clear reminder that people design learning and it is not technology that designs learning. Yet the policy agenda of 'improving what is' has managed to drown out the voices that sought more critical understandings of the role of educational technologies. A call for 'whole new conceptual frameworks' requires a step right back from a vision created by decades of policy rhetoric since the 1970s, of shiny machines to embrace, for the assured enhancement of learning.

### *E-Learning and the Emperor's New Clothes*

During the New Labour period (1997–2007), the rise of a 'network' society more globally and learning via the Internet opened up new avenues for the economics of HE as well as new pedagogical possibilities. A key example was the UK 'E-University' (UKeU). The government invested £55 million in 2000 in the UKeU, relying on the 'marketable' reputation of UK universities, but this project lacked a recognisable brand in a competitive market (Greener & Perriton, 2005: 68). The spectacular failure of UKeU within the New Labour ICT agenda for 'modernisation' of public sector institutions ought to have helped with reviewing the emphasis placed on simply enhancing UK HE, via technology. The discourse of HE policy since then however, tells us otherwise.

In 2003, Clegg, Hudson and Steel described globalisation and e-learning as analogous with 'the emperor's new clothes', suggesting that government inspired policy towards Information and Communication Technologies (ICTs) and education have been shaped by the irresistible power of globalisation and the determining effect of technology (Clegg, Hudson, & Steel, 2003). The argument that HE policy presents a narrative that e-learning should be accepted as inevitable, and the only choice of practitioners is to embrace new media enthusiastically, will be illustrated by the linguistic examples to come. I have already discussed the choices associated with arguments. This means that language in use as discourse is never neutral, but I observe with interest that the important point that no technologies are neutral either, also seems to be repeatedly bypassed across decades of HE policy. As scholars in STS pointed out during the 1970s and 80's, and Clegg, Hudson and Steel argue again here: 'technologies are always the products of real historical social relations, as well as the emergent technical capacities they provide' (Clegg, Hudson, & Steel, 2003). As underlined early in this book, artefacts and commodities become inscribed with all sorts of assumptions through the language in which they are advertised, but politics and power relations are also present throughout the stages of conception, design, manufacture and marketing of any technology.

For example, a recent decision by PepsiCo to launch a new 'lady friendly' version of their corn chips with a 'low crunch' feature and small packaging designed to fit into a woman's handbag illustrates how quickly gendered stereotypes can re-enter globally recognised products (Steafel, 2018). Ironically this delicate marketing of a bag of crisps to meet the fabricated needs of females coincides with the centenary of the suffragette movement, ongoing fights for equal pay for women and the MeToo hashtag campaign against sexual violence (Putnam, 2018). Returning to educational technology, asking any student or lecturer about the features of a virtual learning environment (VLE), that either permit or prevent helpful actions when learning or teaching, will also reveal how design can empower or restrict. VLEs have been adopted by universities since the late 1990s as vehicles for online and blended course design and peer collaboration and discussion. Yet despite the many dynamic functions that might potentially transform learning and teaching, these tools are often underused. VLEs tend to act as repositories of teaching materials and access to recorded lectures. Therefore, rather than changing pedagogical practice in innovative ways, VLEs appear to have reaffirmed traditional transmissive modes of teaching (Flavin, 2017: 8). Flavin argues that 'if we look at what students and lecturers do, rather than what we would like them to do, we will have a firmer evidence base from which to construct technology enhanced learning strategies' (Flavin, 2017: 137). I would add to this observation that if we were to do this, we would no longer refer to educational technology as Technology Enhanced Learning either.

### E-Learning (RIP)

The terminology used to describe educational technology in government policy and reports has varied over the years, offering some hope that Technology Enhanced Learning may not be a fixed buzz phrase. However, the example titles below from a range of reports and strategies about educational technology give an idea of both how terminology has varied (shown in bold), but also how TEL has come to be adopted as a phrase fairly consistently over the last decade:

*Embedding **Learning Technology** Institutionally* (JISC, 2003)
*Towards a Unified **E-Learning** Strategy* (DfES, 2003)
*HEFCE Strategy for **E-Learning*** (HEFCE, 2005)
*Innovative Practice with **E-Learning*** (JISC, 2005)
*Review of the 2005 HEFCE Strategy for **E-Learning*** (HEFCE, 2008)
*Great Expectations of **ICT*** (JISC, 2008)
*Survey of **Technology Enhanced Learning** for higher education in the UK* (UCISA, 2008)
*Effective Practice in a **Digital Age*** (JISC, 2009)
*Enhancing **Learning through Technology*** (HEA/JISC, 2009)
*Transforming Higher Education through **Technology Enhanced Learning*** (HEA, 2009)
*Transformation through **Technology*** (JISC, 2010)
*Transforming Curriculum Delivery through **Technology*** (JISC, 2011)
*Collaborate to Compete* (HEFCE, 2011)
*Survey of **Technology Enhanced Learning** for higher education in the UK* (UCISA, 2012)
*Enabling Innovation in **Technology Enhanced Learning*** (EPSRC, 2013)
*Flexible Pedagogies: **Technology Enhanced Learning*** (HEA, 2014)
*Survey of **Technology Enhanced Learning** for higher education in the UK* (UCISA, 2014)
*Assuring Best Practice in **Technology Enhanced Learning** environments* (ALTC, 2015)
*Survey of **Technology Enhanced Learning** for higher education in the UK* (UCISA, 2016)
*Rebooting Learning for the Digital Age: What Next for **Technology Enhanced Higher Education**?* (HEPI, 2017)

E-Learning was once a popular terminology, with many universities creating e-learning strategies, following the lead of the DfES, in 2003 and HEFCE in 2005:

> E-learning has the potential to revolutionise the way we work and the way we learn. (DfES, 2003)

> E-learning is starting to subsume and replace a number of previously used terms such as communications and information technologies (CandIT or ICT), information and learning technologies (ILT), networked learning, tele-learning or telematics and instructional technology. (Edgehill Strategy, 2005)

By 2008 TEL was clearly taking over, and before long, discourse around e-learning was also something of a distant memory. This change of terminology is reflected in these Joint Information Systems Committee (JISC) comments:

> The concept of e-learning is thus becoming subsumed into a wider discussion of how learning can be enhanced by more effective and far-reaching uses of digital technologies. (JISC, 2009)

> The move from 'e-learning' to 'enhancing learning through the use of technology' is now well embedded and recognized. (JISC, 2012)

What these statements don't reveal is *why?* Instead discussions focus on 'the' concept of e-learning becoming subsumed and 'the' move from 'e-learning' to 'enhancing learning through the use of technology', as if these are universal ideas we all recognise. Yet there is no concrete reason as to why any of these terms should actually absorb another anyway. They do not need to be considered either redundant or hostile, when differing perspectives on terminology and across subject disciplines may yield new understandings (Parchoma & Keefer, 2012). If we can be post-digital and still discuss the digital, then we should be able to be post e-learning, yet still able to explain to each other, why.

### *Embedding Technology Enhanced Learning*

Buzz phrases, it would seem, need to be 'embedded'. If you haven't read a university strategy lately for 'the student experience', 'student engagement' or 'employability' for example, then I invite you to take a look. It won't be long before a little 'embedding' is urged. Buzz phrases concerning educational technology would appear to be no different, but what exactly is being embedded? A few years back we were embedding something called 'e-learning':

> E-learning will be firmly embedded in the curriculum as a means of enhancing the quality of teaching. (Aberystwyth e-learning strategy, 2005–2009)

Now we are embedding the application of TEL:

> To continue to embed the application of technology enhanced learning (TEL). (University of Suffolk Learning Teaching and Assessment Strategy, Vision 2020)

However, TEL as discussed already, is something of a fait accompli. It is a statement about a process already completed by technology that has enhanced learning. How is it possible to embed that? Perhaps taking a course will help. The Staff and Educational Development Association (SEDA) run a taught award entitled: *Leading and Embedding Technology Enhanced Learning*. Alternatively, reviewing policy texts concerning 'the use of technology' and questioning an assumed direct link with 'enhanced learning' might be worthwhile first.

## The Labour of 'the Use of Technology'

### *Examining Patterns of Enhancement via a Corpus-Based CDA*

The corpus of government and university policy and strategy documents for educational technology contains over 1.1 million words drawn from 100 reports. These documents cover the period of 1997–2012, which is perceived as an intensive period of policy making for the role of technology in HE. As such, it is these years and beyond that have directed, shaped and influenced our current understanding of human academic labour, in relation to educational technology. I suggest that what is prioritised in these texts effectively marginalises alternative understandings that might be developed. The corpus includes key strategies for ICT and E-Learning in UK universities as well as for Technology Enhanced Learning. These policy reports were sourced online with the aid of government websites, such as the HEFCE publications list and the Centre for Technology Policy Research (CTPR), as well as individual university websites. Table 4.1 shows some of the keywords and clusters of words and how often these featured in the corpus.

I chose to examine what patterns emerge around 'the use of technology', rather than to narrow examples too specifically to 'e-learning' or 'TEL' alone. However, statements around e-learning and TEL were also revealed via these searches within the corpus, as can be seen in the lines below. A close analysis of the sections of policy statements surrounding these keywords and clusters of words was undertaken in the *Wordsmith* software by highlighting words immediately to the left and right of 'the use of technology'. An indicative extract from the findings from my corpus searches is shown in Figure 4.1 where

TABLE 4.1  Example keywords in the 'technology enhanced learning' corpus

| Keyword | Number of instances |
| --- | --- |
| Learning | 19260 |
| Use | 8131 |
| Technology | 6079 |
| Strategy | 4697 |
| Technology Enhanced Learning | 267 |
| The use of technology | 224 |

70 concordance lines can be observed. These reveal (via the line numbers) just how frequently and closely together these statements concerning 'the use of technology' appear across the many university and government strategies searched. The repetition in itself is striking, but I will proceed to point out some further observations concerning other words that crop up with regularity around this phrase.

5659 **the use of technology** can increase *accessibility and flexibility of learning and support*

5660 **the use of technology** to create *digital archives* to improve *documentation of practice*

5661 **the use of technology** to enhance *front line productivity, management and sharing*

5665 help drive the agenda to enhance *learning and teaching through* **the use of technology**

5667 Developing *strategies through* **the use of technology** to overcome *problems,* circumvent *disability*

5669 an overarching approach to **the use of technology** in support *of core activities*

5670 TechDis offers *particular advice on support through* **the use of technology**

5674 The University has a long history of innovation, in **the use of technology** to enhance *learning*

5675 **The use of technology** has enabled *students to take a more interactive approach to learning*

5677 To produce *resources and advice on* **the use of technology** to enhance *assessment*

5678 Research focuses on **the use of technology** *in higher education*

5680 enhancing *their skills and confidence in* **the use of technology enhanced learning**

5681 to enhance **the use of technology** *in learning and teaching*

5682 to share *information* and drive **the use of technology** to enhance *learning*

5683 to improve *the student learning experience through* **the use of technology**

5684 'best practice' in innovation in **the use of technology** <u>to achieve</u> *effective learning experiences*
5686 support for **use of technology** <u>to enhance</u> *the learning and teaching experience*
5688 much of the evidence <u>supports</u> **the use of technology** <u>*assisted learning and teaching*</u>
5689 The project <u>focused on</u> **the use of technology** <u>to improve</u> *teaching quality*
5690 clear guidance on **the use of technology** *for formative and summative assessment*
5691 Practitioners can easily <u>tailor</u> *learning materials to individuals through* **the use of technology**
5692 <u>focusing</u> *support on* **the use of technology** <u>to ensure</u> *better delivery to the most excluded*
5694 <u>understanding</u> and <u>developing</u> **the use of technology** *in higher education*
5696 a <u>view on</u> *best practice of* **the use of technology** *in teaching*
5698 <u>enhance</u> *core processes of selection, enrolment, and assessment through* **the use of technology**
5699 **the use of technology** <u>can enhance</u> *their learning and teaching experiences*
5701 We aim <u>to support</u> and <u>enable</u> you <u>to enhance</u> *learning through* **the use of technology**
5702 **the use of technology** <u>to provide</u> *flexibility and access, eg in the context of work-based learning*
5703 the case studies <u>provide</u> *testimony of discernible pedagogies emerging which* <u>incorporate</u> **the use of technology**
5704 consider how best to <u>raise</u> *the internal profile of* **the use of technology** <u>to enhance</u> *learning*
5705 consider **the use of technology** in a holistic manner <u>to facilitate</u> *understanding*
5707 **the use of technology** <u>to enhance</u> *the student learning experience, regardless of location*
5708 It aims <u>to optimise</u> **the use of technology** resources *across the public sector*
5709 Research <u>focuses upon</u> **the use of technology** <u>to create,</u> <u>sustain</u> and <u>develop</u> *reflective learning communities*
5711 *shifts in pedagogic approach and the learner–tutor relationship can* <u>result from</u> **the use of technology**
5716 from "<u>embedding</u> *e-learning*" to "<u>enhancing</u> *learning and teaching through* **the use of technology**
5717 Our vision is that <u>enhancing</u> *learning and teaching through* **the use of technology** should be considered
5733 e-Learning <u>includes</u> case studies <u>exploring</u> **the use of technology** <u>to enhance</u> *the student learning experience*
5734 **the use of technology** <u>to support</u> *work-place learning and the transitions between institutions*

5750 taking the HE and FE sectors forward in **the use of technology** <u>to improve</u> *core business*

5752 Our framework <u>focuses on</u> *the broader opportunities offered through* **the use of technology**

5754 <u>Support</u> the needs of managers and practitioners in **the use of technology** <u>to enhance</u> *assessment*

5756 JISC's role is <u>to champion</u> **the use of technology** *where it adds value and builds efficiencies*

5758 <u>widen</u> *participation* by **the use of technology** <u>to encourage</u> *non-traditional groups of students, engage employers*

5762 the move from 'e-learning' to '<u>enhancing</u> *learning through* **the use of technology**' is well <u>embedded</u> and <u>recognised</u>

5764 resources from the Academy and JISC <u>relating to</u> **the use of technology** <u>to enhance</u> *learning, teaching and assessment*

5765 <u>Support</u> *the sector in* **the use of technology** <u>to enhance</u> *learning, teaching and assessment*

5767 **the use of technology** <u>to support</u> and <u>enhance</u> *the business and management functions of educational institutions*

5774 UK literature on 'innovative assessment' <u>includes</u> **the use of technology** <u>to enhance</u> *assessment*

5777 <u>enhancement of</u> *learning, teaching and assessment,* and <u>mainstreaming of</u> **the use of technology** *in all aspects of HE*

5779 **the use of technology** <u>to promote</u> *efficiency and effectiveness through shared public services*

5780 advocacy of **the use of technology** <u>to support</u> *radical change in institutional processes*

5794 our approach to <u>enhancing</u> *learning, teaching and assessment through* **the use of technology**

5795 <u>implementing</u> th*eir own strategies for* <u>enhancing</u> *learning, teaching and assessment through* **the use of technology**

5798 attention on **the use of technology** <u>to enhance</u> *learning and teaching,* <u>to support</u> *all aspects of the institution's business*

5800 This strategy <u>highlights</u> *the government's overall priorities for* <u>enhancing</u> *education through* **the use of technology**

5801 The Academy <u>provides</u> *links to assessment resources* <u>focusing on</u> **the use of technology** *to address plagiarism*

5805 e *learning* towards an <u>appreciation of</u> *the potential* **use of technology** *to address the key challenges facing HE*

5806 **the use of technology** can help <u>make</u> *curriculum design processes more agile and responsive*

5809 published in March 2005 and focuses on enhancing *learning, teaching and assessment through* **the use of technology**

5810 Evidence suggests that **the use of technology** can improve *recruitment and retention*

5812 to synthesise *evidence of effective practice in* **the use of technology** to enhance *learning, teaching and assessment*

5815 *Develop the effective* **use of technology** to enable and support *work-based learning*

5818 **the use of technology** and Statement of Policy on enhancing *learning, teaching and assessment*

5822 from "embedding *e-learning*" to "enhancing *learning and teaching through* **the use of technology**

5830 All staff have opportunities to develop and practice *skills for* enhancing *learning through* **the use of technology**

5832 e-learning focuses on enhancing *learning teaching and assessment through* **the use of technology**

5842 enhancing *learning, teaching and assessment through* **the use of technology**

5844 updated in March 2009 with a new emphasis on *how learning and teaching is* enhanced by **the use of technology**

5849 Develop/use *best practice models for* **the use of TEL** to transform *teaching and learning*

FIGURE 4.1    Concordance lines from the educational technology policy corpus

Across these 70 example lines from the educational technology policy corpus (Figure 4.1) the phrase Technology Enhanced Learning, or TEL, does not appear that often. However, nearly half of these lines refer to an ability of technology to 'enhance', or to the unquestionable 'enhancing' properties of 'the use of technology'. 'Enhance' and 'enhancing' appear in 31 of these concordance lines. In other lines, words like 'increase', 'improve', 'transform' and 'optimise' are adopted too, in relation to 'the use of technology'. There seems to be no room for any doubt in these statements concerning the positive effects of 'the use of technology'. At the start of this set of examples, in lines 5659, 5660 and 5661, 'the use of technology is clearly credited with an ability to 'increase', 'create' and 'enhance' a range of goals. This is a structure that is often repeated looking down the lines. Another common structure to notice is how often processes are accomplished '*through* the use of technology', a phrase that appears in 16 times of these lines.

### *Educationalised and Technologised Social Agendas*

In terms of what 'the use of technology' is credited with amongst academic practices, this includes the ability to improve 'teaching quality' (5689), 'curriculum design' (5806), 'assessment' (5677, 5690, 5698, 5754), 'learning teaching and assessment' (5764, 5765, 5777, 5794, 5795, 5809, 5812, 5822, 5832, 5842) and 'address plagiarism' (5801). However, also notice the number of social agendas that, as well as being educationalised, have also been technologised (Peters, Jandrić, & Hayes, 2018). In these lines, a range of these issues can be noticed, with 'the use of technology' apparently coming to the rescue: 'accessible learning' (5659), 'circumvent disability' (5667), 'better delivery to the most excluded' (5692), 'widen participation' 'to encourage non-traditional groups of students, engage employers' (5758), 'address the key challenges facing HE (5805), 'recruitment and retention' (5810), work-based learning (5815). Reluctant though I am to put the damper on such easy technological 'fixes' for all of these societal matters, but I am not convinced. Where are the long hours spent by academics and students (alongside the technology) working on all of these issues accounted for? The regularity of many of the patterns across these institutional documents seems to reinforce the assumption that: *in exchange for the use of new technology there will automatically be enhanced forms of student learning.* Having noticed these structures were so often repeated within my corpus, I then took a closer look through CDA.

### *Identifying Who Is Acting to Achieve Something*

As mentioned in Chapter 3, the order in which words are placed, alters meaning. Transitivity analysis helps to reveal the types of processes taking place in these statements, but also who is acting to achieve what goal. In lines 5659, 5660 and 5661, 'the use of technology' is the entity that is undertaking a material process to 'increase', 'create' and 'enhance'. However, in the examples below, a few phrases have been picked out from the corpus lines to help shed light on what other processes are 'going on' and who (or what) is undertaking these. 'The use of technology' it would seem has some accomplices. These entities also help enact the mental, verbal and material processes taking place in these statements. For example, in line 5678 below:

5678 Research focuses on **the use of technology** *in higher education*

Here it is 'research' (rather than a person) that, via a mental process, 'focuses' on 'the use of technology'. Again in 5689 a similar pattern can be observed:

5689 The project focused on **the use of technology** to improve *teaching quality*

This time it is 'the project' that, via a mental process, 'focused' on the ability of 'the use of technology' to improve 'teaching quality'. Once more this is repeated in 5832:

> 5832 e-learning <u>focuses</u> on <u>enhancing</u> *learning, teaching and assessment through* **the use of technology**

This time it is 'e-learning', that via a mental process, 'focuses' on 'enhancing' 'learning, teaching and assessment' 'through the use of technology'. E-learning also has some help from 'case studies' in the next example:

> 5733 e-Learning <u>includes</u> *case studies* <u>exploring</u> **the use of technology** <u>to enhance</u> *the student learning experience*

Here 'e-learning', in a material process, 'includes' 'case studies' that are attributed with 'exploring' 'the use of technology' 'to enhance' 'the student learning experience'. Then below 'case studies' now have a role as an actor:

> 5703 the case studies <u>provide</u> *testimony of discernible pedagogies emerging which* <u>incorporate</u> **the use of technology**

Here 'case studies' are the entity that, in a material process, 'provide' 'a testimony'. Don't we do that? Perhaps there will be a chance for humans to speak at some point, if the material and mental processes have been taken care of. Yet that doesn't seem to happen either.

> 5810 Evidence <u>suggests</u> that **the use of technology** <u>can improve</u> *recruitment and retention*

In 5810 it is 'evidence' that is doing the talking, as it *suggests* via a verbal process, that 'the use of technology' *can improve* 'recruitment and retention'. Then next it is the turn of a 'strategy' to do the talking:

> 5800 This strategy <u>highlights</u> the government's overall priorities for <u>enhancing</u> *education through* **the use of technology**

Here it is 'this strategy' that, via a verbal process, 'highlights' the 'government's priorities' for 'enhancing' 'education' through 'the use of technology'. I have to say that right now, I am feeling a little left out of an agenda that concerns me taking responsibility for developing my teaching in conjunction with 'the use of technology'. In these examples, there is not a lecturer in sight, let alone a student.

### Buzz Phrases Collaborating with Each Other

Yet at least there is no need for a buzz phrase to feel isolated, even if I do. Some further examples in the corpus reveal how, in line 5890 'e-learning' meets up with 'the student experience':

> 5890 <u>provide</u> a valid *mechanism for the recognition of excellence in the use and implementation of* **e-learning** <u>to enhance</u> *the student experience*

Again in line 5224, 'e-learning' encounters 'the student experience':

> 5224 *this strategy for e-learning* <u>strives</u> to <u>realise</u> *the following vision to use* **e-learning** <u>to enhance</u> *the student learning experience*

In line 6156 both 'best practice' and 'the student experience' get to sit together:

> 6156 <u>share</u> *best practice in* **the use of technologies** <u>to enhance</u> *the student experience*

### Questioning Policy Values in Relation to Academic Practice

It is worth questioning what kind of paradigm underpins the writing of policy in this way. A paradigm refers to the concepts and thought patterns directing the rational values implicit in these statements. Policy for educational technology does not need to be conceptualised from a paradigm that largely emphasises what 'the use of technology', rather than the practice of humans, is doing. Earlier in this book I questioned the attribution of human qualities and labour to consumer products, such as a car or a hairbrush. Here in concordance line 5704, 'the use of technology' appears to have an 'internal profile' of its own:

> 5704 <u>consider</u> *how best to* <u>raise</u> *the internal profile of* **the use of technology** <u>to enhance</u> *learning*

It is not the only entity to boast a profile, 'examples of TEL' has a profile too:

> 4086 <u>raise</u> *the profile of* **examples of** TEL *for* <u>enhancement</u> *of the student experience and to save staff time*

Before we know it 'the use of technology' and 'examples of TEL' will be awarded my promotion and pay rise, maybe they will also take my place on the Learning and Teaching Committee or perhaps my seat on the commute into work. I doubt though that 'the use of technology' or 'examples of TEL' are going to find themselves asked to comment on my student evaluation feedback, or to be threatened with performance management measures if the scores falter. Not only do these nominalised claims remove any explicit indicator of agency (Simpson & Mayr, 2010: 68), they also remove accountability. This makes it hard to know exactly who makes these choices to write in this way, whether they are consciously enacted or not. In this form of language, human social relations are discussed as if they were 'things', in a form of 'reification' (Lukács, 1971), which then permits them to be traded as objects. Given that so much human labour now involves digital technologies, this must surely interest educators in terms of what this means for students' learning, and indeed instructors' teaching, in universities (Hayes & Bartholomew, 2015).

### A Limiting Discourse

Fundamentally, these transitivity examples reveal how policy discourse can limit people's capacity to manage change. In UK HE (and globally) policy discourse is being shaped by a neoliberal agenda, often playing out as a call for greater marketisation of higher education, as is apparent in the UK Government White Paper: *Higher Education: Students at the heart of the system* (BIS, 2011). Universities have responded to this agenda either by accepting the notion of students as customers of the HE 'offer', or as partners within it. These are two radically different responses (underpinned by different paradigms), but meanwhile, policy discourse is characterised by a tendency to conceal any need for human agency in design, delivery and participation in learning opportunities related to technology (Hayes & Bartholomew, 2015). Transferring agency for 'enhancing student experience' into the hands of technologies is a political activity, which internalises the ideological constructs of both technology makers and policy makers. Power endowed into technological objects is not neutral, as technologies and policies are made by humans and thus reflect their hopes and wishes. Technologies have always promised enhanced opportunities for human learning. Even chalk and a blackboard, may enhance students' experiences, but this cannot be taken as a given because humans perform their encounters with technologies of all kinds in diverse ways. Yet still the complexity of these performances are reduced in media and policy language to reflect a dominant political economy.

### *Moving from a Discourse of 'Nothing' Towards a Discourse of 'Something'*

There are though, alternative ways to frame policy discourse. Whilst policy may guide different forms of practice in universities, surely it is necessary to also ask: *what forms of practice guide policy?* With these ideas in mind, CDA is just *one* way to expose the choices people make (and others may unknowingly replicate) in formulating policy language (Fairclough, 2007). Critically confronting discursive structures in this context is not a negative activity. It helps to point out the inaccuracies that surround simplified statements that credit human labour to buzz phrases in policy discourse. The analysis empowers conversations about the ways in which *technology, language* and *learning* interact. These three constitutive elements are ever-present in learning situations and they intersect across disciplinary borders (Hayes & Bartholomew, 2015). Broadening the way in which we discuss technology for learning, to also consider language, offers a route to restore elements of human practice that are missing from these policy texts.

So whilst this analysis of discourse cannot be claimed to prove or alter anything, it offers a lens through which concrete expressions of an expected 'exchange value' from technology might be noticed, discussed and changed. Massey suggests that discourse of this kind can 'mould identities' (Massey, 2013) in narrow (often economically-based) terms. This can undermine human interactions (including human labour) implicit within dialectical relationships between technology, language and learning. The role of language in constituting the identities of organisations too, such as universities, has been explored by linguists as a principal means through which institutions create their own social reality (Mumby & Clair, 1997: 181). So what possibilities are open to us to ensure that this social reality accurately represents human academic labour?

Firstly, we could each seek to step away from the path of 'least linguistic resistance' (Bleiker, 2009: 5). This would mean making a conscious effort to avoid reinforcing the techno-determinist route discussed in this chapter. A second action would be to support authentic and legitimate student-staff partnerships of discovery about ways in which digital learning is performed and to then re-write and co-write policy together, so that it is easier to apply in everyday practice (Bartholomew & Hayes, 2015). Finally, it is important to note that the lack of human representation in these texts amounts to a loss of power. If we cannot notice our own performance as co-creators with technology, then we are disconnected from our own practice within the policy for TEL. As such, TEL provides a vehicle for political economic agendas to make simplified claims in the name of technology, which can distort the values of human learning communities in higher education. Therefore, any aspirations we may have for human practice to inform policy will struggle to succeed (Hayes & Bartholomew, 2015). It is time for humans to reoccupy this language. If we fail to review and address the assumptions tucked away within TEL, then we will miss a chance to develop a broader theoretical underpinning for educational technology, as an important developing field of knowledge and research (Conole & Oliver, 2002). Right now TEL remains a 'trouble free' policy discourse consisting of 'nothing', because it omits the 'troublesome knowledge' (Mezirow, 1991; Meyer & Land, 2006) concerning human labour that could actually make it 'something'.

CHAPTER 5

# Student Engagement McPolicy

## The Value of Student Engagement

### *Why Student Engagement?*

The term 'student engagement' is now routinely discussed in HE government policy, at the level of institutional strategy, and widely researched in the literature (Trowler & Trowler, 2010; Taylor & Parsons, 2011; Zepke, 2012; Nygaard, Brand, Bartholomew, & Millard, 2013; Zepke, 2014; Macfarlane & Tomlinson, 2017; Hayes, 2018).

Engagement, as a word, concerns forms of captivation and participation, or refers to something absorbing, that engrosses and grips the senses. It would seem to be an entirely apt word to bring into the context of student learning in general. Yet why join the words student and engagement together in this way and not in others? Why not discuss it in the plural and refer to the participation of students, rather than student? Perhaps student engagement is simply easy to point to as a construct, to which expectations can be attached. I will return to this idea a little later, but it is worth observing for now, that just because student engagement includes the word student, it does not necessarily follow that this discourse very often includes students themselves (or even links with staff) or considers inclusivity and diversity of different types of students.

Instead, frequently emphasis is placed on rational statements concerning improving practices within HE, just like Technology Enhanced Learning (TEL), discussed in the previous chapter. Whilst improvement is surely a good thing, as examples will reveal, it is how these approaches are framed that is problematic. Furthermore, a definition of student engagement on which authors agree, does not seem to be readily forthcoming (Taylor & Parsons, 2011).

> Many articles, conference papers and chapters on student engagement do not contain explicit definitions of engagement, making the (erroneous) assumption that their understanding is a shared, universal one. (Trowler, 2010: 17)

If I were to teach a topic to my students, for which I offered no parameters or historical understanding of the title, then I would be failing to meet basic quality requirements. Given so much government policy relates to the regulation of quality in universities and has impact on the lives of students,

I have questioned already why we don't apply similar levels of scrutiny to the discourse of policy texts, as we do to programme approval and evaluation. It would not be unreasonable to require HE policy documents, that relate to student engagement, to clearly explain how this term is being framed and understood, as part of an introductory paragraph. Yet this measure would still only go a small way towards disrupting the now widespread uncritical application of this term, and I suggest that a more radical interrogation of McPolicy on student engagement is needed. This is because, as this chapter will demonstrate, defining student engagement only goes so far. It is only when the words surrounding student engagement in strategy documents are closely scrutinised too, that it becomes possible to see how this term is frequently applied and indeed 'acts' on behalf of students and staff.

### *How Does Student Engagement McPolicy Support a Neoliberal Ideology?*

Even without a working definition, student engagement now has such exposure as a concept, that 'the value of engagement is no longer questioned' (Trowler & Trowler, 2010: 9). Macfarlane and Tomlinson (2017) refer to 'the development of a literature that is heavily influenced by cause-effect framing and a focus on effectiveness' (Macfarlane & Tomlinson, 2017: 5). More recently there have been alternative, critical viewpoints that are drawn from analysis of the effects of neoliberalism. These provide a case 'to shift the emphasis from what and how questions concerning student engagement to consider its broader political, economic and ethical implications as a means of challenging the prevailing policy narrative' (Macfarlane & Tomlinson, 2017: 5).

Zepke argues that student engagement is a 'hot topic' and a 'buzz phrase' (Zepke, 2014: 697) as it connects with student success and performativity, which primarily values what can be produced, observed, measured, recorded and reported (Thomas, 2012: 10; Zepke, 2014: 703). In this way student engagement supports 'a neoliberal ideology' (Zepke, 2014: 698). This position has been contested however by Trowler, who suggests that Zepke's narrative is based on a selective approach to, and interpretation of the literature (Trowler, 2015: 337; Hayes, 2018: 20). Furthermore, Trowler argues that Zepke's narrative 'lacks an explanation of the mechanisms of the relationship between neoliberalism and student engagement' in the form of 'content' (Trowler, 2015: 337).

In this chapter I will draw upon sections from a recent article that I wrote for LATISS journal: *Invisible labour: do we need to reoccupy student engagement policy?* (Hayes, 2018), to offer a form of 'content' (CDA examples from student engagement strategies) to explore the suggested 'gap' in Zepke's thesis. I respond to the Zepke-Trowler debate with an analysis of student engagement policies that illuminate the role of policy discourse, as one mechanism linking neoliberal values with practices of student engagement. Through a corpus-based Critical Discourse Analysis, I will demonstrate once more how a persistent and alarming omission of human labour from university strategy texts takes place around student engagement. The engagements of students and staff are attributed to technology, documents and frameworks. Student engagement is discussed as a commodity to be embedded and marketed back to students in a way that seems to mainly yield an 'exchange value' (Marx, 1867) for universities, rather than students.

Zepke recently examined two distinct readings of student engagement. The first of these is linked to the focus on effectiveness that Macfarlane and Tomlinson have observed. Zepke suggests that this reading 'has an affinity with neoliberal ideas about what should be the business of higher education namely conveying practical knowledge, building performativity and assuring quality through accountability'. This understanding of student engagement 'concerns evidence-based ideas about what works to achieve quality learning and teaching' (Zepke, 2017: 2). The second reading is critical of the first, on the basis of what is 'left out' when student engagement is framed in a largely practical form of reasoning. In the analysis to come, what appears to be left out are people. Just as McDonalds deter loitering, the student engagement discourse in university strategies appears to have cleared out the human presence that could slow down efficiency.

### *Valuing Student Engagement*

How value is expressed in student engagement policy documents is of particular interest in relation to Zepke's question of whether student engagement aligns with and supports a 'neoliberal ideology' (2014: 697). In such an ideology, the maximisation of the economic freedom of individuals within a free market is emphasised. Some would argue that neoliberal ideology routinely redefines citizens as consumers, rewards merit and punishes whatever might be deemed to be inefficiencies (Monbiot, 2016). Yet still, these are only ideas. By closely examining policy discourse about student engagement, patterns can emerge to provide an indication of such ideas and the degree to which they are repeated. This makes it possible to reflect on how pervasive and entrenched these ideas may be across elements of wider communicative behavior. Gibbs suggests that student engagement has been coined in policy to refer to: 'so many different things that it is difficult to keep track of what people are actually talking about' (Gibbs, 2014). In the previous chapter, I examined policy statements that draw attention to an additional form of 'value' that the use of technology-enhanced learning (TEL) is expected to yield (Hayes, 2015; Hayes & Bartholomew, 2015; Hayes & Jandrić, 2014). These texts often omit any *explicit* reference to the human labour required to realise such value. Similar textual patterns might be noticed in educational policy statements around 'student engagement'. The example below shows actions that would usually involve human activities being attributed to non-human entities:

> Develop more sophisticated structures and KPIs to measure the contributions and impact of student engagement. (Student Engagement Policy, Milton Keynes College)

So here, by attributing *contributions* and *impact* to the entity of *student engagement* it is possible to get a sense of where value seems to be placed. Rather than specifically measuring the contributions of people, the sentence suggests that these contributions directly emerge from the concept of student engagement.

### *Embedding Student Engagement*

Frequently, the idea that student engagement is something universal that institutions might *embed* is discussed in student engagement policies:

> The goals of this framework outline the aim to embed a culture and ethos of student engagement. (The University of the West of England Student Engagement Framework)

> This document outlines a strategy to further embed a culture and ethos of student engagement. (Leeds Trinity University Student Engagement Strategy)

Whilst these examples are from two different strategies, written in two different university documents, there are some remarkable linguistic similarities. In both excerpts, there is an assumption that *a culture and ethos of student engagement* is something that can be embedded. A closer look at how these and other policy statements are grammatically structured reveals that the human labour required to enact certain proposals appears to be omitted. Above, through a particular structure of nouns and verbs, it is *the goals of this framework* that are attributed with an aim *to embed* a culture and ethos of student engagement, and it is 'this document' that *outlines* a strategy. Surely these are tasks that require thinking, planning and a vision and would normally be undertaken by people, not by goals within a framework, or attributed to a document. The verb *to embed* suggests that there is work to be done, but there is little indication of who will do it.

## The Labour of Student Engagement

### *Examining Student Engagement via a Corpus-Based Critical Discourse Analysis*

The corpus of U.K. student engagement policy and strategy texts was gathered during 2016–2017 and is relatively small, currently just 62,000 words in total. This is because student engagement policies have only emerged during the last five years or so. All of the policies are freely available on the Internet; they were sourced via searches on 'student engagement policy' and then downloaded from their respective U.K. university websites. In total, twenty documents from twenty universities were used to build the corpus. In order to work with these files in *Wordsmith*, they were converted into text files and then loaded into the software. In Table 5.1 the top keywords in the student engagement corpus are shown.

TABLE 5.1    Example keywords in the 'student engagement' corpus

| Keyword | Number of instances |
| --- | --- |
| Student | 1580 |
| Engagement | 777 |
| University | 514 |
| Framework | 74 |

A close analysis of the sections of policy statements surrounding these keywords was undertaken by highlighting words immediately to the left and the right of the keyword. As mentioned in previous chapters, this reveals how the order of words can affect meaning, and how one can place emphasis on textual constructions rather than on people as enacting academic practices. This provides tangible 'content', as called for by Trowler, to consider the difference between how student engagement is imagined at a policy level in comparison with the contexts in which it is practiced. A small extract from the findings from my corpus searches around student engagement is shown below as concordance lines. This enables the words before and after this term to be noticed and analysed in terms of structure and meaning. The numbering down the left-hand side shows where each concordance line sits in the whole corpus of texts. This makes it easy to return to each example to look at further patterns. The close proximity of the numbering below also indicates that the patterns highlighted in these examples seem to occur with regularity.

1085 **All of this information will help us** <u>to report</u> *on the impact of student engagement*

1088 **Review and monitor** <u>the effectiveness of</u> *Student Engagement opportunities*

1089 **A framework** <u>defines and measures</u> *the remit and impact of student engagement*

1091 **What 'indicators' should be used** <u>to measure</u> *the impact of student engagement activities?*

1097 **The framework also** <u>identifies</u> *a number of features of effective student engagement*

1119 **Goals of this strategy are** <u>to continue to embed</u> *a culture and ethos of student engagement*

1121 **This** <u>will increase</u> *awareness around the impact of student engagement*

1123 <u>Support</u> **our professional services** <u>in embracing and embedding</u> *student engagement*

1125 **what 'indicators' should be used** <u>to measure</u> *the impact of student engagement activities*

1128 **The framework document** <u>highlights</u> *5 key elements of student engagement*

1131 **The University** <u>utilises</u> *a number of mechanisms to engage students*

1133 **Student Partnership Agreements** <u>are developing</u> *the student experience and student engagement*

1134 **A complementary Education Strategy** <u>highlights</u> *the importance of student engagement*

1139 **This partnership agreement is a key aspect** <u>in progressing</u> *specific aspects of student engagement*

1140 **This strategy** <u>aims to further enhance</u> *the continued development of student engagement*

1141 **The College** <u>will provide</u> *student engagement opportunities* <u>which will ensure</u> *equality of access*

1142 **This framework** <u>aims to support</u> *the development of strong student engagement at all levels*

### *Material, Verbal and Mental Processes that Would Usually Involve Humans*

Breaking down the statements in these concordance lines to look at their components is a valuable linguistic tool for noticing who the 'actors' are, and also which 'goals' they are responsible for achieving. The verbs (underlined) reveal different types of labour processes, and the nouns (in bold) tell us who, or what, is actually enacting the processes leading to these goals (in italics). There are some typical sustained patterns that might be said to contribute to an effacing of human labour. For example, in concordance lines (1089), (1097), (1128), and (1142), it is frameworks that are said (through verbal processes) to <u>define</u>, <u>identify</u>, <u>highlight</u> and <u>support</u> aspects of *student engagement*. In concordance lines (1119) and (1140) it is strategies that are said (through material processes) to <u>embed</u> *a culture and ethos of student engagement* and <u>enhance</u> *the continued development of student engagement.* The nouns that are enacting these processes are non-human entities. Thus it is implied that many activities connected to student engagement are conducted by faceless documents, institutions and frameworks, rather than by human beings working together. Taking now some examples from earlier in the corpus, in concordance line (3) below, a mental process is illustrated, yet there are no humans to be identified as enacting it:

> 3 The <u>focus of</u> **student engagement** is <u>to enhance</u> *the quality of learning*

Instead it is suggested that **student engagement** itself (rather than students or staff) has a <u>focus</u> that is <u>to enhance</u> *the quality of learning*. How would we know? After all, having a focus would be categorised as a form of mental process, usually undertaken by a human with whom this focus could be discussed. A person could be asked how the quality of learning is likely to be enhanced. Instead, this statement emphasises performativity, but attributes the labour required to enhance the quality of learning to a disembodied entity, called student engagement.

### *Exchange Value for the University from Student Engagement*

Student engagement is thus presented as offering exchange value, as the demonstrated through the examples below. Firstly, in concordance line (10) interesting insights on where this value is placed are revealed:

> 10 **Student engagement is not just a sector-wide mandatory imperative but also a valued endeavour that** <u>adds to</u> *the quality of University life*

In this sentence, it is student engagement that materially <u>adds to</u> *the quality of university life*, rather than the students themselves. The concept that student engagement is a sector-wide mandatory imperative suggests something compulsory within the concept, with the focus on being a valued endeavour coming secondary. There is also an emphasis on adding to the quality of university life, rather than on enriching the lives of individual students, who would, in practice, 'engage'. In line (29) of the corpus, the emphasis, once again, is on benefits to the university, rather for students and staff:

> 29 **Effective student engagement** offers *a range of benefits to the University*

It is effective student engagement, not people, that offers these *benefits*.

In line (216) it is student engagement again, not staff or students, that is attributed by both the Student Union and the University with enhancing the quality of learning and teaching and the student experience more broadly:

> 216 **The Student Union and the University** acknowledge and welcome the essential role that **student engagement** plays in enhancing *the quality of learning and teaching and more broadly the student experience*

An institutional, rather than a student focus, is clear again in line (141), it is the College that has been successful *in developing* its approaches to student engagement

> 141 **The College** has been successful *in developing* its approaches to **Student Engagement**

In example (64) it is also the college that acts:

> 64 **The College** recognises the importance and value of embedding *student engagement into operating practices and systems within the institution*

Firstly, here it is **the College**, not a human, that (in a mental process) recognises the importance and value of embedding *student engagement*. Secondly, priority is given to embedding student engagement into *operating practices and systems* within the institution, rather than on relating practices of student engagement to people who might benefit. It is not at all clear how the forms of human engagement that students are expected to enact are embedded into institutional operating practices and systems. Again, in line (67), where the ethos of student engagement reaches within *the university* is what is emphasised:

67 **It is important to us that the ethos of student engagement** <u>reaches</u> *every corner of the university*

This emphasis is repeated in line (80) when a **strategy** (in a verbal process) <u>outlines</u> a similar aim <u>to embed</u> *a culture and ethos of student engagement throughout the University:*

80 **This strategy** <u>outlines</u> the aim to continue <u>to embed</u> *a culture and ethos of student engagement throughout the University*

There is a suggestion, via the word 'ethos', that student engagement has a particular character (as opposed to multiple characteristics), and that therefore a rather singular ethos of student engagement should reach across the university.

### *The Impact of Student Engagement*

In both line (185) and line (193), it is **student engagement** that is said to have impact rather than the activities of students and staff:

185 **All of this information will help us** <u>to report</u> *on the impact of student engagement*

193 **This will** <u>increase</u> *awareness around the impact of student engagement* and will <u>ensure</u> *that our quality enhancement work is better informed*

In line (224) it is a framework that <u>defines and measures</u> both *the remit and impact of student engagement*

224 **The framework** <u>defines and measures</u> *the remit and impact of student engagement*

In line (81), it is the wider impact of student engagement, rather than human beings, that makes *a difference.*

81 **Outcome measures** <u>are</u> *measures of* **the wider impact of student engagement** <u>to</u> <u>identify</u> *how* **it** *is making a difference*

Here it is suggested (in what was discussed in Chapter 3 as a relational process) that outcome measures are equivalent to *the wider impact of student engagement*. This is a statement that can also be read in reverse, that *the wider impact of student engagement* is equivalent to outcome measures. The problem is that this reduces student engagement to outcome measures alone. Whilst we are not told in the statement whether this refers to results, employability or what, the assumption that student engagement (as an entity) will have measurable outcomes is a narrow one. Furthermore, if 'engagement' is only considered to be about observable and measurable practices that are expected to have a direct impact on 'the student experience', then 'private, silent, unobserved and solitary practices' of engagement are omitted (Gourlay, 2015: 410).

Given the range of sources that were uploaded to the corpus, it is interesting to consider how much this might reflect and promulgate a particular set of beliefs: these repeated ideas occur across documents generated by a wide range of institutions. For example, we should consider whether student engagement really is a thing that can be measured and embedded. However, it gets worse.

### *Marketing a Packaged Product of Student Engagement*

It seems from the next example that student engagement can even be passed around like a gift. In line (84), student engagement is packaged, marketed and communicated *to applicants, current students and staff*, as if it were any other product or service.

> 84 Packaging, marketing and communicating **student engagement** *to applicants, current students and staff*

I would question how exactly a form of human engagement that students are expected to enact is packaged and then marketed and communicated back to these students, who are in fact those who engage? According to neoliberal ideology, knowledge is a commodity and higher education is a market where knowledge and skills are traded (Zepke, 2014: 702). Universities offer marketable knowledge and skills, as well as supplying marketable services (Codd, 2005), so perhaps the idea that student engagement can be packaged, marketed and communicated is not so strange after all. Yet such 'trafficking in human attributes' (Kopytoff, 1986: 85) undermines the broader purposes of universities. It simplifies the complex human experience of 'engagement', which can take so many forms, into something little different to an Egg McMuffin. As Ritzer points out, a McMuffin is a product that has replaced an entire breakfast (Ritzer, 2015: 68). A cooked breakfast could involve any combination of ingredients, presentation and setting, not to mention who might be consuming this mixture and in what context. If the engagement of a student might be packaged up in this way in policy, as if it were an off the shelf snack, or budget holiday, then the wealth of academic literature written about engaging students student staff partnership may as well be scrapped. Staying with the theme of marketing student engagement, in line (158) then it is a brand and strapline that this time takes credit for promoting student engagement:

> 158 Developing a strong and overarching brand and strapline to promote *student engagement*

### The Labour of a McStudent Engagement Policy

In this last set of examples, human labour is represented by **survey data, frameworks, strategy** and **Student Engagement Policy**. In line (131), it is **student engagement survey data** that has suddenly found a voice and appear to have presented the *opportunities* that are mentioned:

> 131 **Student engagement survey data** has presented *opportunities for enhancement of teaching and learning*

In line (133), it is a student engagement framework that represents our approach to a rather comprehensive set of engagements- *by, with and for students.*

> 133 **The student engagement framework** represents *our approach to engagement by, with and for students*

and in line (442) it is the higher education strategy, not lecturers or managers, that defines its commitment to the development of independent learners and student engagement:

> 442 **The Higher Education Strategy** defines *its commitment to the development of independent learners and student engagement*

In lines (464) and (467) it is The Student Engagement Policy that replaces human voices that would articulate and outline the topics stated:

464 **The Student Engagement Policy** <u>articulates</u> *the mechanisms by which the university facilitates, supports and monitors student engagement*

467 **The Student Engagement Policy** <u>outlines</u> *the range of student feedback opportunities*

What emerges from the sets of examples above is a focus on student engagement as an entity that is linguistically detached from the people with whom it would naturally be connected. It is discussed as something that can be packaged, marketed and promoted, with a distinct emphasis on benefits to the institution from student engagement. Credit too is often given to the university, the college, the framework, data, strategy or policy, rather than to students or staff, for any success and promotion of student engagement. Strategies are provided with powers to outline and articulate plans and to represent people, but in a manner that is universal, rather than contextual and inclusive of diversity. The textual patterns in these examples support the claim made by Zepke that there is 'an approach to knowledge that makes it largely invisible in the engagement discourse, a view of learning that emphasises outcomes and performance, and a view of quality that is informed by accountability measures' (2014: 702).

### *Student Labour, Staff Engagement and the Teaching Excellence Framework (TEF)*

In previous writing (Hayes & Jandrić, 2014), I have drawn on Marxist theory in relation to technology, which like any commodity has 'value' that also represents a quantity of human labour. Marx (1867) distinguished between 'use value' and 'exchange value'. 'Use value' relates to the human social necessities that a technology might fulfil in conjunction with a person's labour. On the other hand, 'exchange value' takes the human labour involved for granted to realise a profit in an economic market. In the same way that new technologies can quickly become subordinated to narratives of exchange value, it would seem that the human labour of student engagement is subject to similar fluid expression within policy language. In relation to students, many of the examples above seem to be about promoting the phenomenon of student engagement as a form of exchange value for the institution. In relation to staff activities, student engagement is said to have powers to enhance quality, learning and teaching, and university processes, but little is said about the many hours of human labour that connect these areas of work.

The labour of academic staff in engaging students also appears to be unaccounted for. In addition to teaching and research, academics undertake a range of activities such as personal tutoring, writing references for students seeking employment, sitting on programme review committees and acting as external examiners, all of which can be described as 'academic citizenship' (Havergal, 2015). While it is important to maintain quality and support pastoral care that universities now commodify and sell to students, this labour is undervalued by institutions and does not bring with it career rewards. Whilst hidden labour may be profitable for institutions, avoiding the costs associated with staff recognition, this also risks hiding from view the very activities of students and staff that would evidence key metrics in a Teaching Excellence Framework (BIS, 2016).

The Teaching Excellence Framework (TEF) is a new ranking system for universities in England. Measurement of teaching quality, the learning environment and student outcomes need to be evidenced through data in institutional TEF responses, and some of this data relates to contact time between teachers and students. In the examples below, taken from the recently published *Teaching Excellence Framework: Year 2 Specification* (BIS, 2016), the office hours that lecturers regularly provide for their students, physically or via Skype, are hidden within statements that objectify situated, social encounters as 'optimum levels of contact time' and 'appropriate levels of contact time'. It is someone's notion of 'optimum' or 'appropriate' quantities of time that then 'acts' to *secure* high levels of engagement and commitment to learning and study from students. There is no mention of the lecturers or other professional colleagues who will personalise provision and provide this time, or indeed of the labour provided by students in using this time, or of the interactions that occur: Optimum levels of contact time, including outstanding personalised provision, *secures* the highest levels of engagement and active commitment to learning and study from students (BIS, 2016: 47), and Appropriate levels of contact time, including personalised provision, *secures* high levels of engagement and commitment to learning and study from students (BIS, 2016: 47).

Instead, a transaction (underpinned by a series of assumptions) takes place between objectified time and high levels of engagement and commitment from students. It is *levels of contact time* that secures engagement from students and not the staff working to commit that time. There is no mention of who decides the levels of contact time that are 'optimum' or 'appropriate'. More importantly still is the problematic positioning of students in each of these texts, which exposes contradictions. Students are not discussed as willing partners in their own learning, nor even as consumers, but as contractors from whom commitment must be 'secured'. The shared labour process that has for centuries closely interconnected academics with their students is effectively eroded away through this discourse. Work undertaken in student-staff partnerships through agencies such as the Joint Information Systems Committee (JISC), the Staff and Educational Development Association (SEDA) and the

Higher Education Academy (HEA) offer alternatives to transactional relationships between teaching staff and students in the form of mutual and collaborative forms of engagement. However, I suggest that a more radical move still in reconsideration of how university and government policy could be rewritten. The shared and intimate practices of engagement between students and staff should not be hidden, but should instead be celebrated. Moreover, a more honest approach needs to acknowledge that these crucial relationships take time and human labour to develop.

### *Learning and the Human Body*

Trowler's challenge is that Zepke's analysis misses out 'content'. He adds that 'the nature of the relationship between ideologies and the social world is simply assumed not theorised' (2015: 337). This criticism calls for a renewed focus on embracing the role of our human bodies in learning and related policy. Academic work within a neoliberal context is strongly constructed (even constricted) around 'managing time in a demonstrably efficient manner' (Walker, 2009: 484). In seeking to justify and 'outsmart' time, there is a tendency to marginalise the role of human bodies in practices of teaching and learning, treating the body 'as relevant only as a vessel that houses the brain' (Ng, 2008: 1). Policy language provides a lens through which to observe the tendency not to credit humans with their own physical and mental labour and to instead discuss processes and systems. This often illogical and contradictory way of writing appears to be widely accepted by institutions and government bodies. One reason for this may be that people have little time to notice, or that noticing these changes is simply not a priority. More generally, Shahjahan suggests that people now just 'set aside' time to focus on the immediate needs of our bodies: to eat, to work out, to sleep. Thus bodies become 'things' to be serviced towards the ends of production and efficiency (2015: 494). In order to undo such a colonisation of our physical being 'we should strive to "embody" ourselves: inhabit our bodies fully, acknowledge an interconnection between mind, body, and spirit, and contest the insertion of the body into the market' (2015: 494).

In the policy extracts discussed above, student engagement was expressed as something which the university *embeds, packages* and *markets* to students. However, when learning is exciting and potentially transformative students and lecturers may feel an intensely personal flow of engagement through their bodies as well as their minds. Rowe (2012: 1034) argues that this powerful sense of connection with the subject matter and with the other people in the classroom promotes a passion for learning. This process can be described as erotic and it can build group resistance to the competitive and divisive forces at the heart of neoliberal education that heavily invest in isolated individuals. The textual examples I have drawn from policy documents, that omit direct references to the labour and emotions of people, would seem to be just a part of a much larger hegemonic knowledge system in modern society. Rather than simply emphasising what staff and students need to do in terms of performativity and accountability alone, these texts seem to also omit the very presence and spirit of students and teachers.

### One Dimensional McPolicy

Vostal, Silvaggi, and Vassilaki (2011) identify a 'one-dimensional' transformation of higher education that 'seeks to meet the imperatives of a capitalist ethos' (2011: 17). One form of resistance to this is to embrace the role of the multidimensional human body in teaching and learning. This helps to replace 'missing content' in a different way. It restores the dimensions of intimacy, self-disclosure, vulnerability and excitement in learning. In policy documents, the placing of the words around student engagement has direct implications for meaning. Certain messages can be repeatedly broadcast that obscure *whose* academic labour is involved with the effect of marginalising human physical, mental and emotional ways of being. Therefore, 'one-dimensional' policy texts that promote mainly economically linked successes of student engagement may appear to serve a global labour market, but they alienate the outcomes of learning and teaching from the human bodies that produce these. Ultimately, 'missing out' this human content, as more embodied forms of learning, may well be self-defeating in reducing, rather than increasing, innovation.

### Rational McPolicy Is Being Unreasonable

Ritzer argues that rational systems of any kind can lose their enchantment and become dehumanising. He refers to this as 'the irrationality of rationality' (Ritzer, 2015: 132), when 'rational systems become unreasonable systems that deny the humanity, the human reason, of the people who work within them or are served by them' (Ritzer, 2015: 132). Ritzer cites examples such as the 'false friendliness' where many workers are expected to engage with customers in a way which actually destroys any engaged human relationships (2015: 136). What I have demonstrated here is a textual version of a similar irrationality, where universities are creating strategies that dehumanise the very relationships they seek to foster. These CDA examples support the case argued by Hayes and Wyngard (2002, 2016) who, as mentioned in the introduction, discuss connections between the forces leading to McDonaldisation and the 'therapeutic turn'. As university management have restructured universities as McBusinesses, these have at the same time become therapeutic universities, with academics failing to see or challenge a new 'student-centred culture' (Hayes &

Wyngard, 2002, 2016). The growth of therapy culture in universities, side by side with marketisation, not only divides students and academics it assumes students to be fragile, in need of a 'Disneyfication' of their 'student experience' (Hayes, 2017: 106). Ritzer discusses numerous ways in which foods and drinks have been delivered in easy forms in recent decades to enable efficient eating, via simplified products (Ritzer, 2015: 68). In a similar way institutions seek to make learning palatable, by breaking it down into small 'bites', not unlike chicken nuggets or other forms of finger food, or five-a-day smoothies. Yet as student engagement is packaged and marketed to students in the bizarre fashion revealed in these strategy texts, it is hard to see how this actually produces engaged students, when it alienates them from their own labour.

### *Reoccupy – Or Risk Being Dismantled into Parts*

Looking ahead to the next chapter, just as student engagement is widely discussed in policy, so is student success and student employability. These universal concepts can be commented on and measured, but do students themselves feel any part of such discourse? It appears to be related much more to student achievement than to student engagement, but achievement for whom? The discourse seems to concern institutions, more than students, in the measuring of outcomes to remain competitive in a global market. Zepke argues that a widespread interest in student engagement research seems to be closely connected to fashioning generic learners within a particular vision of student success and 'the very construct of engagement is generic' (Zepke, 2014: 701). As the next chapter will reveal, the labour of words can go further still. This vision of student success, in the form of employability, appears to involve breaking down what constitutes a student, in terms of sets of attributes and assets. The body is not just alienated, it is dismantled. McPolicy discourse thus sets up the conditions for multiple routes towards marginalisation and fragmentation of human labour. This prompts my final question in this chapter. In the spirit of the Occupy movement of 2011, when people who were 'fed up with Wall Street writing the rules' (Merle, 2016) sought to take over physical spaces, is it now time for both staff and students to protest and collectively rewrite the student engagement discourse to reoccupy our higher education policies?

CHAPTER 6

# Employability McPolicy

## The Value of Employability

### Why Employability?

'Employability', just like 'student engagement', sounds like an unquestionably positive ideal. After investing heavily in a degree, students require support to undertake work placements and to help them to prepare for future employment. Universities seek to demonstrate that their graduates are in demand by employers, so there are vested interests all round. In this chapter, it is not my intention to contest aspirations towards guiding and supporting students to gain meaningful work. This book is about observing *the labour of words in HE,* via scrutiny of policy discourse, therefore the 'work' that a term like 'employability' undertakes on behalf of humans is a main focus. However, when many authors are writing about fundamental societal change that will be wrought through the Fourth Industrial Revolution (Brynjolfsson & McAfee, 2011; Hyacinth, 2017; Aoun, 2017; Peters, Jandrić, & Hayes, 2018; Doucet, Evers, Guerra, Lopez, Soskil, & Timmers, 2018) there are problems to consider if future employment (for any of us) is too narrowly interpreted as 'employability'. This is because the dominant discourse of employability furthers the notion of fragmented labour, in the form of isolated skills students are expected to generate, to 'fit' with the perceived requirements of employers. It does not appear to anticipate how students might be supported in a world without work, where more complex and creative approaches may be needed. Instead a rather 'fixed' vision of student success is expounded. Concepts like 'learning gain' are dialectically intertwined with this understanding, based on a rational calculation of exchange value:

*student learning = gainful employment*

But what if it doesn't? What if all the student engagement in the world doesn't yield employability and these ideals spread by successive governments turn out to be no longer achievable, because work as we know it, has vanished. Whilst 'concerns over the displacement of human labor by machines are as old as capitalism itself' (Means, 2017: 23), there are many writers who believe that this time it will be different, due to the rapid rate of automation that is already upon us. Therefore, a division of society from technology, and severing of human labour from our tools, is a major challenge for the future advancement of humanity, and not just HE (Peters, Jandrić, & Hayes, 2018). Yet surely HE has a stronger role to play than simply serving up students as standardised products with a particular set of features employers are believed to require? We can no longer rely on such narrow human capital models. These tend to reduce, rather than increase, the capacity of formal education to creatively meet the expansive challenges of a potential post-work landscape (Means, 2017: 23).

With these ideas in mind, 'employability' would seem a timely choice of buzz word to examine. University study is now expected to directly 'enhance employability', with strong emphasis on 'the importance of transferable skills' (OECD, 2016). As discussed in Chapter 2, an adaptable and 'enterprising self', a vision grown from the years of the New Labour government, is expected to prepare for an unpredictable labour market. That is, if there is a labour market to prepare for. Now, more than ever before, public opinion about the value of HE is based on emotional appeals and unfounded universal judgments in the form of 'truths' that need closer scrutiny. The rational McPolicy of Employability, as it meets with media rhetoric, would appear to be championing the cause of students, but this is not necessarily the case, as my later analysis in this chapter will reveal.

### *How Does Employability Support a Neoliberal Ideology?*

HE degrees have always been concerned with the development of particular skills and qualities in students. An awareness of a need for graduates to make an effective contribution to the labour market has been around for quite some decades. Both *The Robbins Report* (Committee on Higher Education, 1963) and the *Dearing Report* (National Committee of Inquiry into Higher Education, 1997) linked the importance of education with employability and emphasised the value of students developing core skills and work experience to enhance opportunities for future employment. More recently these ideas have been tailored even more explicitly though to meet the alleged direct requirements of employers, as in the white paper on *The Future of Higher Education* (DfES, 2003). There have also been increased numbers of students in HE leading to competition and university league tables that reveal a perceived success or failure of institutions and individual disciplines to lead to appropriate graduate employment destinations. Therefore, in response institutions now brand and market employability and employment outcomes from individual taught programmes.

Thus, employability has become educationalised across recent decades. This has coincided with a recognition of the economic importance of HE in a global marketplace, rather than a particular drive to empower students. Connecting a country's economic viability with the production of skills through HE to serve employers, has also led to an auditing and accounting of academic performance to achieve targets. At the same time, it has generated a rhetoric that supports a dismantling of the student body into 'parts' that can be taken up to oblige those providing McWork (Hayes & Wynyard, 2002). Increasingly, students are now discussed in terms of 'graduate attributes' or 'assets', as if they were commodities, rather than humans. The concept of employability has been linked to arguments about 'value for money' (VfM) from a university education (Skoulding, 2017) and competition between which university education is most likely to yield 'a good job' (Paterson, 2016). Hayes and Wynyard describe an impoverished experience when education is reduced to consumption and a simple recruiting to McJobs (Hayes & Wynyard, 2002). How well such an approach will support graduates throughout life and in the face of technological unemployment remains to be seen (Peters, Jandrić, & Means, 2019, forthcoming). Widening participation (WP) agendas are also marketing tools for universities. Although increasing access to HE is vitally important in terms of social justice, ideals for inclusivity and diversity in HE policy can become distorted. Jones and Thomas (2005) suggest that the academic strand of the widening access discourse ignores the complexity and multiplicity of obstacles facing people from lower socio-economic groups. It therefore, offers simplistic responses. I argue that the rational discourse underlying these also excludes the very people whose labour is expected to bring about these changes.

Peters and Jandrić argue that neoliberal education is clearly aimed at preservation and further development of a certain type of capitalism (Peters & Jandrić, 2018). Bryan and Hayes (2007) suggest that 'the fact that there are so many policy documents and consultations that require responses may give the appearance of debate, but it is one-sided and controlled (Bryan & Hayes, 2007: ix). So where did the current focus on the role of universities to equip students for the workplace emerge from, and are employability strategies suitable ways to achieve these goals in their current format anyway? With regard to links between a university education and the world of work, Apperley argues that these can be traced back further than the turn of the millennium, when the knowledge-based economy (KBE) and 'lifelong learning' became dominant discourses. As far back as 1976, the Labour Prime Minister, James Callaghan delivered a speech at Ruskin College, Oxford on the future of education, which was no longer to be construed as simply equipping children 'for a lively, constructive, place in society'. Education would now serve another purpose: 'to fit them to do a job of work' (Callaghan, 1976; Apperley, 2014: 735). Indeed, the education system might be considered as failing, if it simply produces 'socially well-adjusted members of society who are unemployed because they do not have the skills' required by prospective employers. Skills that not only comprise the basic tools of literacy, numeracy, respect for others, but also include developing 'an appetite for further knowledge that will last a lifetime.' (Apperley, 2014: 736).

Apperley points out that these two key ideas, that education should serve the interests of the economy, and that learning should be lifelong, have moved to centre stage and were at the heart of the Dearing Report in 1997 (Apperley, 2014: 736). However, Philpott argues that for some 'employability is little more than a buzzword that is more often used than properly understood' (Philpott, 1999). McQuaid and Lyndsay (2005) suggest employability emerged as a central tenet of so-called 'Third Way' policies, as part of the New Labour approach to economic and social policy (McQuaid & Lyndsay, 2005: 197). They raise concerns about the short-term focus now placed on employers' demands for competencies that are specific to their own immediate-term needs (McQuaid & Lyndsay, 2005: 214). They conclude that 'employability as a 'buzzword for welfare to work strategies, adds little to our understanding of the existing debate on supply-side and demand-side explanations of labour market disadvantage' (McQuaid & Lyndsay, 2005: 214).

As raised in the introduction to this book, a clear educationalisation of the issue of employability for over two decades has now caused universities to produce rather similarly worded employability policies, that usually cover a period of around four years at a time. This changes the nature of HE if universities are simply seen in terms of the their contribution to the 'problems to be solved' (Fendler, 2008: 55). This 'new-topic, same-language' approach cannot withstand the global developments in automation described above. A re-think is needed where university policy no longer simply trots out statements of what technology enhanced learning, student engagement or employability will achieve, as if these words were realities that we can 'embed', and not just socially constructed ideas. We now need to confront a cultural shift where we are all implicated in an empty use of language (or to use Ritzer's term 'nothing') about education, technology and employment, that effectively edits out references to the real human labour required to address social issues (Hayes & Jandrić, 2014; Hayes & Bartholomew, 2015; Peters, Jandrić, & Hayes, 2018). Digital technologies have enabled these political values to spread rapidly and become widely adopted across institutions, but in a future without work, is it time to offer a redundancy package to this narrow view of employability?

### *Employability Strategies 2012–2020*
Since around 2012 there has been a surge in the number of strategy documents produced by universities to address the topic of 'employability'. A repetition of

the linguistic patterns already discussed in previous chapters can be noticed in these strategies, which many UK universities produce to cover a certain period, such as between 2015–2020. These texts imply that 'employability strategies', 'attributes frameworks', 'evaluation mechanisms' and even 'module descriptors' are able to address issues related to the future of work for students. These linguistic structures bring to mind Ritzer's concept of 'nothing', because they effectively remove humans from statements about human activities, just as an automated process might mechanically take over the labour of a person.

Students seem to be McDonaldised as McStudents in this language too, in terms of the standardised 'attributes' that they should acquire and bring to the workplace. The more individual and contextual qualities a student might creatively explore or develop appear to be ignored. In this respect the written policy is completely at odds with recent publications by experts who argue that more creative approaches to address global technological unemployment need to be urgently brought into the HE curriculum (Aoun, 2017). The manner in which the strategies are written also fails to acknowledge the considerable progress made in student-staff partnership approaches. As shown already, there are few acknowledgements of who (in terms of people) will perform the labour actions to ensure that what is envisaged for employability actually happens.

Whilst analysing employability texts is open to critique for not actually proving anything, the repeated patterns revealed provide concrete data that can serve as a 'talking point' for discussion in the broader context of the literature on technological unemployment. According to neoliberalist ideology, knowledge is a commodity and HE is a market where knowledge and skills are traded (Zepke, 2014: 702). Universities offer marketable knowledge and skills, as well as supplying marketable services (Codd, 2005). Yet, in relation to critical theory this 'trafficking in human attributes' (Kopytoff, 1986: 85) is problematic in the context of learning (see also Hayes & Jandrić, 2014) and perhaps equally problematic now in the changing context of work and widely predicted technological unemployment.

### The Graduate Attribute Production Line

Therefore, it seems to be a curious thing that, at a time when many writers are predicting that digital technologies are set to destroy more jobs than they create (Brynjolfsson & McAfee, 2011; Frey & Osborne, 2013, 2015), then in universities we respond only to produce repetitive employability strategies that declare the delivery of generic 'graduate attributes' (Peters, Jandrić, & Hayes, 2018: 8). In their 2009 report, *Future Fit: preparing graduates for the world of work*, the Confederation of British Industry (CBI) and Universities UK define 'employability' as:

> A set of attributes, skills and knowledge that all labour market participants should possess to ensure they have the capability of being effective in the workplace – to the benefit of themselves, their employer and the wider economy. (CBI, 2009: 8)

In work undertaken for the Higher Education Academy (HEA), Yorke and Knight (2006) defined employability as:

> A set of achievements – skills, understandings and personal attributes – that make graduates more likely to gain employment and be successful in their chosen occupations, which benefits themselves, the workforce, the community and the economy. (Yorke & Knight, 2006: 3)

In both definitions, personal and societal benefits, including payback for the economy are pinpointed: Universities have responded to these ideas about employability, to seek to provide graduates that 'fit' the 'demands' of employers and the economy:

> Postgraduates can demonstrate the enhanced-level attributes that employers are demanding: attributes that are necessary for our graduates to contribute effectively to our civic, cultural and economic future prosperity. (Anglia Ruskin Employability Strategy, 2015–2016)

### *Pick a Number*

For some universities, this also involves the selection of a certain number of such attributes, or capabilities, as in the examples below where 'five' and 'nine' seem to have been randomly defined:

> Define and articulate five graduate attributes which enable Westminster graduates to thrive in their personal and professional lives as highly employable, socially responsible and globally engaged citizens. (University of Westminster–Employability Strategy, 2015–2020)

> Embed opportunities for students to develop the nine capabilities/ Graduate Attributes of employability and professionalism. (University of Bradford Employability Strategy, 2012–2015)

### *Embedding McEmployability*

In many of the university strategies the aim to 'embed' 'employability skills' into the curriculum and communicate these back to students is expressed:

Evaluate feedback mechanisms and module descriptors to ensure that employability skills embedded in the curriculum are highlighted and clarified to students. (Aberystwyth University Employability Strategy, 2015)

To ensure that the skills, qualities and graduate attributes aligned to employability and enterprise are embedded effectively within the curriculum. (University of Bolton, Employability and Enterprise Strategy, 2014–2017)

Embed the graduate attributes in the learning outcomes across the undergraduate curriculum. (University of Westminster – Employability Strategy, 2015–2020)

### One Size Fits All

There are times when purchasing a 'one-size' garment will do. A scarf is one example or a tie. Maybe some types of hosiery, such as socks, can fit a certain percentage of the population. However, from a consumer point of view, clothing that is made in the correct size for each wearer is usually preferable. It tends to be a manufacturer that reaps the benefits from the rational production of one-size items, via a simplified process, rather than the purchaser. Why then, would there be an assumption by universities that random numbers of generic sets of attributes (in a one-size-fits-all approach) are the best way to equip students for future employment? As later examples and analysis will demonstrate, it is almost as if we are inviting machines to take over from us, by writing in a repetitive manner and discussing the complex, multi-layered practices of learning, as if these were simplistic processes applicable to all.

Unfortunately, whilst these pragmatic approaches may appear to be supporting students towards employment, there are problems in any assumption that the learning of, and ability to apply, such generic capabilities will be evenly experienced by students themselves. Students are a hugely diverse group and given agendas that have encouraged widening participation, their routes into HE, prior experience and their ability to develop these attributes, will vary enormously. Czerniewicz (2018: 1) argues that the intersection of university strategy documents with inequality at an institutional level has received little attention. This is an important point that can be extended to include the intersection where inequality meets with repeated, generic aims that are articulated across university employability strategies. If we are widening participation into HE, then we need to widen participation for all across our university strategies which are aimed at supporting employability. A first step is to review any lack of inclusivity present in the language in which these are written.

## The Labour of Employability

### Examining Employability via a Corpus-Based CDA

A corpus of UK university employability strategies was gathered during 2017. It contains 103,112 words and was constructed from 28 university documents that are freely available to download from institutional websites. In Table 6.1 below, the top keywords are listed. It is not surprising to see that there is a high count for the word 'employability'. However, it is interesting to notice too that whilst both 'students' and 'staff' are present, the word 'staff' has a much small number of instances than 'students'. Given that students are also discussed as 'graduate' and 'graduates' there is an even larger gap between these instances. Yet all student-facing staff in universities are expected to be furthering employability agendas.

TABLE 6.1  Example keywords in the 'employability' corpus

| Keyword | Number of instances |
| --- | --- |
| Employability | 1264 |
| Students | 1125 |
| Work | 603 |
| Support | 589 |
| Learning | 531 |
| University | 495 |
| Skills | 488 |
| Development | 454 |
| Graduate | 425 |
| Develop | 416 |
| Staff | 261 |
| Attributes | 134 |

In the sections to come, I will draw attention to how active processes of labour are constructed and who/what appears to undertake these. Similar patterns to those already identified in the educational technology corpus and student engagement corpus can be noticed again in the employability strategies of universities. There seems to be few acknowledgements of *who* (in terms of people) will perform the labour to ensure that employability goals actually happen.

### Employability Strategies that Forget to Look Both Ways

A response to the threat of technological employment is not explicitly addressed in the strategies I analysed, but what is implied in many is that

EMPLOYABILITY MCPOLICY                                                                         137

people can be moulded and shaped to provide what employers require, to 'add value' to their workforce:

> For employers, we seek to create a university that is responsive to the needs of the labour market, ensuring our students and graduates can add value to their workforce. (University of Bolton Employability and Enterprise Strategy, 2014–2017)

This suggests a rather reactive response, rather than one where a university might also take the lead on advising employers about the implications. Again, in the statement below, it sounds as if the degrees that students are studying are being designed to serve the goal of 'maximum value' to employers:

> Ensure that all courses have the highest available level of professional body accreditation to ensure maximum value of the students' degree to employers. (Anglia Ruskin University, Employability Strategy, 2015–2018)

Aoun argues that whilst universities state they need to match skills to what employers want, a better model would be to work closely with employers but also acknowledge this is not a one-way dialogue. Universities have a role too in developing how employers respond to the unprecedented speed of technological unemployment (Aoun, 2017: 147). Yet currently, it is as if we are simply breaking our students down for 'parts' on the 'graduate attribute production line'.

### *Graduate Attributes*

In the following examples from Employability Strategies written between 2014–2017, the statements below typically demonstrate a trend where students are discussed in terms of the required 'attributes' they should acquire and bring to the workplace:

> 510 **core attributes and capabilities** <u>are identified</u> *by graduate recruiters as indicators of their needs and as hallmarks of* **'graduateness'.**

In line 510, it sounds as though, as an employer recruiting a graduate, you should easily be able to spot what you need when out shopping for a McGraduate. If you don't, then just look out for what sounds like a form of branding or earmarking of these students to fit your requirements. Unfortunately, this sifting of students via 'hallmarks' of 'graduateness' sounds so instrumental a process, that the labour and creativity of graduates themselves in the recruitment process, seems to be unacknowledged. In the next example (line 764), defining the number of 'graduate attributes' to look out for is suggested, but not explained. Does five sound a nice number? Good, let's run with that:

> 764 <u>Define</u> and <u>articulate</u> **five graduate attributes** which <u>enable</u> *our graduates to thrive in their personal and professional lives as highly employable, socially responsible and globally engaged citizens*

It seems then that just five graduate attributes ought to do it. They must be good ones too, as they are going to enable graduates to 'thrive' both personally and professionally. It seems fortuitous that, along with being 'employable', these graduates will also become 'socially responsible' and 'globally engaged' as citizens. How could any institution possibly locate this precise number of enabling attributes, apply them to a diverse student population, yet still be confident that their graduates will emerge as such citizens? Just to pause for a moment to think about this, is this the role of a university anyway?

Perhaps we don't need to worry though, because we can always write an objective for 'all aspects of the curriculum' to handle this for us. Below in line 242, 'the equipping of all graduates with these attributes' has been effectively delegated to five words:

> 242 The equipping of all graduates with these **attributes** <u>is integrated</u> *as an objective of all aspects of the curriculum*

Don't busy lecturers integrate the content of their curriculum, by designing learning outcomes and assessments and seeking the committee approval necessary for any changes to taught content? This is time-consuming work for academic programme teams, yet here it is 'all aspects of the curriculum' that is said to be undertaking this task. By the point of annual performance review to check this objective has been achieved, will these words be able to account for their actions?

### *Linguistically Constructed Unemployment*

In examples so far, the 'irrationality of rationality' is becoming apparent, through the chosen linguistic structures. Having raised the concern earlier of an inadequate response by universities to plan for the potential effects of technological unemployment, there seems to be another less obvious form of reducing people's capacity to undertake work. This is taking place before our eyes in McPolicy, via nominalisation. A form of 'linguistically constructed unemployment' is regularly enacted in rational statements that assign academic labour to non-human entities. In the examples below, a pattern is often repeated, with the actions of humans attributed to 'The Graduate Attributes Framework' or 'the Awards', 'the University' or 'the Employability and Enterprise Strategy'. Line 39 implies that a 'framework' is the actor that is enabling departments to review their taught provision:

> 39 **The Graduate Attributes Framework** <u>will enable</u> all departments <u>to review</u> *their provision* and <u>assess</u> how the **attributes** <u>are delivered</u> *within programmes of study*

Not only does this wording suggest an odd reporting relationship for the academic departments, but this is also not helpful for acknowledging all of the work that university quality teams perform alongside academic staff, when faculty are reviewing taught provision and seeking re-approval of their programmes. Next, it is the turn of 'the awards' to do a little work in line 492:

> 492 **the Awards** <u>will provide</u> *further opportunities for students* <u>to reflect on</u> **attribute development**

So how will 'the awards' communicate this form of reflection to students? Awards don't hold office hours, write feedback or attend graduation, once all of the marking has finally been completed. It is people that do these tasks. Though line 92 would suggest otherwise:

> 92 **The University** <u>has identified</u> *a number of key areas of provision that* <u>directly address</u> *graduate attributes and employability*

It is now 'the University' (rather than a group of named colleagues) that has identified the 'key areas of provision'. However, it sounds as if it is these 'key areas of provision' that will be undertaking the work anyway, to 'directly address' whatever needs to happen concerning 'graduate attributes and employability'. Given that many universities now have large employability teams, I wonder what these staff will be doing? In the next two examples, responsibility to 'ensure' that certain skills, qualities and attributes are embedded in the curriculum and evaluated, falls to both a 'strategy' and the university's 'governance structure'.

> 163 **Key strategic priorities of the Employability and Enterprise Strategy for 2014–2017 are** <u>to ensure</u> that *the skills, qualities and graduate attributes aligned to employability and enterprise are* <u>embedded</u> *effectively within the curriculum*

> 141 **The University's governance structure for education** should <u>ensure</u> *oversight and on-going* <u>evaluation</u> *of the effectiveness and outcomes of the delivery of the strategic framework for employability*

In 163, even 'key strategic priorities', in relation to the curriculum and employability have been delegated to a strategy. It is therefore hard to imagine what the mechanism for actually achieving these important tasks is. In 141, it sounds as if a 'governance structure' is going to be busy undertaking ongoing evaluation of what 'the strategic framework for employability' is undertaking, in terms of 'the delivery'.

### *A Marketing Tool for Universities or a Student-Centred Activity?*

In the next example (174) this pattern continues, but it is the 'coordination of marketing across these functions' that is required to undertake the labour of presentation of a coherent brand to the market:

> 174 **Coordination of marketing across these functions** is required <u>to ensure</u> *the presentation of a coherent brand to the market*

Again, it seems as if a one-way route of universities serving the market is emphasised, rather than the expertise within universities also being called upon to advise the market and employers. Coherence and consistency also seem to be emphasised, in terms of what the university presents and provides, in line 207:

> 207 **employability provision** should be **structurally unavoidable** <u>to tackle</u> *the issue of student non-engagement* and <u>to ensure</u> *consistency of provision.*

Here the term of 'structurally unavoidable' seems to be an odd choice and one that brings to mind an 'iron cage' of employability provision, rather than a collaborative creative response between university colleagues, students and employers.

### Disrupting Rational Choices

Aoun reflects on the popular discourse about universities that has, until now, centred around the question of what sort of education is best. He argues that this is often 'reduced to the dichotomy between learning to live, versus learning to earn a living, or between the value of a liberal arts education, versus the value of a 'practical' course of study that promotes employability (Aoun, 2017: 147). Given that machines will perform the work of some such subjects, he suggests these arguments are now false choices and the roles that human beings will fill will be largely concerned with creativity (Aoun, 2017: 148).

It would seem therefore that the 'ambition' of a university employability strategy now needs to change, to acknowledge the magnitude of what is about to happen in the global digitised world of work. Whilst Aoun argues that 'education is not a panacea for humanity's troubles', he predicts there is a real place for universities in helping individuals to 'brace for change and embrace the technological miracles that lie ahead' (Aoun, 2017: 149). If, as Aoun suggests, we really might approach this future as an opportunity, rather than a threat, then we should begin now. In the next chapter I suggest we begin right away, right where we are, by re-writing human labour back into HE policy. To borrow Ritzer's analogy we need to write ourselves in as a creative 'something' that is rich in distinctive content, in order to replace our current existence as 'nothing' (Ritzer, 2011: 172).

### Reoccupy – Or Risk Being Rendered into 'Cause' and 'Effect'

The idea that education can resolve the problem of technological unemployment is a political construction which has, by and large, failed to deliver its promise (Peters, Jandrić, & Hayes, 2018). As this application of language enacts the so-called 'techno-fix' and 'edu-fix' on our behalf, in a range of contexts in universities, policy documents are materially implicated in educationalisation and technologisation within capitalism. No one seems to be named so that they can be held accountable. The strategy statements tell it the way it is, but who wrote them? Very few of the many documents examined concerning the phrases explored in Chapters 3 – 6 have named authors, let alone any publicised mechanism by which the policy might be updated or changed (Bartholomew & Hayes, 2015: 28). In so many other instances this level of anonymity is simply not an option. How often is a full name required when placing an order online, posting a comment on a blog, booking a hotel or completing quality documents related to teaching. So why is writing policy any different?

It is of course understood that, in order to meet the expectations of accreditation agencies and funding bodies, higher education institutions are required to maintain a growing number of policy documents. The task of writing these documents often ends up though, with academics and administrators who, looking at documents from other institutions, emulate the tone and language of available examples. This means that even more repetition of these structures and unquestioned anonymity takes place. Once written, policy documents get approved at various levels from departmental boards to university senates. Yet as they progress through many different levels of HE management, these texts apparently escape with minimal scrutiny of their actual content. In this sense they are ticking boxes in a 'dispersion of responsibility' (Peters, Jandrić, & Hayes, 2018). In *Risk Society: Towards a New Modernity*, Ulrich Beck links this dispersion of responsibility with the structure of labour:

> Corresponding to the highly differentiated division of labor, there is a general complicity, and the complicity is matched by a general lack of responsibility. Everyone is cause *and* effect, and thus *non*-cause. The causes dribble away into a general amalgam of agents and conditions, reactions and counter-reactions, which brings social certainty and popularity to the concept of system. This reveals in exemplary fashion the ethical significance of the system concept: *one can do something and continue doing it without having to take personal responsibility for it*. It is as if one were acting while being personally absent. (Beck, 1992: 33, original italics)

Beck's comments above on rational systems as a 'generalised other' seem to help explain why these odd linguistic structures may persist. Rationality may sit above blame, but these texts are still constructed by people who are busy 'writing their own labour out'. They are formed as if we are all subject to a natural fate, the 'law of gravitation' of the system (Peters, Jandrić, & Hayes, 2018). With increasing neoliberalisation of the HE sector, the 'law of gravitation' disperses responsibility of academics for actual content of policy documents. This transfer of responsibility seems to be based on two dialectically interconnected utopian ideas:

1. If we provide enough education, work markets will take care of themselves,
2. If we provide enough technology, work markets will take care of themselves.

Peters and Jandrić (2018b) link educationalisation of technological unemployment to the concept of human capital and its main protagonist *homo economicus*. They juxtapose the concept of *homo economicus* (as the main protagonist of the age of industrial capitalism) with the concept of *homo collaborans* (as the main protagonist of the age of digital reason) as follows:

> The assumption of rationality is contradicted in a networked environment as the ontological basis is contained in the relations between entities rather than any one self-sufficient entity that is rationally aware and transparent to itself. The network is a very different kind of epistemic set of relations rather than the individual knowing agent. (Peters & Jandrić, 2018: 343)

My analysis of university strategies therefore has revealed how relations between entities appear to be conducting the 'work' of many of our key labour functions HE.

### Avoiding a Self-Fulfilling Prophecy

So where does this leave the (currently) desperately overworked academics we heard from in Chapter 1? If our educational solutions remain based on the concepts of human capital and *homo economicus* we may well be unable to resolve the impending problem of technological unemployment. It is time to look to an approach based on the figure of *homo collaborans* which fundamentally rethinks the concepts of work, education, and research (Peters & Jandrić, 2018b). If we do not reconsider the way in which we write about our own labour in university strategy, then we encounter a series of risks. Firstly, we risk a self-fulfilling prophecy where we are aiding the process of putting academic labour and human relevance firmly out of the picture. Secondly, universities that might be rich in distinctive human content, risk marketing themselves as 'nothing', through cause-and-effect statements where human labour is no longer present. Students are dismantled into 'parts' that might be assembled to meet an employer's graduate attribute list. However, this rational policy discourse eventually moves institutions towards irrational and conflicting statements that open them to ridicule. History demonstrates that education does not provide a one-size-fits-all answer for the future of work. However, as it becomes increasingly clear that educationalisation of social issues is a site of political struggle, we need to open new discursive spaces for resistance and reimagination. A first step in that direction is to return agency from abstract notions of education, market, and technology, to people, their present needs, and future aspirations (Peters, Jandrić, & Hayes, 2018).

CHAPTER 7

# Re-Writing Human Labour into HE Policy

## What Might Be Learned from the Labour of Words in HE?

### *Running without a Treadmill*

In McDonaldised society, the rationality of fast food has its own corrective responses. These are provided through the logical industries of fitness and exercise remedies to counterbalance excess. Gyms, exercise plans, fitness drinks and vitamins, supported by 'fitbits' and other digital health monitors, offer manufactured alternatives to unhealthy ways of living. I can enrol at a fitness centre, or in the spirit of capitalism, purchase my own exercise bike, treadmill or rowing machine to house at home and use on an individual basis. In HE though, a metaphorical treadmill is increasingly discussed by authors protesting about a neoliberal context of audit, performativity, conflicting metrics and subsequent academic injury. This has pitched colleagues against each other and divided students and staff (Gill, 2010; Hall & Bowles, 2016). Academia is now an accelerated context where the 'stop' button on the treadmill does not seem to be an option and someone else has control of the speed settings. Did someone say, 'it is what it is', but at least there will be recognition and impact along the way? Maybe there will be, but do be aware that respect and acknowledgement are not written into the McPolicy documents that govern the role you currently play in your institution. Do take a little time to notice exactly how your labour is being discussed and marketed. Ask yourself, are your long hour at work represented or attributed?

Policy is an exercise of power and language is used to legitimate that process (Olssen, Codd, & O'Neill, 2004). As such, metaphorically, there are both iron and velvet cages of McPolicy. But what if policy took the shape instead of an open landscape? There are other less automated ways for humans to enjoy running. Getting off the one-directional treadmill and running across fields, lanes and new landscapes provides a different view, helping to nurture a 'sociological imagination' (Mills, 1959) and contest divisive rhetoric. To refresh the view from where we are standing (or running) might lead to a whole new journey. However, it needs to be a journey where the landscape really is viewed with fresh eyes and we can move our legs freely across the uneven territory.

Right now in HE policy discourse, such as 'best practice', 'the student experience' and 'employability', we are human commodities that resemble the distorted shadows in Plato's cave. Academic labour is surely more real than this, because it cannot ever be separated from human voices, emotions, anxiety and happiness. There are some who suggest that taking a more positive and mindful approach is important. This needs to include seeing students as human beings, not data, and building capacity rather than creating dependency (Seldon & Martin, 2017: 15). However, as we continue to seek collective solutions to marketised HE, the rational 'voice' of neoliberalism will also persist in providing us with more answers, in the form of linguistic commodities. These may take the form of *happiness* and *wellness* as industry offerings (Davies, 2015), but these too can become rational 'tools' that employers apply to encourage even greater efficiencies from their workers. Such tools also become necessities as the welfare state has diminished. However, when apathy sets in amongst the workforce in HE, then we do need to be mindful that 'rather than inciting violence or explicit refusal, the mechanisms of contemporary capitalism are just met with a yawn' (Davies, 2015: 105).

### *McPolicy Needs to Be Met with More Than a McYawn in Reponse*

The recent proliferation of authors writing about academic injury and anxiety in HE is, even as I write, in danger of being met with a yawn. It's not 'fake news', it's just old news. I have referenced many of these articles in this book, to draw attention to a critical mass of literature on 'unprecedented levels of anxiety and stress amongst both academic and academic-related staff and students' (Lesnick-Oberstein et al., 2015). Therefore, it is worth putting down the university cafeteria McMuffin you have in your hand, bought in a deal to arrive with your coffee, for just a moment, to take some time to reflect. It is worth pressing 'stop' on the treadmill you are about to set in motion for the day, even to take a photograph of your littered desk as a reminder of how life is, and how it could be. Ask yourself what aspects of your role make you and your students feel alive and consider where your labour is written up explicitly to demonstrate this. Recall the power of *noticing,* as described in Chapter 1. Noticing broader connections within global consumer capitalism is a powerful antithesis to economic agendas that separate people from their own labour and from each other. It can help with recognising more localised instances of rationality within universities and connecting these with a much larger neoliberal project of rationalisation. This is your labour and your words, so don't let 'academic injury' simply become another buzz phrase.

Berg, Huijbens, and Larsen (2016) argue that a 'rise in anxiety must be seen, in part at least, as the result of the neoliberalization of the university'. This was considered in Chapter 2, whereby 'use value is being shifted to exchange value through competition manifest in particular systems of audit and assessment that underpin it' (Berg, Huijbens, & Larsen, 2016: 11). No one in academia sits outside this situation, because our entire society is subject to the governing rationality of neoliberalism 'extending from the management of the state to the soul of the subject' (Brown, 2011: 118). *In The Labour of Words in Higher Education*, I have provided some illumination of one aspect (a confrontation of the discourse of McPolicy) through which to view and review the neoliberal organisation of our universities. It has revealed that, with a similar rationality to that described by Ritzer in his numerous works on the McDonaldisation of Society, even documents, frameworks and many other static buzz phrases can be inscribed with rationality, to enact human labour. This occurs across institutions with a subtle, but alarming, regularity. Smyth argues that dignity should be restored to academics as people and that they should be treated as persons rather than as producers or even as products (Smyth, 2017: 140; Corbett, 2018). If academic work now resembles a production line, then problematic though that is, it is still invested with the human presence of 'producers'. When staff and student producers become 'products', as noticed in Chapter 3, via 'the student experience', the human presence is linguistically extinguished.

### *Exchanging New Values in a Post-Digital Dialogue*

Dialogue is a valuable exchange which continually reaffirms collaborative possibilities for humanity, through discourse. It can take the form of open and insightful interchanges. Or instead, dialogue may be constrained, if language is loaded with economically-based assumptions and individualised agendas, that restrict how we might collectively imagine alternative futures. As discussed in Chapter 4, in educational policy for human learning through technology across recent decades, authentic dialogue to build new knowledge has stalled. A popular discourse (on a global scale) has emphasised instead what technology (not people) 'achieves' and 'enhances' (Hayes & Jandrić, 2014; Hayes, 2015; Hayes & Bartholomew, 2015; Hayes, 2018). This focus in language on an 'exchange value' (Marx, 1867) from technology has hampered more critical understandings of how humans and technologies 'mutually constitute' each other (Mackenzie & Wajcman, 1999). However, a rational political logic that insists technology is an external force able to 'fix' societal issues (Peters, Jandrić, & Hayes, 2018) overlooks three powerful considerations. Firstly, this discourse fails to acknowledge that humans *are* technology. Rikowski reminds us that if 'free-floating technology was a reality' then we could simply halt its entry into our bodies (Rikowski, 2003: 140). Secondly, humans *are* capital, and 'technology is an expression of capitalist social relations' (Rikowski, 2003: 140). Thirdly, language-in-use, as discourse, can either reveal, or conceal, these powerful revelations.

The physical tools that once sustained human lives may have merged with virtual instruments and automation in a digital age, but in contemplating post-digital life, dialogue concerning the distribution of human labour is a constant. The labour power of humans that yields 'value' does not stand apart from people. It can never be attributed to technology alone, in the form of enhancement, despite the persuasive arguments of politicians. Yet the drive to enhance the quality of labour power itself, in the form of surplus value and in the service of capitalism continues, despite the physical limitations of humans (Rikowski, 2003: 148).

We now face a significant challenge to be addressed, as we embark on a 'post-digital' dialogue (Jandrić, Knox, Besley, Ryberg, Suoranta, & Hayes, 2018). This lies in where we choose to place 'value' in our discourse about technology. The technological fruits of human labour now flow through our bodies in unprecedented ways, as we are surgically repaired, enhanced and enabled by the devices humans have created. Yet still we are linguistically separated from our tools. In a sense, the concept of 'post' has resided with us throughout history. Who can say when 'post anything' starts or ends? Yet still the idea of 'post' keeps us hopeful that new possibilities remain. In the post-digital, we now need to open up new dialogues, with an awareness of the value of these exchanges, played out through the 'labour of our words'. If we do nothing further, then let's continue this dialogue and finally disrupt forever, the myth that technology or indeed discourse, acts alone.

### *Choosing to Value Academic Voices*

Much of this book has examined and explored meaning that might be construed from the policy discourse I have labelled McPolicy. This extends a small aspect of Ritzer's McDonaldisation thesis, as applied within the McUniversity. One of the static nominalised phrases that describes a process without acknowledging the student academic labour involved was considered in Chapter 5, through student engagement. Putting these two words together does not suggest an active contextual process. In this form, a dynamic living activity, where human presence cannot be denied, has been shrink-wrapped and preserved as an object to refer to. As Couldry (2010) reminds us, 'human beings can give an account of themselves and of their place in the world'. To treat people as if they lack this capacity, 'is to treat them as if they were not human' (Couldry, 2010: 1).

In the analysis of textual examples of HE McPolicy, my intention has been to demonstrate where value is being placed, in relation to human academic labour. Time and again it was words, not people, who enacted academic processes in these statements from strategies. Thus human presence was hard to locate. Yet these words of McPolicy were still written by humans – humans who failed to value the rich diversity of academic voices. Couldry argues that we are 'experiencing a contemporary *crisis* of voice, across political, economic and cultural domains, that has been growing for at least three decades' (Couldry, 2010: 1). This is linked to the choices made by humans concerning voice as a value. It concerns:

> The act of valuing, and choosing to value, those frameworks for organizing human life and resources that *themselves* value voice (as a process). Treating voice as a value means discriminating *in favour* of ways of organizing human life and resources that, through their choices, put the value of voice into practice, by respecting the multiple interlinked processes of voice and sustaining them, not undermining or denying them. Treating voice as a value means discriminating *against* frameworks of social economic and political organization that deny or undermine voice, such as neoliberalism. (Couldry, 2010: 2)

In other words, we have no time to sit back and merely contemplate. The way in which HE policy is currently written, frequently fails to acknowledge human labour. In so doing, it also devalues the human voices of academia.

### *Resisting Displacement: Looking towards Post-McPolicy*

History has taught us that there is a natural tendency for new technological innovations to displace people. Whilst sometimes violently opposed, displacement can occur in positive ways too, for example a variety of household appliances now reduce repetitive tasks. These machines now even respond to our voices and our mobile phones, as such, our lives are increasingly constituted by our digital devices. Some would argue though that automation is about to present our most difficult challenge yet, as widespread technological unemployment appears to be imminent, due to new global advances in artificial intelligence (Aoun, 2017). Whilst authors debate the pros and cons of a fundamental shift away from work as we know it, through the Fourth Industrial Revolution, another issue of displacement of human labour within higher education is worthy of our attention. This concerns a relatively recent phenomenon, where humans are now routinely displaced and dispersed linguistically in higher education policy. It is the labour of words like 'employability', as explored in Chapter 6, which dismantles students into parts to serve the requirements of industry. No human 'skill' can ever be isolated or reproduced in the same form, except when replicated through automation. Just like best practice, the discourse of 'graduate attributes' gives a false impression. This discourse resembles fake news in a 'value for money' from HE agenda.

The explicit analysis undertaken in this book through CDA cannot eliminate the discourse without the intervention of humans, but I hope that it has gone some way towards 'displacing it' (Savage, 2013: 17) so that new conceptual space to re-imagine alternatives can be envisaged. If the post-digital presents us with an opportunity to resolve a worrying issue of human displacement in the digital, then perhaps the same approach might be applied to HE policy. I suggest we move towards a 'post policy' situation in universities. Just as Cramer (2015) has argued that the prefix 'post', as applied to post-digital, should be understood as still digital, yet also beyond digital, we can regard policy in a similar way to enable new thinking and practices beyond the written policy in its current form.

### Organisation Can Be a Verb as Well as a Noun

In his review of Smyth's *The toxic university: zombie leadership, academic rock stars and neoliberal ideology* (2017), Corbett (2018: 4) argues that 'fragmented rearguard subversions alone or appeals for a return to the good old days will not stop the bleeding in academia'. He makes an observation that nearly 50 years ago, Karl Weick pointed out that 'organisation can be understood as a verb as well as a noun' (Weick, 1969; Corbett, 2018: 4). Corbett suggests the single thing we need to do 'to collectively stop the bleeding' is to 'treat the university as an organising activity rather than an alien organisational structure owned by management' Corbett (2018: 4).

I agree. The university is an organising activity powered by people. However, calls for such collective action need to be accompanied by tangible changes to reflect this insight in written policy. With this in mind, I suggest that having confronted the labour of words in HE policy, through a critical analysis of the discourse, we now have an opportunity to make a fundamental change to support this call from Corbett. If you have been alarmed by the rationality of the policy discourse revealed in this book, it is time to reflect on the problem that it shares your office with you in your university. It subtly governs how you spend your weekend. It fails to credit you with conducting the work you took home with you under one arm, with your fast food take away order under the other. Oh and by the way, when you apply for your next university job or promotion, don't forget that 'the student experience' will be conducting your recruitment, selection and induction – it will later measure your performance too. However, it won't retire on its own, even if you wish it would.

If you are studying in a university and you think that the strategies that have been written concerning your 'experience', 'e-learning', 'engagement' and 'employability' are representing you, then it is time to think again. Some authors have pointed out that, rather than empowering students, a consumerist discourse in HE policy frames students as 'thwarted consumers' and 'vulnerable children' (Brooks, 2017: 3; Hayes, 2017). If that isn't bad enough, your labour undertaken in seminars and tutorials, exams and essays may be discussed in strategy, but you are not acknowledged for this work. It is 'effective student engagement' that has been attributed with having impact and yielding benefits for the university. You may get on well with your lecturers, but it is 'quality assurance and enhancement mechanisms' that drive your student learning experience and 'the University's infrastructure and services' that determine the effectiveness of the teaching you experience. You may have ambitions, but don't get carried away here either, as these will be delivered by a 'strategy' or a little buzz word called 'employability, but not necessarily by you.

Attention needs to be paid to these documents. Not least because contradictory statements around social justice risk cancelling each other out, if widening participation and student retention are enacted by generic statements, projects and technology, rather than diverse staff and students themselves (Hayes, 2018b; Czerniewicz & Rother, 2018). One way to counterbalance this approach is to re-visit the exchange value that underpins university strategies and instead write these as a collaborative endeavor, inclusive and representative of all staff and students. The concept of widening participation in HE has been adopted within narrow margins which can be broadened. It needs to acknowledge that all of us might at times be students, even when we are also staff (Hayes, 2018b). It also needs to acknowledge that barriers to inclusivity, participation and social mobility can occur through the language of policy, as well as well as through the practices of recruitment.

It therefore is time for staff and students, as a collective community, to protest this language and change the way in which divisive forms of HE policy are written. Corbett argues 'we are the university' and 'as citizens of the university, the way forward is to fully engage with the committee structures, with other governance activities at all levels, and with our unions' (Corbett, 2018: 4). Let's add to this list our full engagement to make changes to the way in which our written policies and strategies are constructed. These static documents are communicators, thinkers and actors, but they are not (at least not yet) acting on your behalf.

# References

Ahmed, S. (2014). *Cultural politics of emotion*. Edinburgh: Edinburgh University Press.

Allmer, T. (2018). Precarious, always-on and flexible: A case study of academic working conditions. *European Journal of Communication, 33*(4), 381–395.

Aoun, R. (2017). *Robot-proof: Higher education in the age of artificial intelligence*. London: The MIT Press.

Apperley, A. (2014). Revisiting Dearing: Higher education and the construction of the 'belabored' self. *Culture Unbound: Journal of Current Cultural Research, 6*(4), 731–753.

Baker, P. (2006). *Using corpora in discourse analysis*. London: Continuum.

Ball, S. J. (1993). What is policy? Texts, trajectories and toolboxes. *The Australian Journal of Education Studies, 13*(2), 10–17.

Ball, S. J. (2003). The teacher's soul and the terrors of performativity. *Journal of Education Policy, 18*(2), 215–228.

Ball, S. J. (2012). *Global education Inc.: New policy networks and the neo-liberal imaginary*. London: Routledge.

Barron, L. (2013). *Social theory in popular culture*. London: Palgrave Macmillan.

Bartholomew, P., & Hayes, S. (2015). An introduction to policy as it relates to technology enhanced learning. In J. Branch, P. Bartholomew, & C. Nygaard (Eds.), *Technology enhanced learning in higher education*. London: Libri.

Baudrillard, J. (1993). *Baudrillard live: Selected interviews*. London: Routledge.

Bayne, S. (2014). What's the matter with 'technology-enhanced learning'? *Learning, Media and Technology, 40*(1), 1–16.

Beck, U. (1992). *Risk society: Towards a new modernity*. London: Sage Publications.

Berg, L. D., Huijbens, E. H., & Larsen, H. G. (2016). Producing anxiety in the neoliberal university. *The Canadian Geographer, 60*(2), 168–180.

Bertelsen, E. (1998). The real transformation: The marketisation of higher education. *Social Dynamics, 24*(2), 130–158.

Billig, M. (2008). The language of critical discourse analysis: The case of nominalization. *Discourse and Society, 19*(6), 783–800.

BIS (Department for Business Innovation and Skills). (2011). *Higher education: Students at the heart of the system*. London: TSO.

BIS (Department for Business Innovation and Skills). (2016). *Teaching excellence framework technical consultation*. Retrieved October 1, 2018, from https://www.gov.uk/government/consultations/teaching-excellence-framework-year-2-technical-consultation

Bleiker, R. (2009). *Aesthetics and world politics*. New York, NY: Palgrave Macmillan.

Boles, N. (2017, December 28). How to stop our universities ripping off students AND the taxpayer. *Mail Online*. Retrieved May 24, 2018, from http://www.dailymail.co.uk/debate/article-5216633/How-stop-universities-ripping-students.html

Bothwell, E. (2017, November 15). UK universities forced to axe misleading ranking claims. *Times Higher Education*. Retrieved August 4, 2018, from https://www.timeshighereducation.com/news/uk-universities-forced-axe-misleading-rankings-claims

Bothwell, E. (2018, February 8). Work-life balance survey 2018: Long hours take their toll on academics. *Times Higher Education*. Retrieved August 4, 2018, from https://www.timeshighereducation.com/features/work-life-balance-survey-2018-long-hours-take-their-toll-academics

Bowell, T., & Kemp, G. (2015). *Critical thinking: A concise guide*. London: Routledge.

Brookfield, S. (1986). *Understanding and facilitating adult learning*. Milton Keynes: Open University Press.

Brooks, R. (2017). The construction of higher education students in English policy documents. *British Journal of Sociology of Education, 39*(6), 745–761.

Brown, W. (2011). Neoliberalized knowledge. *History of the Present, 1*(1), 113–129.

Brown, W. (2015). *Undoing the demos: Neoliberalism's stealth revolution*. London: The MIT Press.

Bryan, J., & Hayes, D. (2007). *The McDonaldization of further education. A lecturer's guide to further education*. Maidenhead: Open University Press.

Brynjolfsson, E., & McAfee, A. (2011). *Race against the machine: How the digital revolution is accelerating innovation, driving productivity, and irreversibly transforming employment and the economy*. Lexington, MA: Digital Frontier Press.

Burns, J. (2018, February 22). Universities braced for 14 days of strikes over pensions. *BBC News*. Retrieved March 25, 2018, from http://www.bbc.co.uk/news/education-43140726

Callinicos, A. (2006). *Universities in a neoliberal world*. London: Bookmarks Publications.

Clegg, S., Hudson, A., & Steel, J. (2003). The emperor's new clothes: Globalization and e-learning in higher education. *British Journal of Sociology of Education, 24*(1), 39–53.

Codd, J. (2005). Education policy and the challenges of globalization: Commercialisation or citizenship? In J. Codd & K. Sullivan (Eds.), *Education policy directions in Aotearoa New Zealand* (pp. 3–17). Melbourne: Thomson Dunmore Press.

Coiffait, L. (2018, June 8). There's an app for [insert issue here]. *WONKHE*. Retrieved September 28, 2018, from https://wonkhe.com/blogs/theres-an-app-for-insert-issue-here/

Competition and Markets Authority (CMA). (2015). *UK higher education providers – advice on consumer protection law. Crown copyright*. Retrieved April 4, 2018, from https://www.gov.uk/government/uploads/system/uploads/attachment_data/file/428549/HE_providers_-_advice_on_consumer_protection_law.pdf

Confederation of British Industry and Universities UK. (2009). *Future fit: Preparing graduates for the world of work*. London: CBI.

Conole, G. C., & Oliver, M. (2002). Embedding theory into learning technology practice with toolkits. *Journal of Interactive Media in Education, 8*, 1–28.

Corbett, M. (2018). We are the university. *Pedagogy, Culture and Society, 26*(2), 315–319.

Costea, B., Crump, N., & Amiridis, K. (2007). Managerialism and infinite human resourcefulness: A commentary on the therapeutic habitus, derecognition of finitude and the modern sense of self. *Journal for Cultural Research, 11*(3), 245–264.

Côté, J. E., & Furlong, A. (2016). *Routledge handbook of the sociology of higher education*. London: Routledge.

Couldry, N. (2010). *Why voice matters: Culture and politics after neoliberalism*. London: Sage Publications.

Cramer, F. (2015). What is 'post digital'? In D. M. Berry & M. Dieter (Eds.), *Postdigital aesthetics: Art, computation and design*. New York, NY: Palgrave Macmillan.

Crawford, M. B. (2015). *The world beyond your head: On becoming an individual in an age of distraction*. New York, NY: Farrar, Straus and Giroux.

Crystal, D. (2004). *Rediscover grammar*. London: Longman.

Czerniewicz, L., & Rother, K. (2018). Institutional educational technology policy and strategy documents: An inequality gaze. *Research in Comparative and International Education, 13*(1), 27–45.

Davies, W. (2015). The democratic critique of neo-liberalism. *Renewal, 23*(3), 86–92.

Davies, W. (2015). *The happiness industry: How the government and big business sold us well-being*. London: Verso Books.

Dearing, R. (1997). *Higher education in the learning society: National committee of inquiry into higher education, Leeds*. Retrieved from August 4, 2018, http://www.leeds.ac.uk/educol/ncihe/

Department for Education and Skills (DfES). (2003). *The future of higher education*. London: The Stationary Office.

Dickinson, J. (2018, June 3). *WONKHE. Universities should take back control of the VfM agenda*. Retrieved September 5, 2018, from https://wonkhe.com/blogs/universities-should-take-back-control-of-the-vfm-narrative

Doucet, A., Evers, J., Guerra, E., Lopez, N., Soskil, M., & Timmers, K. (2018). *Teaching in the fourth industrial revolution: Standing at the precipice*. London: Routledge.

Dove, L. L. (2014, September 15). Should I pay any attention to my beer's 'born-on' date? *HowStuffWorks.com*. Retrieved from https://recipes.howstuffworks.com/beer-born-on-date.htm

Edgar, A., & Sedgwick, P. (2002). *Cultural theory: Key thinkers*. Florence: Routledge.

Edgerton, D. (1996). The 'White heat' revisited: The British government and technology in the 1960s. *Twentieth Century British History, 7*(1), 53–82.

European Commission. (2009). *Educating Europe: Exploiting the benefits of ICT*. Retrieved October 10, 2018, from https://ec.europa.eu/digital-single-market/en/news/educating-europe-exploiting-benefits-ict

Fairclough, N. (1989). *Language and power*. Harlow: Longman.
Fairclough, N. (1992). *Discourse and social change*. Cambridge: Polity Press.
Fairclough, N. (1993). Critical discourse analysis and the marketisation of public discourse: The universities. *Discourse and Society, 4*(2), 133–168.
Fairclough, N. (2000). *New labour, new language?* London: Routledge.
Fairclough, N. (2003). *Analysing discourse: Textual analysis for social research*. New York, NY: Psychology Press.
Fairclough, N. (2007). *Global capitalism and change in higher education: Dialectics of language and practice, technology, ideology*. In BAAL Conference 2017, Edinburgh, Scotland.
Fairclough, N., & Wodak, R. (1997). Critical discourse analysis. In T. A. van Dijk (Ed.), *Discourse as social interaction*. London: Sage Publications.
Falkner, N. (2017). What happened to our promised leisure time? And will we find it in the smart city? *The Conversation*. Retrieved October 8, 2018, from https://theconversation.com/what-happened-to-our-promised-leisure-time-and-will-we-find-it-in-the-smart-city-83570
Faruk, A. (2018, January 3). New university regulatory body, office for students, launched. *OxStu*. Retrieved May 20, 2018, from http://oxfordstudent.com/2018/01/03/new-university-regulatory-body-office-students-launched/
Feek, W. (2010). Best of practices? In *A. Cornwall & D. Eade (Eds.), Deconstructing development discourse: Buzzwords and fuzzwords*. Oxford: Oxfam.
Feldman, P. (2018, June 28). Digital skills crucial to the success of fourth industrial revolution. *Jisc*. Retrieved October 8, 2018, from https://www.jisc.ac.uk/news/digital-skills-crucial-to-the-success-of-fourth-industrial-revolution-28-jun-2018
Fendler, L. (2008). Educationalising trends in societies of control: Assessments, problem-based learning and empowerment. In P. Smeyers & M. Depaepe (Eds.), *Educational research: The educationalisation of social problems*. Singapore: Springer Science and Business Media.
Flavin, M. (2017). *Disruptive technology enhanced learning: The use and misuse of digital technologies in higher education*. London: Palgrave Macmillan.
Flood, A. (2016, November 15). 'Post-truth' named word of the year by Oxford dictionaries. *The Guardian*. Retrieved October 10, 2018, from https://www.theguardian.com/books/2016/nov/15/post-truth-named-word-of-the-year-by-oxford-dictionaries
Ford, M. (2015). *Rise of the robots: Technology and the threat of a jobless future*. New York, NY: Basic Books.
Foskett, N. (2011). Markets, government, funding and the marketisation of UK higher education. In M. Molesworth, R. Scullion, & E. Nixon (Eds.), *The marketisation of higher education and the student as consumer*. London: Routledge.
Fowler, R., Hodge, B., Kress, G., & Trew, T. (1979). *Language and social control*. London: Routledge.

## REFERENCES

Fox, C. (2016). *I find that offensive!* London: Biteback Publishing.

Freire, P. (1972). *Pedagogy of the oppressed.* Harmondsworth: Penguin.

Frey, C. A., & Osborne, M. A. (2015). *Technology at work: The future of innovation and employment.* Retrieved September 24, 2018, from http://www.oxfordmartin.ox.ac.uk/downloads/reports/Citi_GPS_Technology_Work.pdf

Furedi, F. (2016). *What's happened to the university? A sociological exploration of its infantilisation.* London: Routledge.

Gee, J. P. (1999). *An Introduction to discourse analysis theory and method.* New York, NY: Routledge.

Gibbs, A. (2001). Contagious feelings: Pauline Hanson and the epidemiology of affect. *Australian Humanities Review.* Retrieved from http://www.lib.latrobe.edu.au/AHR/archive/Issue-December-2001/gibbs.html

Gibbs, G. (2014). Student engagement, the latest buzzword. *Times Higher Education.* Retrieved March 20, 2018, from https://www.timeshighereducation.co.uk/news/student-engagement-the-latest-buzzword/2012947.article

Gill, R. (2010). Breaking the silence: The hidden injuries of the neoliberal university. In R. Ryan-Flood & R. Gill (Eds.), *Secrecy and silence in the research process: Feminist reflections.* London: Routledge.

Gill, R. (2014). Academics, cultural workers and critical labour studies. *Journal of Cultural Economy, 7*(1), 12–30.

Giroux, H. A. (2004). Critical pedagogy and the postmodern/modern divide: Towards a pedagogy of democratisation. *Teacher Education Quarterly, 31*(1), 31–47.

Goffman, E. (1979). *Gender advertisements.* New York, NY: Harper and Row.

Graham, P. (2001). Space: Irrealis objects in technology policy and their role in a new political economy. *Discourse and Society, 12*(6), 761–788.

Gregg, M. (2009). Function creep: Communication technologies and anticipatory labour in the information workplace. *New Media and Society.* Retrieved Auugust 20, 2015, from http://homecookedtheory.com/wp-content/uploads/functioncreepnms.doc

Gregg, M. (2013). *Work's intimacy.* New York, NY: John Wiley and Sons.

Gulli, B. (2009). Knowledge production and the superexploitation of contingent academic labor. *Workplace: A Journal for Academic Labor, 16*, 1–30. Retrieved July 23, 2018, from http://ices.library.ubc.ca/index.php/workplace/article/view/182232

Hall, R. (2018). *The alienated academic: The struggle for autonomy inside the university.* London: Palgrave Macmillan.

Hall, R., & Bowles, K. (2016). Re-engineering higher education: The subsumption of academic labour and the exploitation of anxiety. *Workplace, 28*, 30–47.

Halliday, M. A. K. (1994). *An introduction to functional grammar.* London: Arnold.

Harman, G. (1984). Conceptual and theoretical issues. In J. R. Hough (Ed.), *Educational policy: An international survey.* Sydney: Croom Helm Australia Pty Limited.

Harris, S. (2018). *Subject-level TEF: A done deal or the start of a consultation?* UUK. Retrieved August 3, 2018, from http://www.universitiesuk.ac.uk/blog/Pages/subject-level-tef-done-deal-or-consultation.aspx

Harvey, D. (1996). *Justice, nature and the geography of difference*. Oxford: Blackwell.

Hassan, I., & Hayes, S. (2016). Transforming the relationship between staff and students to effect change. *The Journal of Educational Innovation, Partnership and Change*, 2(1). doi:10.21100/jeipc.v2i1.244

Havergal, C. (2015). Is academic citizenship under strain? *Times Higher Education*. Retrieved March 2, 2018, from https://www.timeshighereducation.com/features/is-academic-citizenship-under- strain/2018134.article

Hayes, D. (2005, June 10). Diploma? Is that with fries? *Times Educational Supplement*. Retrieved July 20, 2018, from https://www.tes.com/news/diploma-fries

Hayes, D. (2017). *Beyond McDonaldization: Visions of higher education*. Abingdon: Taylor and Francis.

Hayes, D., & Wynyard, R. (2002). *The McDonaldization of higher education*. Santa Barbara, CA: Praeger.

Hayes, S. (2015a). Counting on the use of technology to enhance learning. In P. Jandrić & D. Boras (Eds.), *Critical learning in digital networks*. New York, NY: Springer.

Hayes, S. (2015b). A sphere of resonance for networked learning in the 'non-places' of our universities. *E-Learning and Digital Media*, 12(3–4), 265–278.

Hayes, S. (2015c). Encouraging the intellectual craft of living research: Tattoos, theory and time. In P. Bartholomew, C. Guerin, & C. Nygaard (Eds.), *Learning to research: Researching to learn*. London: Libri.

Hayes, S. (2016a). Digital learning, discourse, and ideology. In M. A. Peters (Ed.), *Encyclopedia of educational philosophy and theory* (pp. 1–6). Singapore: Springer.

Hayes, S. (2016b). Learning from a deceptively spacious policy discourse. In S. Bayne, C. Sinclair, M. de Laat, & T. Ryberg (Eds.), *Research boundaries and policy in networked learning*. London: Springer.

Hayes, S. (2017a). Introducing the concept of 'a corresponding curriculum' to transform academic identity and practice. In A. Hørsted, J. Branch, & C. Nygaard (Eds.), *Learning-centred curriculum design in higher education*. London: Libri.

Hayes, S. (2017b). Beyond engagement and enhancement: Piloting a 'digital partnership' with undergraduate students, to teach staff PGDip participants. In J. Branch, S. Hayes, A. Hørsted, & C. Nygaard (Eds.), *Innovative teaching in higher education*. London: Libri.

Hayes, S. (2018a). Invisible labour: Do we need to reoccupy student engagement policy? *Learning and Teaching*, 11(1), 19–34.

Hayes, S. (2018b, June 18). Widening participation and social mobility applies to university staff as well as students. *WONKHE*. Retrieved October 2, 2018, from https://wonkhe.com/blogs/widening-participation-and-social-mobility-applies-to-university-staff-as-well-as-students

Hayes, S., Bale, R., Bhoola, T., Jack, K., Johnsson, C., & Kalyn, B. (2017). Innovative teaching and learning practices using student partnerships. In J. Branch, S. Hayes, A. Hørsted, & C. Nygaard (Eds.), *Innovative teaching in higher education*. London: Libri.

Hayes, S., & Bartholomew, P. (2015). Where's the humanity? Challenging the policy discourse of technology enhanced learning. In J. Branch, P. Bartholomew, & C. Nygaard (Eds.), *Technology enhanced learning in higher education*. London: Libri.

Hayes, S., & Jandrić, P. (2014). Who is really in charge of contemporary education? People and technologies in, against and beyond the neoliberal university. *Open Review of Educational Research, 1*(1), 193–210.

Hayes, S., & Jandrić, P. (2017a). Editorial: Learning technologies and time in the age of global neoliberal capitalism. *Knowledge Cultures, 5*(2), 11.

Hayes, S., & Jandrić, P. (2017b). Resisting the final word: Challenging stale media and policy representations of students' performative technological encounters in university education. In S. Cranmer, N. B. Dohn, M. de Laat, T. Ryberg, & J. A. Sime (Eds.), *Research in networked learning*. London: Springer.

Hayes, S., & Wilson, C. (2018, July 10). Being 'resourceful' in academic engagement with parliament. *WONKHE*. Retrieved October 2, 2018, from https://wonkhe.com/blogs/being-resourceful-in-academic-engagement-with-parliament

Higher Education Funding Council for England (HEFCE). (2018). *Learning gain national conference*. Retrieved October 10, 2018, from http://www.hefce.ac.uk/media/HEFCE,2014/Content/Events/2018/Learning%20Gain%20conf%20agenda%207%20Feb%202018.pdf

Hoey, M. (1991). *Patterns of lexis in text*. Oxford: Oxford University Press.

Hughes, G., Panjwani, M., Tulcidas, P., & Byrom, N. (2017). *Student mental health: The role and experiences of academics*. Retrieved April 20, 2018, from http://hdl.handle.net/10545/622114

Hyacinth, B. T. (2017). *The future of leadership: Rise of automation, robotics and artificial intelligence*. MBA Caribbean Organisation.

Illich, I. (1973). *Tools for conviviality*. New York, NY: Harper and Row.

Jandrić, P., & Hayes, S. (2017). Who drives the drivers? Technology as ideology of global educational reform. In A. Means & K. Saltman (Eds.), *Handbook of global educational reform*. Hoboken, NJ: WileyBlackwell.

Jandrić, P., Knox, J., Besley, T., Ryberg, T., Suoranta, J., & Hayes, S. (2018). Postdigital science and education. *Educational Philosophy and Theory, 50*(10), 893–899.

Jandrić, P., Knox, J., Macleod, H., & Sinclair, C. (2017). Learning in the age of algorithmic cultures. *E-Learning and Digital Media, 14*(3), 101–104.

Janks, H. (1997). Critical discourse analysis as a research tool. *Discourse: Studies in the Cultural Politics of Education, 18*(3), 329–342.

Jarvie, J. (2014, March 3). Trigger happy. *New Republic*.

Jessop, B. (2000). The crisis of the national spatio-temporal fix and the tendential ecological dominance of globalizing capitalism. *International Journal of Urban and Regional Research, 24*(2), 323–360.

Joint Information Systems Committee. (2009). *Effective practice in a digital age.* Retrieved October 2, 2018, from http://www.jisc.ac.uk/publications/programmerelated/2009/effectivepracticedigitalage.aspx

Jones, R., & Thomas, L. (2005). The 2003 UK government higher education White paper: A critical assessment of its implications for the access and widening participation agenda. *Journal of Education Policy, 20*(5), 615–630.

Jorgenson, M. W., & Phillips, L. J. (2002). *Discourse analysis as theory and method.* London: Sage Publications.

Kahane, D. (2011). Mindfulness and presence in teaching and learning. In I. Hay (Ed.), *Inspiring academics: Learning with the world's great university teachers* (pp. 17–22). Maidenhead: Open University Press.

Kernohan, D. (2018, September 30). Plenty ventured but what was gained? *WONKHE.* Retrieved October 10, 2018, from https://wonkhe.com/blogs/plenty-ventured-but-what-was-gained/

Khan, S. (2018, October 4). Opening up student debate on campus. *WONKHE.* Retrieved October 10, 2018, from https://wonkhe.com/blogs/opening-up-student-debate-on-campus/

Kopytoff, I. (1986). The cultural biography of things: Commoditisation as process. *The Social Life of Things: Commodities in Cultural Perspective, 68*, 70–73.

Lea, J. (Ed.). (2015). *Enhancing learning and teaching in higher education: Engaging with the dimensions of practice.* Maidenhead: Open University Press.

Leach, M. (2018, March 9). The enemy within: Why the narrative about universities and students went so wrong. *WONKHE.* Retrieved April 20, 2018, from http://wonkhe.com/blogs/the-enemy-within-why-the-narrative-about-universities-and-students-went-so-wrong/

Lesnick-Oberstein, K. E., Burman, I., Parker, S., Grech, R., House, P., Abbs, P., Ainley, P., et al. (2015, July 6). Let UK universities do what they do best – teaching and research. *Guardian Online.* Retrieved October 10, 2018, from https://www.theguardian.com/education/2015/jul/06/let-uk-universities-do-what-they-do-best-teaching-and-research

Lukács, G. (1971). *History and class consciousness.* London: Merlin.

Luppicini, R. (2005). A systems definition of educational technology in society. *Educational Technology and Society, 8*(3), 103–109.

Macfarlane, B., & Tomlinson, M. (2017). Critiques of student engagement. *Higher Education Policy, 30*(1), 5–21.

Malabou, C. (2008). *What should we do with our brain?* New York, NY: Fordham University Press.

# REFERENCES

Marx, K. (1867). *Capital: A critique of political economy*. Retrieved October 10, 2018, from https://www.marxists.org/archive/marx/works/download/pdf/Capital-Volume-I.pdf

Massey, D. (2013). Vocabularies of the economy. *Soundings, 54*, 9–22.

Matthewman, S. (2011). *Technology and social theory*. New York, NY: Palgrave.

Mautner, G. (2005). The entrepreneurial university: A discursive profile of a higher education buzzword. *Critical Discourse Studies, 2*(2), 95–120.

McKie, A. (2018, June 7). Minister attacks 'threadbare' courses at English universities. *Times Higher Education*. Retrieved October 10, 2018, from https://www.timeshighereducation.com/news/minister-attacks-threadbare-courses-english-universities

McQuaid, R. W., & Lindsay, C. (2005). The concept of employability. *Urban Studies, 42*(2), 197–219.

McRae, A. (2018, February 22). What does 'value for money' mean for English higher education? *Times Higher Education*. Retrieved October 10, 2018, from https://www.timeshighereducation.com/features/what-does-value-money-mean-english-higher-education

Means, A. (2017). Education for a post-work future: Automation, precarity, and stagnation. *Knowledge Cultures, 5*(1), 21–40.

Merle, R. (2016, May 24). The occupy movement has grown up – and looks to inflict real pain on big banks. *Washington Post*. Retrieved October 10, 2018, from https://www.washingtonpost.com/news/business/wp/2016/05/24/the-occupy-movement-has-grown-up-and-looks-to-inflict-real-pain-on-big-banks/

Meyer, J. H. F., & Land, R. (2006). Threshold concepts and troublesome knowledge: Issues of liminality. In J. H. F. Meyer & R. Land (Eds.), *Overcoming barriers to student understanding: Threshold concepts and troublesome knowledge*. London: Routledge.

Mezirow, J. (1991). *Transformative dimensions of adult learning*. San Francisco, CA: Jossey-Bass.

Mills, C. W. (1959). *The sociological imagination*. London, Oxford, & New York, NY: Oxford University Press. (Online resource) Retrieved from http://www-rohan.sdsu.edu/~psargent/Mills_Intell_Craft.pdf

Millward, C. (2015, September 22). HEFCE seeks the measure of learning gain. *HEFCE*. Retrieved March 3, 2018, from http://webarchive.nationalarchives.gov.uk/20150708130628/http://blog.hefce.ac.uk/author/chris-millward/

Molesworth, M., Scullion, R., & Nixon, E. (Eds.). (2011). *The marketisation of higher education*. Oxon: Routledge.

Molloy, D. (2018, March 6). What is populism, and what does the term actually mean? *BBC News*. Retrieved April 2, 2018, from http://www.bbc.co.uk/news/world-43301423

Monbiot, G. (2016, April 15). Neoliberalism: The ideology at the root of all our problems. *The Guardian*. Retrieved October 10, 2018, from https://www.theguardian.com/books/2016/apr/15/neoliberalism-ideology-problem-george-monbiot

Morley, L. (2003). *Quality and power in higher education*. Maidenhead: McGraw-Hill Education.

Morrish, L. (2015, July 10). The paradox of the 'under-performing professor'. *Academic Irregularities: Critical University Studies, Discourse, and Managerialism Blog*. Retrieved from https://academicirregularities.wordpress.com/2015/07/10/the-paradox-of-the-underperforming-professor

Morrison, K. (2006). *Marx, Durkheim, Weber: Formations of modern social thought*. London: Sage Publications.

Mulderrig, J. (2003). Consuming education: A critical discourse analysis of social actors in new labour's education policy. *Journal for Critical Education Policy Studies, 1*(1), 1–20.

Mulderrig, J. (2009). *The language of education policy: From Thatcher to Blair*. Saarbrucken: VDM Publishing.

Mulderrig, J. (2011). Manufacturing consent: A corpus-based critical discourse analysis of new labour's educational governance. *Educational Philosophy and Theory, 43*(6), 562–578.

Mumby, D. K., & Clair, R. P. (1997). Organizational discourse. *Discourse as Social Interaction, 2*, 181–205.

Ng, R. (2008, November 7–9). *Toward an integrative embodied critical pedagogy through Qi Gong*. Paper presented at the Scope of Interdisciplinarity Symposium, Athabasca University, Edmonton.

Nudzor, H. (2009). Re-conceptualising the paradox in policy implementation: A postmodernist conceptual approach. *Discourse: Studies in the Cultural Politics of Education, 30*(4), 501–513.

Nygaard, C., Brand, S., Bartholomew, P., & Millard, L. (2013). *Student engagement: Identity, motivation and community*. Oxon: Libri.

O'Byrne, D., & Hensby, A. (2011). *Theorising global studies*. New York, NY: Palgrave Macmillan.

Olssen, M., Codd, J., & O'Neill, A. M. (2004). *Education policy: Globalization, citizenship and democracy*. Thousand Oaks, CA: Sage Publications.

Olssen, M., & Peters, M. A. (2005). Neoliberalism, higher education and the knowledge economy: From the free market to knowledge capitalism. *Journal of Education Policy, 20*(3), 313–345.

Organisation for Economic Co-operation and Development (OECD). (2016). *Enhancing employability: Report prepared for the G20 employment working group*. Retrieved October 10, 2018, from https://www.oecd.org/g20/topics/employment-and-social-policy/Enhancing-Employability-G20-Report-2016.pdf

Papert, S. (1973). *Uses of technology to enhance education* (MIT Artificial Intelligence Memo No. 298). Cambridge, MA: The MIT Press.

Parchoma, G., & Keefer, J. M. (2012). *Transdisciplinary research in technology enhanced/ networked learning practices*. In Proceedings of the 8th International Conference on Networked Learning 2012, Maastricht, The Netherlands.

Paterson, K. (2016, May 5). Revealed: The unis most likely to get you a good job. *Student News*. Retrieved October 2, 2018, from https://www.savethestudent.org/news/revealed-the-unis-most-likely-to-get-you-a-good-job.html

Pennycook, G., Cannon, T. D., & Rand, D. G. (2018, May 3). Prior exposure increases perceived accuracy of fake news. *Journal of Experimental Psychology*. Retrieved from https://ssrn.com/abstract=2958246

Peters, M. (2009). Education, enterprise culture and the entrepreneurial self: A Foucauldian perspective. *The Journal of Educational Enquiry, 2*(2), 58–71.

Peters, M. A., & Jandrić, P. (2018). Neoliberalism and the university. In D. Cahill, M. Koenings, & M. Cooper (Eds.), *Sage handbook of neoliberalism*. London: Sage Publications.

Peters, M. A., Jandrić, P., & Hayes, S. (2018). The curious promise of educationalising technological unemployment: What can places of learning really do about the future of work? *Educational Philosophy and Theory*, 1–13. doi:10.1080/00131857.2018.1439376

Peters, M. A., Jandrić, P., & Means, A. J. (Eds.). (2019). *Education and technological unemployment*. Singapore: Springer.

Philpott, J. (1999). *Behind the 'buzzword': Employability*. London: Employment Policy Institute.

Pokorny, H., & Warren, D. (Eds.). (2016). *Enhancing teaching practice in higher education*. London: Sage Publications.

Polianskay, A. (2018). Student sues Anglia Ruskin university for 'Mickey Mouse' degree that hasn't helped her career. *The Independent*. Retrieved October 10, 2018, from http://www.independent.co.uk/news/education/education-news/student-anglia-ruskin-university-mickey-mouse-degree-pok-wong-tuition-fees-a8250441.html

Pope, E., Ladwa, N., & Hayes, S. (2017). Improving retention. In *Where next for widening participation and fair access?* Retrieved October 10, 2018, from http://www.hepi.ac.uk/2017/08/14/next-widening-participation-fair-access/

Prevent Strategy. (2011). *H M government*. London: The Stationary Office. Retrieved October 10, 2018, from https://assets.publishing.service.gov.uk/government/uploads/system/uploads/attachment_data/file/97976/prevent-strategy-review.pdf

Price, L., & Kirkwood, A. (2010). Technology enhanced learning – where's the evidence? In C. H. Steel, M. J. Keppell, P. Gerbic, & S. Housego (Eds.), *Curriculum, technology and transformation for an unknown future. Proceedings ASCILITE Sydney* (pp. 772–782).

Retrieved March 30, 2015, from http://ascilite.org.au/conferences/sydney10/procs/Price-concise.pdf

Putnam, P. (2018, February 6). Do today's tweeting feminists have anything in common with window smashing suffragettes? *Curator's Blog*. Retrieved October 10, 2018, from https://blog.hrp.org.uk/curators/todays-tweeting-feminists-anything-common-window-smashing-suffragettes/

Quality Assurance Agency (QAA). Retrieved from http://qaa.ac.uk

Relph, D. (2016, April 29). Eyes on the prize: Time for university leaders to rethink civic engagement. *WONKHE*. Retrieved October 2, 2018, from https://wonkhe.com/blogs/comment-eyes-prize-civic-engagement

Rikowski, G. (2003). Alien life: Marx and the future of the human. *Historical Materialism, 11*(2), 121–164.

Ritzer, G. (1993). *The McDonaldisation of society*. Thousand Oaks, CA: Pine Forge Press.

Ritzer, G. (1993/2018). *The McDonaldisation of society: Into the digital age* (9th ed.). Thousand Oaks, CA: Sage Publications.

Ritzer, G. (1997). *The McDonaldisation thesis: Explorations and extensions*. London: Sage Publications.

Ritzer, G. (1998). The Weberian theory of rationalization and the McDonaldisation of contemporary society. *Illuminating Social Life: Classical and Contemporary Theory Revisited*, 37–61.

Ritzer, G. (2004). *The globalization of nothing*. Thousand Oaks, CA: Pine Forge Press.

Ritzer, G. (2008). *The McDonaldisation of society 5*. Thousand Oaks, CA: Pine Forge Press.

Ritzer, G. (2010). *Enchanting a disenchanted world: Continuity and change in the cathedrals of consumption*. Thousand Oaks, CA: Pine Forge Press.

Ritzer, G. (2011). *Globalization: The essentials*. New York, NY: John Wiley and Sons.

Ritzer, G. (2015). Prosumer capitalism. *The Sociological Quarterly, 56*(3), 413–445.

Ritzer, G., Jandrić, P., & Hayes, S. (2018). The velvet cage of educational con(pro)sumption. *Open Review of Educational Research*, 1–17.

Ritzer, G., & Jurgenson, N. (2010). Production, consumption, prosumption: The nature of capitalism in the age of the digital 'prosumer'. *Journal of Consumer Culture, 10*(1), 13–36.

Rowe, A. C. (2012). Erotic pedagogies. *Journal of Homosexuality, 59*(7), 1031–1056.

Savage, M. (2013). The social life of methods: A critical introduction. *Theory Culture Society, 30*(4), 3–21.

Scott, J. (2012). *Sociological theory: Contemporary debates*. Cheltenham: Edward Elgar.

Scott, M. (1997). PC analysis of key words: And key, key words. *System, 25*(2), 233–245.

Scott, P. (2014, February 4). Student experience is the new buzzword, but what does it mean? *The Guardian*. Retrieved April 2, 2018, from http://www.theguardian.com/education/2014/feb/04/university-education-not-just-about-student-experience

Seldon, A., & Martin, A. (2017). *The positive and mindful university* (HEPI Occasional Paper No. 18). Oxford: Higher Education Policy Institute.

Selwyn, N., Gorard, S., & Williams, S. (2001). The role of the 'technical fix in UK lifelong education policy. *International Journal of Lifelong Education, 20*(4), 255–271.

Sennett, R. (2006). *The culture of the new capitalism*. New Haven, CT: Yale University Press.

Shahjahan, R. A. (2015). Being lazy and slowing down: Toward decolonising time, our body and pedagogy. *Educational Philosophy and Theory, 47*(5), 488–501.

Shore, C., & Wright, S. (1999). Audit culture and anthropology: Neo-liberalism in British higher education. *Journal of the Royal Anthropological Institute, 5*(4), 557–575.

Shore, C., & Wright, S. (2011). Conceptualising policy: Technologies of governance and the politics of visibility. In C. Shore, S. Wright, & D. Però (Eds.), *Policy worlds: Anthropology and the analysis of contemporary power* (pp. 1–26). New York, NY: Berghahn Books.

Shore, C., & Wright, S. (2015). Governing by numbers: Audit culture, rankings and the new world order. *Social Anthropology, 23*(1), 22–28.

Shulock, N. (1999). The paradox of policy analysis: If it is not used why do we produce so much of it? *Journal of Policy Analysis and Management, 18*(2), 226–244.

Simpson, P., & Mayr, A. (2010). *Language and power*. Abingdon: Routledge.

Skoulding, L. (2017, May 5). Report: The UK universities offering best value for money. *Student News*. Retrieved April 5, 2018, from http://www.savethestudent.org/news/revealed-which-universities-offer-students-best-value-for-money.html

Slaughter, S., & Leslie, L. (1997). *Academic capitalism*. Baltimore, MD: John Hopkins University Press.

Slaughter, S., & Rhoades, G. (2004). *Academic capitalism and the new economy: Markets, state, and higher education*. Baltimore, MD: The Johns Hopkins University Press.

Smart, B. (1999). *Resisting McDonaldisation*. London: Sage Publications.

Smyth, J. (2017). *The toxic university: Zombie leadership, academic rock stars and neoliberal ideology*. London: Springer.

Spelman, E. V. (1989). Anger and insubordination. In A. Garry & M. Pearsall (Eds.), *Women, knowledge and reality: Explorations in feminist philosophy*. Boston, MA: Unwin Hyman.

Steafel, E. (2018, February 5). Doritos' 'lady friendly' crisps prove its crunch time for sexist marketing. *The Telegraph*. Retrieved April 4, 2018, from http://www.telegraph.co.uk/women/life/doritos-lady-friendly-crisps-prove-crunch-time-sexist-marketing/

Stecula, D. (2017). The real consequences of fake news. *The Conversation*. Retrieved July 1, 2018, from http://theconversation.com/the-real-consequences-of-fake-news-81179

Taylor, L., & Parsons, J. (2011). Improving student engagement. *Current Issues in Education, 14*(1). Retrieved October 10, 2018, from http://cie.asu.edu/

Thomas, L. (2012). *Building student engagement and belonging in higher education at a time of change.* London: Paul Hamlyn Foundation. Retrieved October 9, 2018, from https://www.phf.org.uk/wp-content/uploads/2014/10/What-Works-Summary-report.pdf

Thompson, G. (2013). *Introducing functional grammar.* London: Routledge.

Toffler, A. (1980). *The third wave.* New York, NY: William Morrow and Company.

Travers, A. (2001). Public technologies, radical pedagogy. *CAAP*.

Trowler, P. (1998). *Education policy: A policy sociology approach.* Eastbourne: The Gildridge Press Limited.

Trowler, P. (2001). Captured by the discourse? The socially constitutive power of new higher education discourse in the UK. *Organization, 8*(2), 183–201.

Trowler, P. (2015). Student engagement, ideological contest and elective affinity: The Zepke thesis reviewed. *Teaching in Higher Education, 20*(3), 328–339.

Turp, M. (2001). *Hidden self-harm: Narratives from psychotherapy.* London: Jessica Kingsley.

Universities UK (UUK). (2017). *Review of the teaching excellence framework year two: Process, results and next steps.* Retrieved October 2, 2018, from http://www.universitiesuk.ac.uk/policy-and-analysis/reports/Documents/2017/review-of-the-teaching-excellence-framework-year-2.pdf

University of Gloucestershire. (2016–2020). *Student employability and employment strategy 2016–2020.* Retrieved July 5, 2018, from http://www.glos.ac.uk/docs/download/student-employability-and-employment-strategy-2016-2020.pdf

University of Stirling. (2017–2021). *Employability strategy 2017–2021.* Retrieved October 10, 2018, from https://www.stir.ac.uk/media/stirling/services/internal/careers-and-employability/employability/documents/Employability_Strategy.pdf

University of Winchester. (2016–2020). *Employability strategy 2016–2020.* Retrieved October 10, 2018, from https://www.winchester.ac.uk/about-us/leadership-and-governance/policies-and-procedures/?download=trueandid=215

Van de Velden, G. (2018, January 30). What if we were serious about students at the heart of the system? *WONKHE*. Retrieved March 12, 2018, from http://wonkhe.com/blogs/students-at-the-heart-of-the-system-what-if-we-were-serious-about-that

Wagner, P. (2012). *Modernity: Understanding the present.* Cambridge: Polity Press.

Wajcman, J. (2002). Addressing technological change: The challenge to social theory. *Current Sociology, 50*(3), 347–363.

Walker, J. (2009). Time as the fourth dimension in the globalization of higher education. *The Journal of Higher Education, 80*, 483–509.

Watts, M. (2008). Higher education and hyperreality. *Educational Research: The Educationalisation of Social Problems*, 141–155.

# REFERENCES

Weber, M. (1905/1958). *The protestant ethic and the spirit of capitalism.* New York, NY: Scribner.

Weber, M. (1930). *The protestant ethic and the spirit of capitalism.* London: Allen and Unwin.

Webster, G. (2003). Corporate discourse and the academy: A polemic. *Industry and Higher Education, 17*(2), 85–90.

Weller, S. (2016). *Academic practice: Developing as a professional in higher education.* London: Sage Publications.

Winn, J. (2015). Writing about academic labour. *Workplace: A Journal for Academic Labor, 25,* 1–15. Retrieved October 2, 2018, from http://ices.library.ubc.ca/index.php/workplace/article/view/185095

Winn, J., Hall, R., & Erskine, C. (Eds.). (2017). *Mass intellectuality and democratic leadership in higher education.* London: Bloomsbury Publishing.

Winner, L. (1980). Do artifacts have politics? *Daedalus, 109*(1), 121–136.

Worthington, F., & Hodgson, J. (2005). Academic labour and the politics of quality in higher education: A critical evaluation of the conditions of possibility of resistance. *Critical Quarterly, 47*(1–2), 96–110.

Zepke, N. (2014). Student engagement research in higher education: Questioning an academic orthodoxy. *Teaching in Higher Education, 19*(6), 697–708.

Zepke, N. (2016). *Student engagement in neoliberal times: Theories and practices for learning and teaching in higher education.* London: Springer.

Zepke, N. (2017). Student engagement in neo-liberal times: What is missing? *Higher Education Research and Development, 37*(2), 433–446.

# Index

Academic labour   vii–ix, xiii, 1, 2, 4–7, 9, 11, 12, 14, 16, 20, 22, 26, 27, 29, 30, 32, 44, 46–48, 50–53, 55–58, 61–65, 69, 71–73, 76, 86, 87, 90, 93, 96, 102, 111, 127, 139, 143, 147
Ambition   8, 23, 65, 141
Audit culture   ix, 19, 47, 48, 51

Best practice   viii, 1–4, 6, 19, 20, 28, 32, 44, 52, 69, 73, 80, 84, 85, 104, 106, 109, 144, 148
Buzz phrases   viii, 2–5, 9, 11, 14, 17, 19, 22, 37, 41, 47, 61, 62, 65, 71, 73, 74, 76, 93, 111, 146

Commodities   7, 8, 13, 41, 42, 51, 95, 99, 131, 144
Concordance   79–81, 84, 85, 103, 106, 109, 117–119
Con(pro)sumer   95
Consumer culture   viii, 1, 4, 5, 8, 9, 12, 32, 33, 49, 51, 88
Consumers   2, 7, 8, 21, 25, 28, 29, 32, 35, 37, 38, 45, 72, 93, 95, 97, 115, 125, 150
Consumption   7, 12, 13, 21, 28, 38, 44, 47, 60, 71–73, 78, 93, 95, 96, 98, 131
Corpus   ix, 5, 14, 24, 25, 33, 76, 77–80, 82, 84, 102, 106, 107, 109, 115, 117, 119, 120, 122, 136
Critical Discourse Analysis   ix, 5, 14, 24, 25, 33, 76, 77, 115, 117

Dearing   1, 47, 58, 65, 71, 130, 132
Digital   xi, 14, 22, 23, 28, 51, 87, 89, 91, 101, 103, 110, 111, 133, 142, 144, 146–149
Discourse   vii, xii, 2–5, 10–12, 15–21, 24–27, 29, 30–35, 41–48, 51–55, 57, 59, 60–62, 64–69, 71–74, 76, 77, 80, 87, 90–94, 96, 98, 99, 101, 110–115, 124, 125, 128, 129, 131, 141, 143, 144, 146–150
Diversity   vii, 3, 5, 15, 46, 87, 113, 124, 131, 147

Educationalisation   20, 71, 132, 141, 143
Employability   viii, 2, 3, 5, 13, 14, 19, 21–23, 28, 37, 54, 58, 61, 62, 75, 78, 101, 122, 128–136, 139–141, 144, 148, 149

Fairclough, N.   11, 25, 32, 60, 65–67, 76–78, 91, 111

Graduate attributes   2, 9, 36, 131, 133–135, 138–140, 148

Human labour   vii, ix, xii, 2, 4, 8, 9, 18, 22, 25, 28, 30, 31, 35, 37, 40–44, 47, 60, 71, 82, 83, 88, 91, 93–96, 110–112, 115, 116, 119, 123, 124, 126, 128, 130, 132, 141, 143, 146–148

Iron cage   28, 45, 71, 72, 94, 140

Language-in-use   146
Learning gain   9, 16, 32, 36–39, 42, 43, 129
Linguistics   vii, 10, 24, 72, 77, 78, 80

Marx, K.   12, 28, 35, 36, 40–43, 62, 71, 93, 94, 115, 124, 146
McDonaldisation   vii, xiii, 3–6, 14, 15, 17, 25, 29, 33, 40, 45, 51, 58, 62–64, 71–73, 83, 127, 146, 147
McPolicy   vii–ix, xiii, 2–10, 15, 26, 27, 29–34, 38–40, 45, 46, 51, 54–57, 58, 60–62, 71–74, 76, 92, 93, 114, 127, 128, 130, 139, 144–148
McStudent   74, 75, 123
McUniversity   4–7, 11, 28, 33, 51, 60, 72, 74, 83, 95, 96, 147
Mills, C. Wright   viii, 34
Mulderrig, J.   xii, 66, 68

Neoliberal   2, 11, 12, 15, 16, 24, 30, 39, 40, 43, 46, 53, 56, 60, 61, 63, 66, 67, 71, 90, 92, 110, 114, 115, 122, 126, 130, 131, 144–146, 149
Nominalisation   4, 83

Office for Students   viii, 19, 32, 50, 75, 88

Post-digital   89, 147, 149
Prosumer   20, 26, 28, 34, 40, 48, 93, 95

# INDEX

Rationalisation   15, 16, 25, 28, 30, 33, 44–46, 52, 53, 59, 62, 73, 83, 145

Rationality   ix, 7, 16, 17, 21, 24, 30, 32, 38, 40, 44, 46–48, 51, 56, 59, 61, 62, 67, 88, 92, 94, 127, 138, 143–146, 149

Reoccupy   ix, 112, 114, 128

Ritzer, G.   vii, ix, xiii, 3–7, 12, 14, 17, 19–21, 24, 26, 28, 33, 34, 38, 40, 45, 46, 51, 62, 64, 72, 73, 75, 83, 88, 93–95, 122, 127, 132, 133, 141, 146, 147

Snowflake   xii

Sociological imagination   viii, 33, 34, 40, 51, 144

Strategy   5–7, 9, 16, 22, 23, 30, 52, 55, 59, 60, 64, 68, 71, 75, 78–80, 83–85, 89, 101, 102, 105, 108, 109, 113–118, 121, 123, 124, 128, 132, 135, 140, 141, 143, 150

Student engagement   viii, 2, 3, 9, 14, 17, 19, 21, 23, 28, 37, 61, 62, 75, 78, 92, 101, 113–124, 126–129, 132, 136, 147, 150

Teaching Excellence Framework   32, 45, 124, 125

Technologisation   11, 32, 91, 141

Technology enhanced learning   3, 5, 61, 62, 75, 78, 89, 90, 93, 94, 100, 102, 103, 132

*The student experience*   viii, 2–6, 13, 15, 16, 18–20, 29, 32, 39, 42, 48, 51, 52, 54, 55, 71–75, 79, 80, 82–87, 94, 101, 109, 110, 118, 120, 122, 144, 146, 149

Transitivity analysis   78, 81, 82, 84

Value for money   viii, 3, 32, 48, 62, 71, 73, 86, 87, 131, 148

Wordsmith   78, 79, 102, 117

Printed in the United States
By Bookmasters